The
Mormon
War

The
Mormon
War

ZION AND THE MISSOURI
EXTERMINATION ORDER OF 1838

Brandon G. Kinney

WESTHOLME
Yardley

Frontispiece: "The Extermination of the Latter Day Saints from the State of Missouri in the Fall of 1838," an illustration from the *Missouri Republican* newspaper. Officers of the Missouri State militia met Mormon leaders outside of their stronghold of Far West, Missouri, to negotiate their surrender and expulsion to Illinois.

Westholme Publishing, LLC
904 Edgewood Road
Yardley, Pennsylvania 19067
Visit our Web site at www.westholmepublishing.com

ISBN: 978-1-59416-363-0
Also available as an eBook.

Printed in the United States of America.

CONTENTS

Preface vii

• ONE •

FOUNDATION 1

• TWO •

MISSOURI 11

• THREE •

KIRTLAND, OHIO 22

• FOUR •

EXPULSION 33

• FIVE •

ZION'S MARCH 46

• SIX •

THE SAFETY SOCIETY BANK 58

• SEVEN •

FAR WEST 73

• EIGHT •

THE ELECTION BRAWL 85

• NINE •

CONFLICT 95

• TEN •

MILITIA ON THE MOVE 108

• ELEVEN •

THE DeWITT STAND-OFF 118

• TWELVE •

THE RAID ON GALLATIN 133

• THIRTEEN •

MASSACRE AND CAPITULATION 152

• FOURTEEN •

EXODUS 174

• FIFTEEN •

NAUVOO 187

Notes 205

Bibliography 241

Index 253

Acknowledgments 265

PREFACE

In 1820 in Palmyra, New York, Joseph Smith, Jr., like many others, joined the revival of faith in America. A great awakening had occurred and the country was seized by religious fervor with preaching and proselytizing. There is no record of what attracted Smith to explore the spiritual life; he was later to write that he "became interested in theology at the age of twelve." Perhaps the adolescent farmer was drawn to the evangelist revival meetings in order to experience God in a direct sense, much like his parents may have with religious folk magic or Christian mysticism.[1] He may have simply regarded the revivals as a way to earn a living, being impressed by the passion and offerings generated by itinerant preachers. Regardless of his motivation, on his way to get religion, Smith claimed he had received a revelation:

> One of them spake unto me, calling me by name, and said, (pointing to the other) "This is my beloved Son, hear him." . . . I asked the personages who stood above me in the light, which of all the sects [churches] was right, and which I should join. I was answered that I must join none of them, for they were all wrong. . . that all their creeds were an abomination in his sight; that those professors were all corrupt.[2]

Smith established the Church of Jesus Christ of Latter Day Saints, or Mormon church, as a purified and refined version of Christianity with the intent of replacing all other forms.[3] Although he was charismatic, he found it difficult to convert people in New York to his religion. In 1831, Smith therefore moved his church to Kirtland, Ohio, where his skills as a prophet were put to the test when dissension among the faithful and a disastrous banking enterprise threatened to destroy the fledgling organization.

In January 1838, Smith resolved to relocate the church's main headquarters to the town of Far West, Missouri, despite the Mormons being violently driven out of their first gathering place in Independence in 1833. Upon settling in the young state his message was clear: dissenters and those who doubted Smith's revelations must be forced from the church or true believers would never inherit the favor and blessings of God. Western Missouri at this time was populated by mostly proslavery settlers who farmed and ranched. It was also a place where the political upper hand could be readily gained, particularly with a large emigration of like-minded converts as voters. Smith developed an ambitious plan for his church to dominate the political landscape as a way to allow the laws God provided through him to become the supreme law of the land.[4]

In due course the Mormons suffered from the prejudices of the local settlers who were wary of both the Mormon's abolitionist leanings and their non-mainstream Christian beliefs. Once Smith began his plan of political control and the number of Mormons grew—bolstered by waves of Canadian and English converts, his followers became emboldened and clashes erupted between Mormon and non-Mormon groups. Despite the destabilizing threat to the state, Missouri Governor Lilburn Boggs did nothing for some time, allowing the tension between the Mormons and their neighbors to devolve into a shooting war. When the governor finally took action, he mobilized the state militia and issued an extermination order, perhaps one of the most infamous official acts in United States history, an order to either kill or forcibly remove all those of the Mormon faith from the state.

Known as the Mormon War, the Missouri Mormon War, and the Mormon War of 1838, the conflict is better characterized as a clash of ideologies and the ultimate expression and defense of First Amendment rights, rather than as a full-fledged series of battles between armies. However, the Missouri Mormon War is a major event in American history, despite its lack of popular notoriety. Here in 1830s Missouri, we have the seeds of the Civil War, challenges to core American beliefs in freedom, and an outcome that shaped the future of westward migration. It is also a stark lesson in the damages of prejudice, a problem that our country has continued to struggle with throughout its history. It is an event charged with controversy and emotions that are still felt today. Even the names used to describe the participants can indicate a bias. Mormon sympathizers use terms like "saints" and "martyrs" for Mormon participants and the term "mob" and "villains" to describe those against them, while the anti-Mormon side of the story refers to the Mormons as "fanatics" and "dupes." These terms appear within accounts written at the time that are included in this book, but throughout I refer to the Latter Day Saint participants generally as Mormons and the Missouri citizenry as volunteers, settlers, or residents.

In order to relate the history of the Mormon War it is necessary to explore the origins of Mormonism and the movements of its leaders and followers that led them ultimately to Missouri. Since one of the main charges levelled at the Mormons was their arrogance and dishonesty when interacting with non-Mormons, it is important to discover the nature of these claims. Much of what we know about the inner workings of the early church and its history up to the death of Joseph Smith, Jr., outside of official church histories, comes from affidavits and other claims by persons who were excommunicated from the church. Sometimes these persons ended up recanting their statements taken under oath when they were reconciled with the church at a later date; others stood by their statements as spoken or written. Mormon literature tends to discredit or discount contrary accounts, which is to be expected. Nonetheless, without judging the veracity of these records, they contributed to the received information of persons who came into contact with Mormons. From the moment the church was first revealed to the greater public in April 1830, newspaper accounts and books criticizing Mormonism appeared in great frequency.

I am a lawyer by profession and have brought that expertise to my interpretation of the reports and court transcripts in an effort to understand the legal proceedings and claims of governmental authority. In addition, I have traveled to the sites of many of the events of this book and include descriptions of these places to help the reader visualize the events of the Mormon War. My goal is to provide a general history of a fascinating, but tragic event in American history and one that can provide lessons for our day-to-day interactions with fellow citizens of different faiths, cultures, and circumstance.

* ONE *

FOUNDATION

IN THE EARLY NINETEENTH CENTURY, the United States was
at a crossroads where Christianity met mysticism, and
most Americans were friendly to both practices and considered them compatible. There were few churches in
many areas and travel could be hazardous; as a result,
around 1800 only about one in ten Americans was a regular churchgoer.[1] Many Americans therefore adopted folk
magic beliefs in order to express their spirituality.[2]

From 1790 to 1830 large numbers of settlers from rural
Pennsylvania and New England, including the family of
Joseph Smith, Jr., the founder of the Mormon church,
moved into upstate New York between the Adirondack
Mountains and Lake Ontario. These immigrants brought
with them a variety of religious experiences, as well as folk
practices and implements, including scrying, the use of
objects such as stones in order to obtain spiritual visions,
and divining rods. The region soon became known as the
"Burned-over District," a term popularized by the traveling revivalist Charles G. Finney, to describe the extraordinary religious exuberance that swept through the area like
a forest fire.[3] Besides Mormonism the Seventh Day
Adventist faith and other millennialist movements
emerged in upstate New York around this time. American
protestant sects, such as the Methodists, Baptists, and
Presbyterians, all saw their memberships increase here,

and the rival Universalist Church that denied evangelical warnings of eternal damnation also became popular.[4]

Although protestant faiths held revivals, most of the traveling proselytizing in upstate New York during this time incorporated some variation of folk magic.[5] During the late 1700s and early 1800s, revivalists frequently claimed divine instruction, and conversion stories regularly included a theophany or vision from God. Many Protestants considered these traveling revivalists to be bewitched and of dubious character. In 1810 one orthodox Lutheran minister claimed that any direct communication between the spiritual and human was magic and should not be practiced. This view formed the official position of mainline protestant faiths toward theophanies, despite the acceptance of the practice by a majority of the memberships. This disapproval extended to nearly all conversion narratives that included some form of angelic ministration.[6]

Several tales of theophanies were popular throughout the Northeast during this time. The theophany of Richard Brother was published in New Hampshire in the same town where Hyrum Smith, Joseph Smith, Jr.'s older brother, attended school. The 1821 theophany of fourteen-year-old Benjamin Putnam was published in Vermont, the state where Joseph was born. The library in Palmyra, New York, where young Joseph spent much of his youth, had an 1817 edition of the popular and influential theophany of Emanuel Swedenborg.[7]

The Smith family had an interest in both mainstream and folk religions, although it probably was not much greater or varied than what was typical of the time in the Burned-over District.[8] Smith's parents, Joseph Smith, Sr. and Lucy Mack-Smith, are claimed to have practiced various forms of folk magic and both were also associated with protestant churches.[9] In 1811, according to Lucy, her husband experienced his own vision in which God communicated with him directly.[10] Again in 1819 Joseph, Sr. claimed he received visions from spirit guides.[11] His brother was so concerned about Joseph, Sr.'s practices that he wrote a strongly worded letter telling him to give up his magic ways.[12] Joseph, Sr.'s visions appear to have had a major influence on Joseph Smith, Jr. and his formation of the Mormon church.[13]

Among the magic devices employed by Joseph Smith, Sr. were divining rods.[14] While the Smith family lived in Vermont, Joseph, Sr. and his friend William Cowdery, the father of future Mormon church leader Oliver Cowdery, may have been members of a religious group founded by Nathaniel Wood known as the Fraternity of Rodsmen.[15] The group thought that the hazel rod contained a magic powerful enough to answer hidden questions and locate buried treasure. They received their training in the craft of divining from a member named Winchell, who also taught Rodsmen other secret methods which could be employed in treasure digging.

The Rodsmen, according to Wood, believed that they had descended through their faith from the Israelites and that they would rightfully inherit America.[16] This tenet would find its way into the Mormon theology as well. Wood also preached that a small town in Vermont would be delivered into the Rodsmen's hands on January 14, 1802, for their control and use according to the power of God. When the Rodsmen confronted townspeople on the day appointed by Wood, they were driven from the area and forced to disband. The event was known as the "Wood Scrape."[17]

In 1816, the Smith family moved to Palmyra, New York. The Smiths were having financial difficulties at the time and it is probable they left on their own accord rather than being "warned out" by local authorities.[18] (Warning out, a kind of municipally sponsored expulsion, was a process whereby the town council identified an individual it wanted removed from the community for any number of reasons, which could include poverty, nefarious activities, or the town's simple distaste for strangers. Thereafter the council authorized the constable to notify said individual that he or she was no longer welcome in the community and should leave immediately.[19] Reverend Wood, having received his notice, relocated to New York shortly after the Scrape.) Winchell and Cowdery followed the Smiths to Palmyra in 1819; though they would not have left due to having been warned out as the technique was outlawed in Vermont in 1817.[20]

In Palmyra, both Josephs, Sr. and Jr., became involved in treasure digging for hire.[21] This was not an unusual activity at the time, and was competitive. Someone wishing to hire a treasure seeker, such as the Smiths, would designate the land, and the seeker would determine the proper incantations to enable the party to locate the treasure and confuse any spirits that guarded the same. A split hazel divining rod was used. If the rod moved, this indicated the location of treasure and digging began. Treasure seekers were compensated regardless of whether treasure was found. Generally the Smiths' endeavors ended with their employers empty-handed.[22] Joseph Smith, Jr. would later state in an interview with church historians that he had never earned much at money-digging, as he called it. He preferred the life of a prophet.[23]

Like many adolescents in America in the early 1800s, Joseph, Jr. experienced visions of God. Joseph, Jr. once said he "became interested in theology at the age of twelve."[24] In his first theophany Smith wrote: "I was filld with the spirit of God and the Lord opened the heavens upon me and I saw the Lord and he spake unto me saying Joseph my son thy Sins are forgiven thee."[25] This type of theophany was consistent with visions recorded by other children his age and similar to those in books at the local library.[26] Soon after his first vision, Smith embarked on his religious career.

In September 1819 Smith became a seer, a term interchangeable with magician or prophet.[27] It was at this point after successfully envisioning and locating his first seeing stone that he spoke of his seer status.[28] The stone as revealed to Smith was a whitish, glossy, and opaque rock buried in the neighboring land of a girl named Sally Chase. Chase was also a seer, and it was with her stone that Smith was able to determine the location of his own stone. The stone fit comfortably in his hand, but it was Smith's practice to place the stone inside his hat and peer into the hat to make his prophecies, which led many witnesses to call it his "peep stone." The use of this and other stones would be the methodology by which Smith is said to have translated the Book of Mormon. Shortly thereafter he began to offer his seer services in the Palmyra area.[29]

In his career as a seer Smith received better pay; after one successful job Smith was paid seventy-five cents. His client, Mr. Vanderhoof, asked him to look into his white stone to locate a stolen mare. After consulting his stone Smith envisioned the man's horse on a lake shore about to be taken to Canada. Smith was referring to the area's well-known horse smuggling route across the border, and on further investigation Vanderhoof located his mare in Canada. Smith's neighbors readily accepted his seer abilities and he quickly developed a steady flow of work.[30] Throughout the 1820s Smith continued to grow in prestige and extended the range of his services from Palmyra to Harmony, Pennsylvania, about thirty miles southeast of Binghamton.[31] In 1827 Smith's announcement of his discovery of what became the Book of Mormon would make him the most famous of the Palmyra area seers.

By 1825, Smith located two additional seer stones, adding to his collection and his prestige.[32] That same year Smith met his future wife, Emma Hale, while seeking treasure for her father in Harmony.[33] The two would marry in January 1827 in New York.

Smith was prosecuted in March 1826 for treasure digging in Bainbridge, New York.[34] He was tried as a "disorderly person," which was defined as a person who falsely "tells fortunes, or where lost or stolen goods may be found."[35] Certain area citizens had complained to the constable that Smith "was about the country in the character of a glass-looker: pretending to discover lost goods, hidden treasures, mines of gold and silver, etc."[36] In his defense Smith explained he had "a certain stone" with which he could locate "where hidden treasures in the bowels of the earth were."[37] Smith was eventually acquitted based on his own testimony and the supporting testimony of his father and Josiah Stowell, a client of Smith's, who both confirmed Smith's ability.[38]

It did not require a seeing stone to notice the multitudes of Indian mounds that dotted the landscape in western New York.[39] In the early 1800s most people in the area had theories about the race of people that created the mounds, their origin, and their extinction.[40] It was commonly believed that these "moundbuilders" were an agrarian people skilled in metal workings and the arts. Most locals, including Smith, believed the moundbuilders to be a peace-loving, more civilized race of Indians that were wiped out by the menacing and bloodthirsty forebears to the modern Indians during the course of a vicious war and an epic final struggle. According to legend the moundbuilders' final battle may have even occurred near the Smiths' farm.[41] A similar version of this tale appears in the text of the Book of Mormon when the Nephite tribe is destroyed by the Lamanite tribe.[42] In 1821, it was reported that diggers of the Erie Canal unearthed metal engravings described as "brass plates."[43] Joseph Smith, Jr. shared another story with a friend which reported that plates described as "a history of the Indians" were found at the base of a hollow tree in Canada.[44]

No one was more interested than Smith in the mystery of the moundbuilders, which fueled his imagination.[45] Lucy Mack-Smith, Joseph's mother, remembered that prior to 1823 her son began creating entertaining stories about the moundbuilders and their history for his family. At some point between 1820 and 1827 Smith determined to compile a written history of the moundbuilders basing his work on the popular theories of the day.[46]

According to his friend and neighbor Peter Ingersoll, Smith, having heard about the Canadian "brass plates," was inspired one day in 1827 to stop along his way home and filled his frock with white sand.* When he arrived home Smith announced his clothing concealed "the golden Bible." To his surprise Smith's family believed him and asked to see the plates. Even his younger brother William Smith, who would later follow Joseph to Missouri, put aside the sibling rivalry because of the intriguing revelation. Smith quickly made an excuse as to why the plates could not be exposed; he explained that if viewed with the naked eye the viewer would surely die. Again his family believed him and even left the room when he offered to show the plates despite the grim warning. Smith purportedly confided in Ingersoll that the "golden plates" never existed but were made up as a joke to fool his family.[47]

Soon everyone wanted to know how the young man found these golden plates, not readily viewable with the naked eye. Smith claimed that in 1823 a spirit revealed to him that he should possess and translate an ancient text on golden plates created by the moundbuilders which would be the completion of God's holy word. According to Smith, due to an unfortunate series of delays and deviations the spirit would not allow him to recover the plates for four years. Finally in 1827 the spirit guided Smith to a hill not far from his father's farm and permitted him to retrieve the golden Bible.[48] It has been suggested that Emanuel Swedenborg's theophany, a book in Smith's hometown library, was an inspiration for Smith's own plate discovery.[49] In it, Swedenborg, too, is visited by a spir-

---

*This and other first-person accounts of the Smith family and early Mormon history were collected under oath by disgruntled ex-Mormon Philastus Hurlbut in 1833. These accounts were widely circulated and continue to be used in interpreting the origins of Mormonism, with their details being used both to support the faith and to discredit it.

it who wishes to deliver sacred writings to mankind: "on a certain night, a man appeared to him in the midst of a strong shining light, and said, 'I am God the Lord, the Creator, and Redeemer; I have chosen thee to explain to men the interiour and spiritual sense of the sacred writings. I will dictate to thee what thou oughtest to write.'"[50]

Smith immediately began to translate the plates with the use of his seer stone. By 1828, however, the work became difficult because it was widely rumored around Palmyra that Smith had unearthed a great treasure, and everyone wanted to see it.[51] It was not long until rival treasure diggers attempted to locate the golden Bible and steal it from Smith. The thieves were unable to find the plates; Smith later explained he had foreseen the attempted theft and moved them from their hiding place. Despite these setbacks and the fact that no one had yet seen the plates, Smith was able to secure a local farmer, Martin Harris, as his patron to finance their translation.[52]

It soon became evident to Joseph, Jr. that he could not work at his parents' house owing to the eagerness of his family and neighbors to view the unseen plates and the translation process. He moved to the house of his wife's parents in Harmony in order to continue the translation.[53] His wife, Emma, became Smith's first scribe. She did not actually see the plates but said they often lay on the table wrapped in a small linen tablecloth while Joseph worked on the translation. The process required only that Smith stare into his seer stone to translate the text, which was written in "reformed Egyptian."[54]

In April 1829 Joseph, Jr. met Oliver Cowdery, the son of William Cowdery. Shortly thereafter Oliver replaced Emma as Smith's scribe and the two began collaborating on the translation of the gold plates.[55] Cowdery, Harris, and David Whitmer, an acquaintance of Cowdery's, stated that they were able to see the gold plates through an angelic vision. In addition to these three witnesses, eight others, members of the Smith and Whitmer families, claimed to have seen and handled the actual plates at the invitation of Joseph Smith.[56] Once the translation was completed, Smith related that he returned the plates to the angel who had originally given them to him.

Smith's golden Bible would later be called the Book of Mormon, named for a character in the book who ensured that the text was saved for future readers. Followers of Smith's new religion would also carry the name Mormons for this reason. In 1831 Hyrum Smith begged his brother to elaborate on the finding of the plates, but Smith refused to do so until 1838, more than a decade after their discovery. In that year he described finding the plates as follows:

> He [the spirit] had on a loose robe of most exquisite whiteness. . . . His hands were naked and his arms also, a little above the wrist, so also were his feet naked, as were his legs, a little above the ankles. His head and neck were also bare . . . his whole person was glorious beyond description, and his countenance truly like lightning. . . . He called me by name, and said unto me that he was a messenger sent from the presence of God to me and that his name was Moroni; that God had a work for me to do; and that my name should be had for good and evil among all nations, kindreds, and tongues, or that it should be both good and evil spoken of among all people. He said there was a book deposited, written upon gold plates, giving an account of the former inhabitants of this continent, and the sources from whence they sprang. He also said that the fullness of the everlasting Gospel was contained in it, as delivered by the Savior to the ancient inhabitants; also that there were two stones in silver bows—and these stones, fastened to a breastplate, constituted what is called the Urim and Thummim—deposited with the plates; and the possession and use of these stones were what constituted "Seers" in ancient or former times; and that God had prepared them for the purpose of translating the book.[57]

On April 6, 1830, three years after discovering the gold-
en Bible, Smith established his church and copies of the
Book of Mormon were distributed.[58] Evangelism was part
of the church's ministry, and Smith sent converts out as
missionaries to gain new members. With this publicity
came rapid condemnation in newspapers from far afield.
On April 16, the *Rhode-Island American* reported:

> The following singular evidence of human credulity or
> knavery, appears in the *New York Rochester Republican*:
> Blasphemy—"Book of Mormon," alias The Golden
> Bible.
>   The "Book of Mormon" has been placed in our
> hands. A viler imposition was never practised. It is
> evidence of fraud, blasphemy and credulity, shocking
> to the Christian and moralist. The "author and pro-
> prietor" is one "Joseph Smith, Jr."—a fellow who, by
> some hocus pocus, acquired such an influence over a
> wealthy farmer of Wayne county, that the latter mort-
> gaged his farm for $3000, which he paid for printing
> and binding 5000 copies of the blasphemous work.
> The volume consists of about 600 pages, and is divid-
> ed into the books of Nephi, of Jacob, of Mosiah, of
> Alma, of Mormon, of Ether and of Helaman. "Copy
> right secured!"[59]

Joseph Smith anticipated the negative reaction to his
claims, already noting in his preface to the Book of
Mormon that "many false reports have been circulated
respecting the following work, and also many unlawful
measures taken by evil designing persons to destroy me
and also the work." In less than a year, Smith and his followers would begin a series of flights westward.

TWO

MISSOURI

T HE TERRITORY THAT EVENTUALLY became known as Missouri was first explored by the French in the seventeenth century. The French sought silver but instead found a plentiful supply of lead ore. Lead mined in southeast Missouri was used for bullets throughout the struggle for America. Control over the territory was transferred between the French and Spanish crown until the rights were finally purchased by the United States from France in 1803.[1]

As the War of 1812 ended, many soldiers made their way west to settle the new territory and a land rush began in Missouri. When Missouri petitioned to enter the United States of America on January 18, 1818, it was the twenty-third most populous state out of twenty-six. Missouri had more residents than Illinois or any of the other seven states added to the union since the original thirteen colonies.[2] According to the April 16, 1821, edition of the *Missouri Intelligencer,* the population statewide was 66,604 and by the end of the year had reached 70,647.[3] Missouri was admitted to the union on August 10, 1821.[4] During its first decade as a state the population doubled and by 1830 Missouri's population reached 140,304.[5]

St. Louis was the population center of Missouri during this time. The outlying portions of the state were mainly wilderness or small settlements. The first settlers who migrated to the Missouri Territory in large numbers came from Virginia, Kentucky, Tennessee, North and South Carolina, and Georgia.[6] In later years more Americans from the New England regions also began to migrate to Missouri.

The political climate in the United States from 1818 to 1821 was divided. Having just defeated the British Empire, Americans turned their focus westward and toward expansion. The thorny issue of slavery, which the founding fathers had avoided in order to preserve the fragile union, would once again be debated as the U.S. border continued its westward movement.

When the nation was formed there were seven free states and six slave states. In order to balance the voting powers among the states, a policy was implemented that would alternate between admitting a slave state and a free state. Alabama was admitted in December 1819, despite having applied for statehood after Missouri. By allowing Alabama to enter before Missouri, Congress created a dilemma in that the next state into the Union must be a free state. Slavery was allowed in its state constitution so Missouri's petition for statehood upset the balance of power and was thus passed over until March 6, 1820. When the petition was finally taken up, New York Representative James Tallmadge introduced a resolution to allow Missouri in as a free state with several conditions, which would require a ban on slavery in the state.[7]

Within Missouri there was a debate over the issue of slavery. Whatever their beliefs, all Missourians were outraged and disappointed to see Congress delay their application for statehood. The *Missouri Gazette* expressed the sentiment of many Missourians about Tallmadge's resolution, contending that the issue of slavery in Missouri should be decided only by Missourians, not dictated by Congress. If Missouri was to be admitted as a state then it should be able to make its own decisions regarding how to deal with the issue of slavery.[8]

The issue was the political topic of the day and was debated throughout the country. Ministers even weighed in. The Baptist Association went as far as to agree that although slavery was bad, it was an issue for the people of each state to decide.[9] Former President Thomas Jefferson was seriously concerned over the issue of Missouri's admission. In December 1819 at the age of seventy-six he wrote to retired President John Adams saying: "The banks, bankrupt law, manufacturers, Spanish treaty are nothing. Those are occurrences which like waves in a storm will pass under the ship. But the Missouri question is a breaker on which we lose the Missouri country by revolt and what more God only knows. From the battle of Bunker Hill to the treaty of Paris, we never had so ominous a question."[10] Later Jefferson wrote another friend, Hugh Nelson, stating that: "The Missouri question is the most portentous one which ever yet threatened our Union. In the gloomiest moment of the Revolutionary War I never had any apprehension equal to what I feel from this source."[11]

By the time Maine petitioned to be a state in December 1819 it was proposed in the Senate that Maine enter as a free state and Missouri enter as a slave state. However, by this point the majority of northerners in the House of Representatives felt Missouri should be compelled to enter the Union as a free state.[12] The Speaker of the House, Henry Clay of Kentucky, took the side of Missouri and pointed out that it was unfair to dictate the terms of Missouri's constitution when no such restriction was being imposed upon Maine.[13] Equality was equality, Clay argued, no matter from which part of the country one came. Clay's argument for equality among states while contemporaneously supporting the subjugation of one race by another in slavery seems ironic if not contradictory. Nonetheless, his support was applauded and appreciated by the people of Missouri.

A compromise was reached whereby Missouri and Maine would both be allowed into the Union and that the parallel 36°30 (roughly the border between Tennessee and

Kentucky) would mark the northern limit of slavery in the western territories. When the Missouri Compromise was finally put to a vote in the House it passed 134 to 42. Virginia Congressman John Randolph was outraged, insisting slavery laws should be decided at a state level, and asked that the bill be reconsidered. Speaker Clay blocked the re-vote by claiming that procedurally the motion of Congressman Randolph was out of order. While other issues were addressed that morning, Clay signed the bill and delivered it to the Senate where it easily passed. On March 6, 1820, President James Monroe signed the bill into law allowing Missouri to become a state.[14]

But it was not yet part of the Union. On March 2, 1821, President Monroe passed a resolution adding a restriction that Missouri could only become a state as long as it never tried to enact a law to enforce section 26 of its constitution, which provided that free blacks and mulattoes from other states could not live in Missouri. Despite their bravado the governor, state legislature, and state senate were not about to lose the approval of Missouri's statehood over a technicality.[15] They approved Monroe's restriction on June 26, 1821, and Missouri officially entered the Union on August 10, 1821, after Monroe finally ratified its admission.[16]

While the Missouri Territory was still a possession of Spain, an edict was executed that forbade the importation of slaves to its borders. The Spanish monarch believed that the threat of slave uprisings, like those experienced by the French in Haiti, outweighed the benefit of the labor they provided. As a result the slave population in St. Louis was never large.[17] In fact, during the territorial days many blacks were freed for good service. Free blacks were allowed to own real estate and 1805 records indicate there were many black landowners in St. Louis.[18] Despite the liberal attitude toward African Americans in St. Louis, in the remainder of the state whites were unkind toward free blacks and sought to exclude them.

A homestead in Missouri around the year 1832. (*Library of Congress*)

During the national controversy of Missouri's admission, emigrants continued to pour into the state from Illinois, Kentucky, and Virginia, bringing with them trains of slaves.[19] Slave owners tended to be the best educated of the emigrants to the state. Despite the growing number of pro-slavery residents during the statehood controversy, a significant anti-slavery sentiment remained in much of Missouri. The Tallmadge Act, which sought to impose emancipation as a condition for Missouri's admission to the Union, steeled the resolve of the Missouri General Assembly that no restrictions on slavery would be included in Missouri's constitution.[20] Missourians generally felt that Congress's restrictions on the state constitution were unjust and unreasonable. Despite the putative progress mandated by Monroe's restrictions on the Missouri constitution and the abolitionist sentiments of many St. Louisians, conditions in Missouri were so bad for people of color that few chose to come to the state.[21]

Due to the debate over slavery during the admission process, all anti-slavery candidates were for a time defeated in Missouri state elections.[22] However, by 1828, the anti-slavery movement again gained traction in Missouri. Present at a secret conference were such leading politicians as Democrat Senator Thomas Hart Benton, a man opposed to mainstream Jacksonian Democrats and who would later oppose Jackson-groomed successor President James K. Polk, and Judge David Barton, a Whig. It was resolved by both Democrats and Whigs that the parties should work together to eliminate slavery. The meeting resulted in the preparation of a pamphlet supporting emancipation to be distributed to voters. Just before the pamphlet's release, Missourians became outraged by news that in New York a politician allowed his daughter to entertain several African American gentlemen in his home. The populace once again became polarized; the pamphlets were shelved.[23]

Perhaps because of their support of the anti-slavery movement, the Missouri constitution prohibited all "bishops, priests, clergymen or teacher of any religious persuasion" to be a member of the General Assembly.[24] One such clergyman was Elijah Lovejoy, a pro-Whig supporter of Henry Clay. Lovejoy had moved to Missouri from Maine and begun his career as a teacher and journalist. He converted to the Presbyterian Church in a religious revival in 1831-1832.[25] In 1834 he declared he was against slavery and turned his journalistic talents to preaching the evils of slavery. Just outside the St. Louis region, on November 7, 1837, Lovejoy was killed by an angry mob that had come to destroy his printing press in an effort to silence the emancipation message.[26]

Missouri's early economy was tied to fur trade with the native peoples and a lead mining boom in what is today southeastern Missouri. The lead deposits initially supplied bullets to the French, who used them during their expansion in North America, including the defeat of General Edward Braddock and his aide-de-camp George Washington during their march on Fort Duquesne in 1755 at the start of the French and Indian War. Later the colonists would rely upon its supply during the revolution for ammunition used to win their freedom from the

British. By 1838, a Prussian immigrant by the name of Hagan had invented a smelting system whereby the worthless and leftover bits of ore could be reclaimed to make useable lead. It revolutionized the lead mining in Missouri and the industry was reborn.[27]

While the fur trading posts were the economic heart of the St. Louis community, the grist mills served this function in rural parts of Missouri.[28] They were where the local populace gathered to trade news, goods, and information.

In 1832, President Andrew Jackson vetoed a bill to renew the Bank of the United States's charter and sent the country into a cash flow shortage.[29] As the U.S. Bank would no longer be printing its own money, each state would be required to take on the responsibility of either chartering a state bank or allowing private institutions to issue paper currency. Other alternatives included trading goods in kind or using precious metals. Missouri wanted to keep its branch of the United States Bank and anti-Jackson sentiment ran high in response to the veto.

Initially Missouri relied on a banking company from Cincinnati for its banking needs, but it did not take long for Missourians to demand a local moneylender.[30] By 1837 the St. Louis Chamber of Commerce sent a petition to Congress demanding a National Bank. When the request fell on deaf ears, Missouri chartered its own bank, which soon became the standard bearer in the United States for safe and secure banking and currency.[31] The Bank of Missouri was one of the only banks in the United States that produced a currency accepted beyond its geographical region.[32] This was in large part due to the strict and conservative standards for lending imposed by John O'Fallon, the bank president.[33] O'Fallon had faithfully run the Missouri branch of the United States Bank since 1815. He was well liked and well respected in St. Louis. It had taken the Missouri branch of the United States Bank two years to raise the capital from within the state in order to operate, but the state-chartered bank took only two months.[34] This confidence was a direct reflection of the state's belief in O'Fallon's ability as a banker.

It was vital for Missouri's economy that the bank stay strong. St. Louis was a huge importer of Spanish goods by means of the Santa Fe Trail, which by 1825 passed through Independence, Missouri, on its way to its final destination. Once in St. Louis Spanish goods and silver were traded or sold.[35] The Spaniards brought silver dollars and the Missourians exchanged bank notes drawn on the Bank of Missouri.[36] Each caravan would exchange between $10,000 and $100,000 worth of silver dollars in a single journey. Banking regulations were so tight that by 1839 the Bank of Missouri accepted only its own bank notes or precious metals. This practice proved wise when the nation was beset by a three-year depression. During that time over $600 million in debt was discharged in bankruptcy and values declined by approximately $2 billion. Throughout it all the Bank of Missouri survived.[37]

Yet the stability and security of Missouri's financial institution did not reflect the general atmosphere in the State at that time. During its territorial days, Governor William Clark (the expedition partner of Meriwether Lewis) was the longtime leader of the region. After obtaining statehood, Alexander McNair defeated Clark in an election for governor. McNair declined a second term and was followed by a rapid succession of subsequent governors. Frederick Bates died of pleurisy during his term. His successor, Abraham J. Williams, served only five months. John Miller became the next governor, and in 1832, his lieutenant governor, Daniel Dunklin, the Jacksonian candidate, won in a close vote despite the unpopularity of Jackson's bank charter veto.[38]

The capital of Missouri was moved in 1826 from St. Charles to present-day Jefferson City due to a requirement in the first constitution requiring the capital to be located on the Missouri River within forty miles of the mouth of the Osage River.[39] The Capitol building burned in 1837 and was not rebuilt for three years. The government was in dire need of funds and in 1831 it legalized gambling in the form of state-authorized lotteries. The state was also wracked by the specter of dueling, a phe-

"6 cents. Humbug glory bank." This fake note was issued in satirical response to the financial panic of 1837 when hard currency alone was generally accepted around the country to counter the financial speculation of paper bank notes whose values were not guaranteed by bullion. Missouri Senator Thomas Hart Benton was a hard-money advocate and therefore this note is payable to "Tumble Humbug Benton." The panic and subsequent depression caused hundreds of private and state banks to close across the country in the late 1830s, including the Kirtland Safety Society Bank founded by the Mormon Church. (*Library of Congress*)

nomenon among the wealthy and influential that was so out of control that by 1822 the legislature considered a bill that made death from a duel chargeable as murder. The bill also would have banned those who participated in such events from holding a public office. The proposal seems reasonable considering the number of early Missouri government leaders involved in the practice. Among them were the brother of Governor Bates and Senator Thomas Hart Benton. Ironically, when Bates was presented with a bill that would punish duelists with lashes by a cat'o-nine-tails, he refused to sign it.[40]

The French had good relations and almost continual peace with the Indians during the time they controlled the Louisiana Territory. The territory, which encompassed Missouri, was controlled by the French from 1682 to 1763 when they ceded it to Spain, only to regain it again briefly from 1800–1803 before selling it to the United States as the Louisiana Purchase.[41] Like the French, the Spanish

also had a good relationship with the native peoples in the
area. Groups of Delaware and Shawnee, Algonquian tribes
originally from Pennsylvania and Ohio who were driven
west by the British, ended up settling in Missouri in the
late eighteenth century. The Spanish decided to relocate
them to the St. Louis region to act as a buffer between the
Spanish settlers and the wilder western peoples.[42] The
Americans under Territorial Governor Clark treated the
American Indians well when they assumed control of the
Louisiana Territory.[43] Each year during Clark's tenure,
after the first thaw Indians from all over the Missouri
Territory would make an annual pilgrimage to St. Louis
where they honored Clark. This loyalty proved decisive
during the War of 1812 when British agents attempted to
turn them against the Americans.[44]

Missouri's fortunes changed after the war and Clark's
departure from office. More immigrants moved to the area
and this increased the tension between the Indians and
the settlers.[45] Moving forward, constant strife and distrust
burned between the native peoples and the Missourians.
Indian groups who had been forced to migrate from the
east such as the Osage, Shawnee, and Delaware were well
acquainted with the settlers and caused few problems. It
was the northern peoples such as the Sac, Fox, Iowas, and
Pottawatomies who, with British encouragement, would
often travel south hundreds of miles to attack settlers
along the Missouri River and stir up trouble.[46] Even after
the War of 1812, British agents continued to entice
Indians friendly to them to attack American settlers.[47] The
British relied heavily upon the Sac for their support in
these efforts.

In July 1829, Sac Chief Big Neck was involved in what
was later described as the Big Neck War. In fact his group
was mistakenly attacked by settlers who believed them to
be a war party. Chief Big Neck ordered his warriors to fight
back in defense and the ensuing struggle was labeled further proof of Indian aggression against the Anglo settlers.
General David R. Atchison, a future U.S. senator, took part
in bringing Chief Big Neck to trial, where he was eventu-

ally acquitted of any wrongdoing. Nonetheless, the so-
called war exhibits the uneasiness of Missouri frontiers-
men and their inclination to react to any outside group,
whether benign or not, as a threat.

Ultimately Missouri began to press for the removal of
American Indians from its borders. The Osage were
removed to the Indian Territory, now known as Oklahoma,
and in 1829 the Shawnee and Delaware were relocated to
the Leavenworth region, in present-day Kansas.[48] The legislature annexed certain lands set aside for Indians called
the Platte, an area which today makes up the northwest
corner of Missouri. These Indians were also pushed into
Kansas and Oklahoma to make room for continued settler
expansion.

By the 1830s Missouri was dominated by a majority of
slave-owning southern immigrants. It was soon beset by a
new wave of immigrants whose differences with Missouri
residents revolved less around slavery than religion.

* THREE *

KIRTLAND, OHIO

JOSEPH SMITH, NOW TWENTY-SIX YEARS OLD, relocated his
church's headquarters to Kirtland, Ohio, in February
1831.[1] The town was about 300 miles southwest of Palmyra
along Lake Erie, not far from Cleveland. The move came
after Smith was once again indicted on charges of disorderly conduct, specifically the performance of an exorcism
on Newel Knight in Colesville, New York, on June 27, 1830,
during a church meeting.[2] Many guests were convinced by
Smith's display of spiritual authority and were baptized as
new converts on that Sunday evening.

The New York authorities arrested Smith the next day
before the new converts had received their confirmation
ceremony. The trial began on Tuesday the 29th at 10 A.M.
in South Bainbridge, New York. Smith's trial lasted two
days and two nights before he was acquitted by Justice of
the Peace Joseph Chamberlain of disorderly conduct at
midnight on June 30.[3] Smith's attorney John Reid was so
exhausted that when Smith was rearrested on July 1 on
separate charges of disorderly conduct, he seriously considered declining the representation.[4]

The subsequent case was heard by three justices and
Smith was again acquitted after a trial lasting one day and
night.[5] Following his second acquittal, an angry mob

formed to harm him. With the assistance of his lawyer and the town constable, Smith was able to escape.[6] In a few days Smith and Cowdery returned to the home of Newel Knight to confirm the new church converts. The pair came after nightfall feeling emboldened by Smith's latest revelation that they would be delivered from their enemies. Not long after they had arrived, word spread and vigilantes gathered, intent on capturing Smith; Cowdery and Smith immediately evacuated the premises.[7] The posse followed Smith and Cowdery through the night but the two successfully evaded them and returned to their homes at dawn.[8] This was the final straw for Smith, and he received a revelation to take his handful of New York followers, approximately twenty-seven members—most of whom were friends and relations—to Kirtland, Ohio, where a recent convert, Sidney Rigdon, a former Campbellite minister, had converted his entire congregation to the Mormon church.[9] Smith believed Mormon religious practices would not be interfered with there.

Once settled in Kirtland, Smith began a series of revelations and took steps to consolidate his rule and the inner workings of the church. In an early Mormon text, the Book of Commandments, Smith encouraged a communistic approach dubbed the "Kirtland Order." Smith instructed his followers to "consecrate" all their property to the church. This included deeding their real property and giving all their income to his church, which would then be responsible for providing for all its members. The Kirtland Order was intended to eliminate poverty by ensuring that all Mormons were provided for. The congregation was not wealthy to begin with, and since it had to support Smith and his chosen leaders at some cost, it began to take a financial toll on the struggling Mormon population of about 200 persons.[10]

Initially, Smith was viewed as a prophet among potentially many prophets. A prophet was responsible for receiving and revealing God's instructions to his people and held great prominence in the congregation. An article in the *Painesville* (Ohio) *Gazette* from February 1831, states that,

They [the Mormons] profess to receive sensible demonstration of the Deity. A few days since, a young man gave information to some of his brethren that he was about to receive a message from heaven. They repaired to the spot designated, and there as they solemnly assert, a letter descended from the skies, and fell into the hand of the young man. The purport was to strengthen his faith and inform him that he would soon be called to the ministry. They declare their solemn belief that this letter was written in heaven by the finger of God. The style of writing was round Italian, and the letters of gold. The favored youth immediately attempted to copy the communication, but as fast as he wrote, the letters of the original disappeared until it entirely vanished.[11]

Seeing no limitation on the number of prophets allowed under church law, Hiram Page, brother-in-law of the Whitmers and one of the eight witnesses who swore to having handled the golden plates, began using a seer stone and introducing new revelations affecting Smith's church and "the golden Bible." Threatened by Page's interference, Smith put a quick stop to the putative prophet's efforts by revealing word that God had made Smith the exclusive prophet of the new church. Even though Page was no longer considered a prophet in the church, Smith also smashed Page's seer stone to ensure that he could no longer use it to impede Smith's control over the organization. Smith's revelation declared, "no one shall be appointed to receive commandments and revelations in this Church excepting my servant Joseph Smith, Jr., for he receiveth them even as Moses."[12]

Another revelation received at this time which helped Smith to consolidate his hold on the young church was as follows: "There is none other appointed to you to receive commandments and revelations until he be taken. If he abide in me . . . none else shall be appointed unto this gift except it be through him [Smith] for if he be taken from him he shall not have power except to appoint another in his stead."[13]

Essentially this revelation confirmed Smith as the sole prophet of the church and that this role could not be usurped by another unless and until Smith authorized it. This rule applied even if Smith became a "fallen" prophet; that is, if he lost God's authority to receive and reveal instructions to the church, he would have the power to "appoint another in his stead." How Smith could become fallen is not clear. Nonetheless, with this revelation Smith guaranteed his authority to determine his successor. This particular clause would have great significance during the aftermath of the Mormon War. The revelation contradicts an 1829 revelation recorded in the Book of Command-ments, which states that Smith "has a gift to translate the Book of Mormon, and I [God] have commanded him that he shall pretend no other gift, for I will grant him no other gift."[14] All but a few copies of the Book of Commandments were destroyed by fire when the Mormons were run out of Jackson County, Missouri, in 1833, however. Smith issued the Doctrine and Covenants in 1835 without the contra-diction. The new text was changed as follows: "and you have a gift to translate the plates; and this is the first gift that I bestowed to you; and I have commanded you that you should pretend no other gift until my purpose is ful-filled in this; for I will grant unto you no other until it is finished."[15]

It was not until his son Joseph Smith III wrote a trea-tise on the discrepancies between the Book of Command-ments and the Doctrine and Covenants that they were explained. The younger Smith wrote that the Doctrine and Covenants was authorized by the church and God but the Book of Commandments was not, and therefore the Doctrine and Covenants was controlling.[16] David Whitmer, a leader in the church and New York convert, explained that "In a few years they had gone away ahead of the written word, so they had to change the revela-tions." Early church historian Orson Pratt writing in the 1870s also acknowledged the retroactive changes the Doctrine and Covenants made from the Book of Commandments.[17] These changes were necessary to make the original revelations consistent with Smith's new role as church president with exclusive right to announce revelation. Smith used these changes in order to consolidate his power and prevent charismatic upstarts from threatening his organization and authority.[18]

One such threat was a young convert by the name of Philastus Hurlbut, who was four years Smith's junior, and in June 1833 was excommunicated from the church by Smith for "unchristian conduct with the ladies."[19] Some suggest that the true reason Smith sought to silence Hurlbut was his rival's knowledge of and wish to broadcast the early occult and magical origins of Smith's church, while Smith hoped that by discrediting Hurlbut he could bury the non-Christian origins of his church and draw in more converts.[20] After his excommunication, Hurlbut made it his goal to learn more about the beginning of the church and expose Smith for the fraud he believed him to be. Hurlbut claimed to have evidence that the Book of Mormon was copied from an unpublished historical novel about the mound-building ancestors of the Indians written by Solomon Spaulding in the early nineteenth century. Hurlbut also interviewed many people familiar with the origins of the church from Palmyra.[21] In late 1833 Hurlbut began lecturing in Kirtland and surrounding towns about his research and findings. He taught that Smith was deeply involved in the occult and that he had made up the story of the "golden Bible" and simply stolen the story from Spaulding's writings. His church, according to Hurlbut, was built on a foundation of lies and manipulations. Many of the New York Mormons were superstitious and believed in witchcraft, but this information did not play well to the Ohio audience.[22]

The lectures caused a furor. Orson Hyde, a church leader, wrote: "They had fired the minds of the people with much indignation against Joseph and the Church." Another leader, Heber Kimball, wrote that reported enemies "were raging and threatening destruction upon us [the church] and we had to guard ourselves night after night and for weeks were not permitted to take off our clothes."[23] Problems were arising not just from outside the church. Apprehensive converts began questioning church leaders like Martin Harris and Oliver Cowdery to get more details about the "golden plates." Harris had the misfortune to have reported that Smith had drunk too much liquor while translating the Book of Mormon and was nearly excommunicated from the church himself. Realizing his mistake, Harris changed his story to state that Smith's consumption of liquor was simply before and not during the translation process.[24] The effect of the lectures was so profound that Smith became concerned about the effect on his followers. Realizing that the rumor mill would eventually destroy his grip on power, Smith decided on a counteroffensive against Hurlbut.[25] Smith obtained a copy of every affidavit published by Hurlbut against him and read them aloud to his followers, denouncing the statements as the work of Satan.[26] Sidney Rigdon began to publicly attack Hulburt's character with an unusual flair for obscenity.[27]

Hurlbut was so enraged by these tactics that he threatened to take Smith's life. With witnesses to substantiate Hurlbut's actions, he was charged with threatening murder, and tried and convicted in April 1834. He served six months in jail. The effect of the conviction was to shatter Hurlbut's influence permanently. He cut his losses and sold his material to local newspaper editor Eber D. Howe for five hundred dollars. Howe published Hurlbut's finding in a volume under his own name called *Mormonism Unvailed*, and continued the assault on Smith. Smith survived the Howe storm as well, simply telling his church the contents were all lies. His followers took Smith at his word, without further question on the subject. Even those who suspected that the Hurlbut allegations were true took the position that it didn't matter what Smith had done because the spiritual doctrine would save them.[28] Despite the controvery, the church had a message, the faithful believed, that was directly from God and would therefore save their souls.

The first general conference of Smith's church in Ohio was scheduled in Kirtland June 3 through 6, 1831. The general conference was held once a quarter during the early days of the church and is now an annual gathering where church membership comes together to celebrate, learn, teach, and preach. During a conference, it is not unusual for new revelations to be published or church-wide events to be announced. On the first day of the conference Smith was said to have healed a deaf man. Approached by a man with a deformed hand the same day, Smith was unable to heal it, but it was still a popular belief during this time that physical afflictions were a manifesta-tion of sin and therefore not always reponsive to faith healing. Smith sent his leaders on a mission to find more injured or sick people to bring before him. One convert with a deathly ill child was discouraged from seeking medical treatment by the church elders so that Smith could demonstrate his skills. Smith could not cure the child, who soon died. (Earlier, Smith had lost his own twins, Thaddeus and Louisa Smith, who had died on the day of their birth, April 30, 1831.) The child's death soured the mood of the conference and some attendees turned hostile toward Smith.[29]

Newel Knight, previously an exorcism subject and now a leader in the church, brought startling news on the sec-ond day of the conference: Ohio converts Leman Copley and Ezra Thayer were rescinding their generous gifts to the church of real estate in Thompson, Ohio. Thompson was sixteen and a half miles from Kirtland and was selected as the future site of the Mormon temple. Furthermore the two intended to evict the New York "trespassers." This was just the first of many such rescinded gifts. After the setbacks of the first two days, Sidney Rigdon dismissed the conference a day and a half early to avoid further turmoil.[30]

Joseph Smith's next revelations had a profound effect on the history of his church. Right after the first general conference, Smith and Rigdon traveled to Missouri. Here, Smith revealed, was Zion, and the town of Independence in Jackson County was the centerplace for the Mormon temple. Smith would call all believers to Missouri. Returning to Ohio, Smith instructed a large group of converts led by Edward Partridge, who had recently arrived from New York, to be the first to settle the new land.

Having followed the Kirtland Order, many converts began to worry after the failed June conference because they had deeded their property to the church. On October 25 and 26, 1831, Smith held another general conference at the home of Sirenes Burnett with close to one hundred members in attendance. Acting quickly to encourage members not to continue to rescind their gifts to his church, Smith announced his recent revelations from God. He instructed his followers that the Mormons were spiritually descended from the Israelites and would be given their own kingdom just like the Israelites when they left bondage in Egypt. God's new chosen people, the Mormons, were to go to the land of their inheritance, Zion. Zion was the location where God's Kingdom would return to earth from heaven. It would occur, Smith said, in Independence, Missouri.[31] According to Oliver Cowdery, "the direction in which himself and David Whitmer," his fellow believer, or brother in Mormon usage, "had received this morning respecting the choice of the twelve [apostles] was that they would be ordained and sent forth from the land of Zion."[32] Smith promised any property that Mormons gave to his church in Ohio would be returned to them tenfold in Missouri. The revelation revived the excitement among his followers, and preparations began to settle the land of Zion.

Smith believed that the frontier, which Independence certainly was at the time, would be the ideal place for his church to succeed because no one there could have deep roots and the relative isolation would force cooperation between believers.[33] Smith announced that the next conference would be in Independence where a glorious temple to the Lord would be built.[34]

Despite the dramatic revelation, with the failed June conference still in recent memory, many church members

delayed in leaving for the Missouri frontier. Smith consequently issued a prophecy threatening those who would
not go.[35] Most went, but some left the church. Among
those who traveled first to Missouri were Oliver Cowdery,
Frederick Williams, and Peter Whitmer (David and John's
brother), whose specific mission was to convert the
Indians to Mormonism.[36] The Indians were seen as progeny of the Lamanites described in the Book of Mormon
and thus the Mormon people's spiritual forebears.[37]

On March 8, 1832, Smith appointed counselors Jesse
Gause, originally a Quaker and Shaker from Pennsylvania,
and Sidney Rigdon to be the number two and three leaders in the church behind Smith.[38] Gause was sent back
east to proselytize to his Shaker brethren about
Mormonism. By August that year Gause was an utter failure as a missionary; he had not even been able to convince
his wife to convert. Gause decided to leave the church and
was excommunicated.[39] While Gause was back east, Smith
traveled to Missouri to view the progress in establishing a
new foothold for the church. Rigdon was left in charge of
Kirtland during this time. Tiring of his role as third in
command, Rigdon attempted to take control of the church
in Smith's absence. He shared a revelation that the
"Kingdom" had been taken from the church and given
directly to Rigdon. He soon had the Ohio congregation
following his orders. Smith's brother Hyrum, who had
stayed behind in Kirtland, raced to Missouri with news of
Rigdon's actions.[40] The coup was short lived, and when
Smith returned on July 2 he stripped Rigdon of his powers in the church. By the 28th the two had mended the rift
and Rigdon was ordained to the "High Priesthood." Smith
explained the move by saying that Rigdon had earned a
second chance after he repented "like Peter of old."[41]
Smith also appointed Dr. Frederick G. Williams to replace
the wayward Gause as the second in command counselor.[42] Williams was originally from Connecticut but by

1830 he was living in northern Ohio and was among the earliest converts to the Mormon faith in the area.[43] Smith dubbed the leadership arrangement as the "Presidency and Two Counselors." In March 1833, a year after its creation, Smith confirmed the institution of the Two Counselors was coequal to him acting alone as president.[44]

Much controversy arose when Oliver Cowdery, Smith's first nonfamily member convert and Book of Mormon scribe, was not chosen to replace Gause as the second in command of the church. Smith told Cowdery that he was not appointed due to his "acts of adultery," without further elaboration.[45] By 1834 Cowdery had redeemed himself and on December 4 he was conferred the title of assistant president. His new role, though technically not higher than Williams or Rigdon, was administratively more powerful than the other two leaders. Smith and Cowdery were understood to have joint control over the church.[46] Joseph Smith, Sr. was also given a role in the new leadership hierarchy as patriarch.[47] Never veering far from his occult roots, Smith, Sr. would later, in his official capacity, declare that treasure digging was sanctioned and encouraged by the church.[48] Despite his close relationship with the prophet, Cowdery never got over initially being passed over for church leadership because of an apparent double standard. Cowdery would later be excommunicated when he publicly discussed as fact Smith's affair with Fanny Alger from 1833 to 1836.[49]

Following the events of the first conference and the revelation of Zion, Smith revealed that the conduct of all forms of government—including local, regional, and national—were within his control as the head of the church.[50] Unlike Thomas Jefferson's one-time vice president Aaron Burr, who intended to establish a second country west of the Mississippi River, the Mormon plan given subsequent events was simply to take control through the existing political framework. However, once duly elected to power in the United States, Smith intended to replace the republic with a theocracy with himself at the head.[51] By March 1832 Smith's approach to government domination, which he would attempt again in Missouri, led to mob violence. In Kirtland, vigilantes led by former church members targeted Mormon leadership. Rigdon and Smith were attacked in their homes in the middle of the night.[52] Neither man, nor his family, was harmed and they were allowed to stay in their homes and keep their property; but the message had been sent: stay out of politics.

Not to be intimidated, Smith made a bold revelation on theocracy. He instructed Mormons to be and act as one in all things, stating that any dissent was now contrary to God's will.[53] Two years later, Kirtland voters elected Mormons without church leadership roles to civil office in April 1834. Smith was so confident of his success that in October of the same year he began his intended climb to political power when he ran for a minor political role as county coroner; he lost 62 to 2.[54] Smith took the loss hard and did not run for office again until he was confident the Mormons comprised virtually the entire local voting bloc. After his first foray into political candidacy, his attentions returned to his church. Smith created a concept called "theocratic ethics" which would give him the right to declare the laws of the state and country as unethical and void. He used this concept to violate Ohio law when he officiated at the marriage between Newel Knight and an already married woman who did not know the whereabouts of her lawful husband.[55] Smith would rely heavily on theocratic ethics in the future war with Missouri.

* FOUR *

EXPULSION

ON FEBRUARY 4, 1831, AFTER HAVING moved his church to Ohio, Smith appointed recent convert Edward Partridge as bishop of the church. By the summer of 1831, following Smith's revelation about Zion, Partridge and other church members were ordered to Missouri to lay the groundwork for Mormon settlements in the state, which began in Jackson County. Partridge was given total control over the financial affairs of the Missouri believers. Partridge proved to be an able and loyal church leader, but perhaps because of Smith's concern with the threats against his authority after Rigdon's recent uprising, he issued several revelations warning Partridge not to exceed his position or he would be replaced. Nonetheless, by 1835 Partridge was commended for his faithful service and remained bishop until the church was forced out of Missouri.[1]

Missouri in the 1830s was inhabited by Indians, traders, missionaries, and settlers. The region was wild and life was arduous. The majority of inhabitants were brave and adventurous, and often also illiterate, spendthrift, and antisocial. They preferred hunting to farming and would often pack their bags and move on as soon as a neighbor moved within gunshot.[2] Under normal circumstances these "old settlers" would no doubt have moved on to new areas when an influx of Mormons began to arrive. However, President Jackson established a firm boundary for the Indian frontier, which made it impossible for long-time settlers to press their expansion onto adjacent lands to the west. Even if it were not for legislation preventing such expansion, the Great Plains were inhospitable due to their lack of forests, water, and the threat of Indian attack. The mindset of the original settlers to move away was in stark contrast to the communal farming approach of the Mormons.

The Mormon population was comprised mainly of Northerners without slaves. Most original Missouri settlers hailed from the South and many were slave-owners: 20 percent of Missouri's population in 1830 was enslaved individuals. Most Jackson County residents believed that Mormons were attempting to stir up sedition among the slaves and cause a revolt. These opposing interests set the stage for a struggle between the early settlers and the new Mormon immigrants.[3] The anger and resentment among the Missourians toward the Mormons was not based merely on the settlers' lack of education or savageness. Even the more educated classes were agitated over the influx of Mormons. Lawyers, doctors, editors, and especially clergymen saw the Mormon migration not only as a threat because of the unorthodox beliefs it represented but for its potential to upset the proslavery voting bloc.[4]

The Mormon community was soon served by its own monthly newspaper, *The Evening and the Morning Star*, edited by William W. Phelps. The July 1833 edition included an article explaining the Missouri law requirements to free blacks who had converted to Mormonism and might wish to immigrate to the state. In the article Phelps even referenced the possibility of an end to slavery.[5] The article triggered an immediate outcry. That same month a committee of Jackson County citizens resolved to issue a statement condemning the presence of Mormons in the county:

We believed them [Mormons] deluded fanatics, or weak and designing knaves, and that they and their pretensions would soon pass away; but in this we were deceived. The arts of a few designing leaders amongst them have thus far succeeded in holding them together as a society; and since the arrival of the first of them, they have been daily increasing in numbers; and if they had been respectable citizens in society and thus deluded, they would have been entitled to our pity rather than to our contempt and hatred; but from their appearance, from their manners, and from their conduct since their coming among us, we have every reason to fear that, with but very few exceptions, they were of the very dregs of that society from which they came, lazy, idle, and vicious. This we conceive is not idle assertion, but a fact susceptible of proof, for with these few exceptions above named, they brought into our country little or no property with them and left less behind them, and we infer that those only yoke themselves to the "Mormon" car who had nothing earthly or heavenly to lose by the change; and we fear that if some of the leaders amongst them, had paid the forfeit due to crime, instead of being chosen ambassadors of the Most High, they would have been inmates in solitary cells. But their conduct here stamps their characters in their true colors.[6]

Anti-slavery candidates were repeatedly defeated in elections, and the Jackson County ruling elite were intent on maintaining the status quo.[7] Articles were published voicing the growing anxiety over an anticipated conflict between the two stances, including this one in the *Western Monitor*:[8]

The day is not far distant . . . when the sheriff, the justices and the county judges will be Mormons, or persons wishing to court their favor from motives of interest or ambition. What would be the fate of our lives and property, in the hands of jurors and witnesses, who do not blush to declare, and would upon occasion not hesitate to swear, that they have wrought miracles, and have been the subjects of miraculous supernatural cures, have conversed with God and His angels, and possess and exercise the gifts of divination and unknown tongues, and fired with the prospect of obtaining inheritances without money and without price—may better be imagined than described.[9]

The populace of Missouri would not have to wait long to experience the situation described in the article.

The reaction is understandable: Mormons frequently informed all who would listen that the land of Jackson County was holy land that would be taken from its current owners in some undisclosed fashion and handed over to Mormons as an "inheritance." When questioned about the method by which this land would end up in the hands of Mormons, they never could agree. Perhaps it would be accomplished by a destroying angel, the judgment of God, or an "arm of power."[10] None of these explanations gave landowners much comfort.

As soon as Oliver Cowdery arrived in Jackson County he immediately went to work among the Delaware Indians preaching and teaching. He instructed them "they should be restored to all their rights and privileges; should cease to fight and kill one another; should become one people; cultivate the earth peace, in common with the pale face."[11] This teaching incensed the settlers who had worked to subdue the Indians and keep them docile and separate from the white settlements. Cowdery and his preaching were not appreciated by the Missourians, and despite his message of restoration, he had very little success among the Indians.

Jackson County residents also believed that the encouragement of free black Mormons to immigrate to the state would corrupt the slaves and touch off bloodshed. The residents resolved that the Mormons must leave the coun-

William Wines Phelps, left, was the editor of the Mormon newspaper *The Evening and the Morning Star* which ran an article about African American immigration to Missouri that touched off a firestorm among the pro-slavery settlers. Edward Partridge, right, was the first bishop of the Mormon Church and was the leader of the first Mormon community in Jackson County, Missouri. (*Public Domain*)

ty and that they should be forcibly removed if they would not go voluntarily. Removing the Mormons from Jackson County was the goal of their petition, known to the Mormons as the "Mob Manifesto." The petition was signed by such leaders of the community as the judge of the court, the county clerk, the constable, and the jailer.[12] The plan allowed for compensation for their property, but remaining was not an option.

On July 16, 1833, after the first meeting of the Jackson County Committee but before they issued their petition, Phelps ran a retraction to clarify what was said in his paper and repair the damage his earlier edition had caused.[13] He stated in his retraction that the church wanted to stop immigration of the free blacks entirely and would also discourage them from joining the church.[14] Ignoring the retraction, five hundred settlers met in Independence and drafted five demands in their Petition to the Mormons:

Manifesto of Five Orders to Mormons
First, no Mormon settle in Jackson County in the future;

Second, that those already settled promise to sell
their lands and leave;

Third, . . . the Mormon press, storehouse, and shops
close, immediately;

Fourth that the leaders stop all immigration from
Ohio; and

Fifth, those who fail to comply with these requisitions
be referred to those of their brethren who have the
gift of divination, and of unknown tongues, to inform
them of the lot that awaits them.[15]

After the demands were read aloud at the meeting
there was a great shout from the audience and it was
determined the settlers would immediately go and serve
the demands on the Mormon leaders. A group quickly
formed and proceeded directly to Bishop Partridge's
house just west of Independence. He was given fifteen
minutes to agree to the demands. When he asked for more
time he and another Mormon leader, Charles Allen, were
tarred and feathered. The settlers destroyed the printing
press, burned furniture, and razed the two-story brick
building that housed the newspaper. Nearly all copies of
the Book of Commandments printed and stored there
were either seized or burned.[16]

Partridge ordered that no one retaliate against the settlers. The Mormons felt as though they were being persecuted for their faith like the early Christians. Three days
later the group returned, threatening the leaders with one
hundred lashes—a death sentence—unless they agreed to
leave Jackson County. The leaders responded that half the
colony would leave by January 1, 1834, and the rest before
spring.[17]

Oliver Cowdery delivered the news of the Mormon expulsion from Zion to Joseph Smith. Smith immediately
issued a revelation ordering Mormons in Independence to
maintain the peace and abstain from violent retaliations

The expulsion of Mormons from Jackson County, Missouri in 1833 depicted by Carl C. A. Christensen who painted a widely reproduced series of episodes in the history of the Mormon Church during the 1870s. The original series is in the collection of Brigham Young University Museum of Art.

against the settlers and to be patient for the time when they should inherit the land. Smith also appointed two men to petition Governor Daniel Dunklin for restitution for the value of the destroyed Mormon property. Privately, Smith suggested the believers in Independence had brought the calamity down upon themselves.[18]

The Missouri converts' only immediate act of self-defense was to vigorously petition Missouri Governor Dunklin for troops, which would maintain order while they sued for compensation for their property damage. The governor replied in late October expressing his sympathies but instructing the Mormons to first exhaust their remedies in the local courts before appealing to his office. Church leaders hired four local attorneys to petition for Mormons' rights in the courts. The four attorneys, William T. Wood, Amos Rees, Alexander Doniphan, and David R. Atchison, worked vigorously for their clients.[19]

On October 31, 1833, a contingent of fifty men arrived at the outlying homes of the Mormon colony just west of the Big Blue River in Jackson County, intent on sacking

them. The intruders unroofed and partly demolished ten
cabins. They whipped and threw stones at the men and
drove the terrified women and children screaming into
the woods. These acts of aggression were repeated on suc-
cessive nights with the intent of driving every last Mormon
from the county.[20] Smith reversed his earlier instruction
of nonviolence after learning of the continued aggression
in Missouri. A revelation was released that stated after
being attacked four times it was permissible for Mormons
to defend themselves by force.[21] The Mormons immediately moved to organize a defense. They broke into small
bands, each with its own leader, and then patrolled near
their settlements to prevent further incursions by Jackson
County residents. David Whitmer led one of the bands.[22]

One late afternoon in November 1833 a Mormon storehouse was sacked by ruffians. One lone vandal had
remained behind to hurl one final brick through the
storehouse door, when a group of hastily armed Mormons
rushed upon the scene. They arrested the man and proceeded directly to the justice of the peace to have the man
charged with destruction of property. The settler claimed
that he had been wrongfully detained, and the justice to
the Mormons' surprise had them arrested and jailed on
false imprisonment charges. A Mormon participant, John
Corrill, said, "although we could not obtain a warrant
against him [the vandal] for breaching open the store, yet
he had gotten one for us by catching him at it."[23]

Just days after the arrest of the Mormons, David
Whitmer's patrol clashed with marauders. The groups
exchanged gunfire and one Mormon and two settlers were
killed.[24] The escalation of violence enraged Jackson
County residents. Some threatened to murder the
Mormons being held in jail.[25] The settlers feared the
Mormons would kill or drive out all non-Mormons in
Jackson County.[26]

Believing there was nothing he could do to end the turmoil in Independence, Smith went north with Rigdon to
Canada to preach and convert new followers. His only
advice to Missouri Mormons was to leave until things qui-

eted down if they felt they were in
danger. He gave specific instructions, however, that they were not
to sell their land. Smith sent
Cowdery to New York to purchase
a new printing press and asked
him to become the new editor in
chief of the Mormon newspaper,
but told him to publish in Ohio
instead of Missouri. In November,
upon his return from preaching
in Canada, Smith was quick to
avoid further bloodshed by noting that "we are informed, however, that those persons [the Jackson
County settlers] are very violent,
and threaten immediate extermi-

David Whitmer, one of the
Three Witnesses to the gold-
en plates, was eventually
excommunicated from the
church. (*Public Domain*)

nation upon all those who profess our doctrine. How far
they will be suffered to execute their threats, we know not,
but we trust in the Lord, and leave the event with Him to
govern in His own wise providence." Smith believed that
pressure might be relieved by a change in philosophy. He
immediately dictated a revelation wherein the communal
system was laid aside and replaced by a more capitalistic
approach so that members would have their own stake in
the future of the church. On April 10, 1834, the Kirtland
Order was dissolved and communal land divided among
the church leaders.[27] Mormons were now allowed to own
private property.

Lieutenant Governor Lilburn Boggs, a southern emigrant
and slave-owner, lived in Independence and was one of
the wealthiest landowners in all of western Missouri. A
man with much to lose from a change in the voting bloc
due to an influx of northern nonslave-owning Mormons,
he volunteered to help Governor Dunklin resolve the
issues with the Mormons. Boggs was home at the time the

violence erupted between Mormons and non-Mormons.
After the November 4 gun battle, Boggs called out the
militia to restore order. He appointed Colonel Thomas
Pitcher, a signer of the Manifesto of Five Orders to
Mormons, to head the militia.[28] The Jackson County residents, emboldened by this appointment, made plans to
execute the Mormons being held in the jail.

When the Mormons learned of the residents' intention,
they gathered forces just west of Independence with the
objective of freeing the prisoners from jail. Colonel
Pitcher proceeded directly to their encampment to
demand they surrender and disband. Pitcher further
required that some of the members who took part in the
November 4 shooting be surrendered to county authorities to stand trial for the deaths of the two non-Mormon
participants. Initially, the Mormons declined these
demands.[29]

After Pitcher's failed attempt to negotiate peace terms,
Lieutenant Governor Boggs came to the Mormons and
personally urged them to lay down their weapons and
submit to Colonel Pitcher's authority. He promised to
make Pitcher also disarm the settlers that had organized
and had been terrorizing the Mormon colony.[30] Based on
Boggs's assurances, the Mormons voluntarily laid down
their arms. Boggs in turn approached Colonel Pitcher and
asked him to disarm the settlers. Colonel Pitcher ignored
the lieutenant governor. Boggs took no further steps to
force the issue and the settlers kept their weapons. That
night they returned to the Mormon colony, now completely defenseless, and sacked every Mormon home. The total
Mormon population at the time was slightly more than
1,200 people and comprised approximately one third of
the overall population of the county.[31] The settlers beat the
men and drove out the women and children. By morning
the entire colony had been forced from their homes. The
same night a great winter storm blew into the area to further harass and punish the Mormons as they huddled
together under the cottonwood trees along the river bank
and prayed for deliverance. Many Mormons traveled north

to Clay County where they were received with kindness
and compassion. The majority remained along the river,
without food, weapons, or a leader, and praying for a mir-
acle and awaiting further instruction from their prophet.[32]
On November 13, the waiting Mormons saw a huge meteor
shower (now known as the Leonid meteor shower, an
annual event) and took it as a signal from God that both
their deliverance and the end of the world were close at
hand. Ironically, the same shower was seen by local settlers as a sign to push the Mormon community out.[33]

The newspapers throughout the state and the nation
decried the outrageous acts of the Jackson County citizens
against the Mormons. The *Missouri Republican* wrote:

> It is possible to forsee what is to be the result of this
> singular and outrageous violation of the laws. We fear
> that the party opposed to the Mormons will think
> themselves placed so far beyond the pale of the law as
> to continue utterly regardless of it. . . . There may be
> many worthless and intolerable members of the
> obnoxious sect; but the laws are equal to the punish-
> ment of all those who are guilty of violating them. The
> Mormons are as much protected in their religion,
> their property, and persons, as any other denomina-
> tion or class of men.[34]

The scathing editorials were indignant that the
Mormons had been forcibly dispossessed of their lands
and property.[35] The Mormons' lawyers vehemently petitioned Governor Dunklin for some redress to the injustice
rained down on their clients at the hand or with the passive approval of state authority. They asked the governor to
provide a military escort to protect the Mormons so they
could return to their homes and even applied for public
arms so the Mormons could form their own militia.

In light of the negative publicity, the governor granted
most of the Mormon demands. However, he told the
Mormons the state could not provide a standing guard to
protect them after they returned to their homes. The lack
of continued protection made the prospect of returning to
Independence a terrifying proposition, and many

Mormons declined to return to their homes for fear of immediate and repeated reprisals by angry non-Mormon citizens. Instead they instructed their lawyers to file actions with the local court for redress of their suffering. Until the Mormon witnesses hazarded the trip to the courthouse, which they did with a militia escort, the cases were continued indefinitely until finally they were dismissed for lack of prosecution.[36] The Mormons would have to look elsewhere for justice.

It took one month for news of November's renewed violence in Missouri to reach Joseph Smith. He received accurate reports of events that had been prepared by Phelps and Hyde on November 6–7, 1833, but he also received a report from non-Mormon sources that twenty Missourians had been killed. Smith began to doubt his decision to call his followers to settle in frontier Missouri.[37]

On December 5, 1833, Smith wrote to the Missouri Mormons that the Ohio believers were dubious as to the actual events because they had received conflicting reports and that no monetary aid would be forthcoming because they were strapped for cash themselves. He concluded by reminding them that all of Christ's followers would be persecuted.[38] His followers wondered why Mormons had not inherited their holy land as predicted, and Smith searched for a logical answer. Just days later on December 17 Smith revealed that the Missouri Mormons had brought this misery on themselves due to their lack of faith and unchristian living.[39] This revelation, a nonbeliever could suggest, effectively passed the blame for the Zion failure from Smith to his followers; it was a scheme Smith would repeatedly use in the future when other problems arose.

This last revelation passed in the mail with a letter from Phelps who inquired on December 15 what the "honest in heart" Missouri Mormons should do to help themselves in their plight. When they received word from Smith that he blamed them for their problems, they became distraught and gave up on Jackson County. Many Mormons by this time had moved north to Clay County, where they continued to be received warmly. Smith was sure to instruct his followers not to sell their lands, as he believed that with ample petitioning of the governor the matter would ultimately be resolved and Mormon property would be returned. Smith also personally petitioned President Andrew Jackson, demanding that the Mormons be reinstated to their lands. Smith included his most recent revelation, which included a curse against any nation that would not vindicate the Mormons. His demand to the president went unanswered.[40]

FIVE

ZION'S MARCH

The Mormons in Ohio could not understand Smith's delay or his inattentiveness to the plight of the believers in Missouri. In February 1834, two Missouri Mormons arrived in Kirtland intent on raising an army to avenge the atrocities in Jackson County. One of the men, Lyman Wight, was a bellicose and ardent believer whose goal was to bully any opponents of his plan of revenge. He was accompanied by Parley Pratt, who possessed a silver tongue and considerable powers of persuasion. Wight's zeal and Pratt's eloquence roused the entire Kirtland colony to anger and action.

Wight and Pratt intended to make the Mormon restoration of arms in Jackson County coincide with the arrival of an army of Mormons from Ohio. With the reinforcements the Mormons in Missouri could defend their holdings until enough money could be raised to buy out the settlers.[1] The plan was well received and Smith could not argue with such popular sentiment.

In order to add some divine authority to the revenge plans and secure his position as its leader, Smith issued a revelation. "Redemption of Zion must . . . come by power. Therefore, I will raise up unto my people a man, who shall lead them like Moses led the children of Israel. For ye are the children of Israel, and of the seed of Abraham, and ye must . . . be let out of bondage by power, and with a stretched out arm."[2] In another revelation Smith stated that at least one hundred soldiers were called, and "whoso is not willing to lay down his life for my sake is not my Disciple."[3] After Smith's revelations, the Kirtland colony flew into a flurry of preparations. The editor of the *Painsville Telegraph* newspaper described the scene:

Old muskets, rifles, pistols, rusty swords and butcher knives, were soon put in a state of repair and scoured up. Some were borrowed and some were bought on credit if possible, and some were manufactured by their own mechanics. . . . Old men, invalids and females who could not endure the trials and hardships of a pedestrian excursion of 1,000 miles, felt it to be a great privilege to contribute liberally in the way of funds and the materiel of war. Poor fanatical females, who could save no more than a shilling per day, by their exertions, there in all they could raise, for the purpose of helping on with the expedition, and as they supposed, thereby securing the smiles and blessings of the Lord.[4]

Smith also sent out his leading elders to recruit soldiers and funds for the mission to Missouri. He hoped to raise an army of five hundred. By the end of April, after weeks of recruiting, the army raised was scarcely two hundred soldiers and the Kirtland colony had raised a mere $100.[5] Fortunately, when the elders returned from back east they brought $250. It was a promising start, but Smith's army needed more money and as fast as possible. If he could leverage the equity in the church's property, the crisis would be solved. Shortly thereafter another revelation was given that authorized the church to mortgage its lands to finance the military mission to Missouri.[6]

Despite the initial rush of activity in Kirtland, many setbacks discouraged Smith and the church leadership. In addition to the shortage of funds in Ohio, continued vigilante justice in Jackson County and restricted access of

Mormons to the courts were disturbing. The Mormons' lawyers had filed suits to restore them to their property and land, but the level of intimidation was so severe one of the attorneys, Captain (and future general) Atchison, had to provide a military escort to the courthouse.[7] Despite the depressing news from Independence and the obstacles to preparing the Mormon military response, work continued. By May, the Mormon army of two hundred men was ready to depart for Independence.

On Sunday, May 4, 1834, the Mormon army met in Kirtland to hear an address by Sidney Rigdon. He promised the glory of Christian martyrs and victories of ancient Hebrew legions and he urged them to achieve deeds of valor.[8] The Mormon army was divided into twelve-man companies, each of which selected its own leader (Brigham Young was one company leader). All army job duties were then assigned by the company leaders. On May 5 the army left Kirtland, Ohio, bound for battle, or so it thought.

In order to surprise their enemy, Smith instructed the soldiers to evade all questions from outsiders and to treat strangers as spies and horse thieves. Under no circumstances was the final destination of the army to be disclosed. When approaching a town of significant size the soldiers were to split up into their smaller contingents and go through or around the town if need be to pass unnoticed.[9] Smith hoped that by following this procedure the entire army would cover the thousand-mile trek undetected.

Lyman Wight was selected to be the army's general and Joseph Smith was quartermaster and treasurer. Frederick Williams, Sidney Rigdon, and Joseph's brother Hyrum stayed behind to manage church affairs in Kirtland. The expedition would suffer poor supply due to Joseph Smith's mismanagement of funds, but in May hopes were high as they departed to liberate Zion.

The first half of the journey passed uneventfully with excitement fueling the march. Nearing the halfway point, Mormon troops paused in Salt Creek, Illinois, for three

days to drill and rest their horses.
The soldiers polished their
weapons and were pleased to see
Joseph Smith, Jr., their prophet,
demonstrate his prowess as an
excellent marksman and rider. It
was commonly believed by many
of the men that due to Smith's
lame leg he would not be adept
with a rifle or horse. (As a boy
Smith had developed a severe
infection in his leg, and after several surgeries the surgeons finally
succeeded in extracting the portion of bone that was infected.
The surgery saved young Joseph's
life but left him with a permanent
limp.)[10] Despite his apparent
skills, Smith had no stomach for

Lyman Wight, who became a
member of the Quorum of
Twelve Apostles, was eventually excommunicated for
challenging the succession of
church leadership. (*Public
Domain*)

war and no ambition to be a great warrior. His goal instead
was to make a show of force which would scare Jackson
County residents and demonstrate to them that his followers were formidable. He then planned to sue for peace on
favorable terms. His men in contrast were spoiling for a
fight, and these divergent interests would later create a
trying situation for the Mormon leader. Smith was also
concerned that he would be identified by non-Mormons
and singled out for punishment so he developed a pseu-
donym, Captain Cook. He also kept a large and savage
English bulldog, which the men detested. After crossing
the Mississippi River, Smith finally demanded a contingent of twenty men to act as his private bodyguards.[11]
Despite all the precautions, people all along the route
noted that the Mormons passing by seemed intent on
killing the Missourians and taking back their property.[12]
Some locals sent word ahead to warn the Missourians
what was coming.[13] The Missourians were on high alert
waiting for the Mormons to arrive and made it known they
intended to "dispute every inch of ground, burn every

blade of grass, and suffer their bones to bleach on their hills rather than the Mormons should return to Jackson county."[14]

Along the Illinois River an Indian burial ground was discovered and Smith immediately examined the grave. He proclaimed that he had found a great Lamanite warrior chieftain named Zelf and that because of that discovery the Mormons would enjoy success in their campaign.[15] Each night Smith blew a blast on the sacred ram's horn, and he and his men would kneel together and pray for God's guidance and provision.[16]

Smith was not a talented bookkeeper and the men were in agreement by the halfway point that he was the wrong man to plan a thousand-mile march. Within two weeks of their departure from Kirtland their funds were running low and there were food shortages. The only company with bread was Brigham Young's, due to his resourcefulness and thoughtful planning. At this point in the journey the weather turned on them and they marched through intense heat. Soon thereafter rain turned the roads into quagmires and wreaked havoc on the wagons. The men suffered blisters on their feet which began to bleed. Under worsening road conditions the wagons began to break down and get stuck, and the only foodstuffs available to the men were johnnycakes and corn dodgers.[17]

Tensions were running high and a disagreement broke out between Parley Pratt, who asked another man, Sylvester Smith, for some of his bread. Sylvester refused and they began to fight. Joseph Smith broke up the fisticuffs. The next day all the troop's horses became sick. Joseph Smith declared that the sickness was a punishment from God for their bickering and discontent. He further stated that unless their attitudes changed their horses would not recover. All the horses except for Sylvester Smith's survived. After the prophet's display of power, the men were in awe of him and the discontent died down.[18]

Back in Missouri, by May 1834, Governor Dunklin learned of Colonel Pitcher's insubordination to the orders of the lieutenant governor to make the settlers surrender their weapons and provide protection to the unarmed Mormons. Dunklin had Pitcher arrested and investigated for the unlawful seizure of Mormon weapons.[19] The governor also took the Mormons' request for protection into account. He realized that his militia forces, which were temporary in nature, could not perform a permanent guard duty in Jackson County. When disbanded, the forces went back to their normal occupations and could not be imposed upon for long periods of time in the absence of a war. Looking for an alternative, the governor secured approval for a federal arsenal to be built in Jackson County. The arsenal would come with a garrison of federal troops who could permanently provide security to the Mormons.

The governor was also seriously considering dividing Jackson County in half and allowing the Mormons one half and original Jackson County residents the other. This would allow the two groups to coexist without bothering one another, or so the governor imagined. On May 2, 1834, Governor Dunklin gave orders to General Lucas to restore the Mormons their firearms. This order incensed the Jackson County residents. At this moment, news of Smith's army from Ohio reached Jackson County. In order to prevent Mormons in Jackson County from arming themselves to join Smith, residents of Jackson County stormed the Independence jail and seized the Mormon weapons.[20]

For an entire week beginning April 24, residents burned 150 Mormon houses to challenge the return of Mormons to the area. The governor's attention was diverted however from the vigilantes in Jackson County and focused instead on the invading army from Ohio. Militiamen from Jackson and four surrounding counties gathered to form a common defense against the Mormon army. The incursion by Smith and his armed force destroyed any empathy the governor held for the Mormons. Sensing that releasing additional weapons to Mormons or resettling them among non-Mormons would only make matters worse, Dunklin took the official posi-

tion that it was impracticable to restore the Mormons to
their weapons or homes at that time.[21] In Clay County,
Mormons began to organize a homemade arsenal in order
to defend themselves. Many believed that as soon as Smith
arrived with his army of Ohio Mormons, all-out civil war
would ensue.

"Zion's Camp" was the name Joseph Smith assigned to
the Ohio Mormon expedition to aid the Jackson County
Mormons. The force not only suffered from depleted
funds and supplies; Zion's Camp was also plagued by
widespread dissension. Its source was stress created by
the overwhelming distance of the march, the uncertainty
of the outcome, and the inept leadership. Lack of cohesion
spread from the lowest soldier to those in charge, and its
ultimate expression was a disagreement over strategy
between Lyman Wight and Joseph Smith. Smith attempted to usurp the military strategy from Wight and was
called out for it. Wight and Smith finally resolved their
issues and Wight begged Smith's forgiveness. Smith forgave Wight but required him to swear an oath of strict
obedience.[22]

Wight was not the only problem for Smith; Sylvester
Smith also denounced Joseph Smith. He was quoted as
saying, "You have stamped out liberty of speech! You
prophesy lies in the name of the Lord! You've got a heart
corrupt as hell!" Smith was so angry with Sylvester that he
threw a holy relic at him.[23] Despite the contentiousness
among the men in ranks, the group inched closer to their
final destination.

As the Mormon army came within a few days' march of
Independence, influential Jackson County residents
began working on a peace proposal to avoid disaster.
Judge Ryland brought the list of compromises to Liberty,
Missouri, where they were read aloud to a gathering of
both Mormons and non-Mormons. The terms of the compromise were that Jackson County residents would buy
the Mormon land at twice the appraised value, which was
to be determined by a panel of three disinterested arbitra-
tors agreed upon by the Mormons and the settlers. The

purchase price was to be paid within thirty days of agreement, and Mormons would agree not to resettle in the county. The reverse offer was also placed on the table which would allow the Mormons to buy out the non-Mormons under the same terms.[24] Unfortunately, due to the larger holdings of land by the settlers and the impoverished state of the Mormons, it was impossible for the Mormons to buy. The Clay County Mormons felt like the offer would force them to sell out like Esau.[25] They would no longer be able to build a temple to the Lord on the site designated by revelation. The generosity of the offer was doubtful since the structures to be valued were in ashes at the hands of the buyers.[26]

This image of Joseph Smith, Jr., is claimed to be either an actual photograph or a photograph of a painted portrait of the founder of Mormonism. The image was donated to the Library of Congress by his son, Joseph Smith III. (*Library of Congress*)

Under the leadership of W. W. Phelps, the Clay County Mormons rejected the offer but promised to present a counterproposal, and said that the Mormon army from Ohio would not cross into Jackson County until an agreement was reached.[27]

Three days after the dispute in the Mormon ranks, Smith halted his troops on the Clay County side of the Fishing River. He decided to wait until the next day to pass over into Jackson County. Later that day cholera broke out among the troops and they were unable to proceed. It struck sixty-eight of the two hundred Mormon soldiers; fourteen would later die of the illness. The prophet instructed his followers to humble themselves before God so that they would be spared from the disease, but that the cholera outbreak was God's will.[28] The frontier treatment for cholera was to drench the infected person with water and feed them a mixture of flour and whiskey.

What exactly Smith had done to stop this cholera outbreak is unknown. In St. Louis multitudes of people estimated at some seven thousand had died of cholera
between 1833 and 1834.[29] It is likely the Mormons had
contracted the disease while crossing the Mississippi
River near St. Louis and not some mysterious plague.
While tending to their sick, Clay County sheriff Cornelius
Gilliam arrived in the Mormon camp with news of the
Jackson County residents' offer to settle.[30]

Some Missouri residents wanted to kill Smith rather
than negotiate peace.[31] On June 17, 1834, James Campbell
led a group of eleven settlers on a raid to attack the
Mormons. He and seven others drowned in the Missouri
River as they tried to cross it. Two days later a group of 200
settlers tried to make it across the same river and attack.
Forty made it to the other side successfully but the others
could not and so they turned around and left. On June 21,
1834, Sheriff Gilliam returned with news that if the
Mormons crossed the river the governor would consider it
an insurrection and send out the militia.[32]

Gilliam informed Smith that the Mormons could either
buy the land at two times its value or sell it at two times its
value per the Jackson County residents' earlier terms, but
they could not remain in the state under arms. Smith
assured the sheriff that his army would not attack or move
during negotiations but they did not consider the terms
offered fair. Instead, Smith countered that the Mormons
would buy the land of the Jackson County settlers at a
price set by twelve disinterested men payable within twelve
months and that the loss of value suffered by the Mormons
as a result of the ruffians' acts of aggression would be
deducted from the sale price.[33] This counteroffer was flatly
refused. The *Liberty Enquirer* published an editorial within
a few days of the event stating that Jackson County residents would rather burn every inch of ground and die
fighting than suffer one Mormon to return to their home.[34]

A new revelation that came to Smith that day told the
Mormons not to fight and that God would fight their battles. The Mormon army was brought to Missouri as a test

of faith.[35] God's new instructions were to return to Kirtland, Ohio, and receive their reward. Zion could not be redeemed until all its elders had been so blessed. And so Smith informed Sheriff Gilliam that the residents' terms would be accepted. The Mormons were infuriated that Smith surrendered without a fight. Lyman Wight was especially mad that his men had suffered the long march from Ohio with nothing to show for it. They were not pacified until they read the revelation for themselves.[36] Smith promised that within three years the Mormons would return to Jackson County and that no one would stop them.[37] The date of "the redemption of Zion," as Smith called it, would occur no later than September 11, 1836,[38] In the meantime Smith returned to Kirtland to raise enough money to buy all the settlers' land in Jackson County. He even ordered the Missouri leadership to return to Kirtland so they could retrieve the money and bring it back with them. The *Liberty Enquirer* noted after Smith's departure the excitement was gone and that the "war" was over.[39] No military action was taken, the peace terms were still dictated by the settlers despite the presence of Zion's Camp, and the Mormons lost the sympathies of the governor for their cause. Overall the expedition was an utter failure for Smith and the Mormons. With the goals of the expedition unmet, Smith returned again the one thousand miles to Kirtland, Ohio.

Clay County residents had received Mormons with kindness and respect under the assumption that their residence would only be temporary. But the influx of Mormons from outside the state continued to flow into Clay County and it became obvious the Mormons had no intention of leaving. Colonel William P. Penniston began making speeches and taking steps to raise the resentment of Clay County settlers against their Mormon neighbors in an effort to force them out. Residents predictably grew agitated and by 1836 vigilantes once again began forming to forcibly remove Mormons from their homes.[40]

This reaction was due in part to the Mormons' continued assertions that God would favor them over the settlers
and that Mormons would receive all the settlers' lands.
One Clay County resident, Joseph Thorp, reported an
exchange with one Mormon who said his people would
"literally tread upon the ashes of the wicked after they are
destroyed from off the face of the earth."[41] Another settler
reported that the Mormons said that "this [land] was theirs
by a gift of the Lord and it was folly for them (Missourians)
to improve their lands, they would not enjoy the fruits of
their labor; that it would finally fall into the hands of the
saints."[42]

In an effort to prevent further violence, the Clay County
leaders approached the Mormon leaders with a proposal
to relocate the Mormons from Clay to a new county of
their own. State Representative Alexander Doniphan,
General David R. Atchison, and Judge Elisha Cameron
sympathized with the Mormons whom they perceived to
be unjustly persecuted in Jackson County. The leaders
offered to help the Mormons scout an area for the group's
relocation. They rode out from Liberty and found an
appropriate site in a remote portion of northern Ray
County. Thereafter, Representative Doniphan introduced
legislation to create a new county called Caldwell, which
would be dedicated for Mormon relocation.[43]

When the settlers already in that area learned of the
Mormon relocation proposal, they too began forming vigilante groups to oppose the move. These residents had
never been in direct conflict with the Mormons but feared
they would experience the same problems as the Jackson
and Clay county residents had.[44] Violence was averted
when both sides agreed to a compromise. The Mormons
would cede a six-mile tract of land near Crooked River
from the proposed southern portion of Caldwell County
to northern Ray County.[45] In addition the Mormons would
relinquish certain settlements along the eastern border of
Caldwell and allow the formation of Livingston County on
the east.

Although the Mormons were disappointed at the decrease in the total land mass granted, they were nonetheless ecstatic to come into their own territory and make it home. The cessation of hostilities and agreement on boundaries brought about a great rapprochement between Mormons and non-Mormons over the next eighteen months. The local population of non-Mormons greeted the move by supplying necessities and aiding in the settling.[46] Mormon newspaper editor William Phelps, who had only recently been tarred and feathered by Jackson County dissidents, was quick to comment on the warmth of the Mormon reception in Caldwell. The "settlers are generally very honorable, and more hospitable than any other people I ever saw, you are in most instances, welcome to the best they have," he wrote to his brethren in Ohio.[47] Relations would remain friendly and stable until Joseph Smith's return in 1838.

SIX

THE SAFETY
SOCIETY BANK

B Y THE TIME JOSEPH SMITH reached Kirtland, Ohio,
there was an angry crowd waiting to receive him.
Dissenter Sylvester Smith had spread the news of the failure of Zion's Camp and the inability of Joseph Smith to
manage the company's finances. The church president
defended himself before the council for six hours. He
defeated this most recent opponent just as he had all previous ones; with his tongue. By the time Smith was done
with the council they demanded Sylvester Smith's apology to the prophet and had leveled an investigation aimed
at excommunicating the dissenter.[1]

Joseph Smith's gospel had grown into a force beyond
his ability to control. From 1829 until 1834 he had issued
over one hundred revelations, but over the next ten years
he dictated only a dozen. When Smith switched from seer
stones to revelation it increased his influence and prestige
among the followers. Likewise, changing from continual
new revelation to relying on older revelation allowed him
to reinforce the confidence of his followers.[2] Despite his
determination to rely on old revelations, such as the Book
of Mormon, an opportunity to explore new revelations
presented itself in July 1835 when an Irishman with
Egyptian artifacts arrived in town.

Although hieroglyphics had been deciphered recently, the details were not commonly known, and Smith believed he had an opportunity to employ his seer stones to unravel the ancient texts. Smith immediately purchased the ancient scrolls and claimed to be able to dictate the inscriptions.[3] Smith proclaimed that the text was about Joseph of Egypt and Abraham from Genesis. He took this opportunity to introduce new doctrines such as plurality of gods, eternal progression to godhood, and the preexistence of men's spirits.[4] Many of these concepts had emerged in the "Burned-over District" back in New York, and it is probable that Smith was first exposed to these ideas there. After its initial publication in the Mormon newspaper *Times and Seasons*, the texts were included in the Mormon book identified as the *Pearl of Great Price*.[5] The original scrolls were thought lost in the great Chicago fire of 1871.[6] It was not until May 1966 that University of Utah Professor Aziz S. Atiya recognized the remnants of the text in the collection of the Metropolitan Museum of Art in New York City as the same used in the *Pearl of Great Price*.[7] The scrolls were acquired by the Church of Jesus Christ of Latter-day Saints in Utah and were translated. It was discovered that the papyri contained nothing more than a funeral text about a man named Hor. Although reference is made to fifteen gods and goddesses in the script, there is no mention of Abraham, Joseph, or the Hebrew God.[8] However, in 1835 Joseph Smith's prestige was restored almost overnight; he called the papyri "The Book of Abraham."[9] The church accepted the prophet and his new inspired gospel.[10]

The second prong of Smith's comeback was to make Kirtland and not Missouri the new focal point of his religion. He therefore announced the construction of a great temple in Kirtland. This temple became the hope and anticipation of all his followers and quickly replaced Zion as the primary symbol of Mormonism.[11] All converts who visited Kirtland were reminded of the temple's construction and encouraged to mortgage or sell any property they owned to buy building materials. Those without property

were given manual labor duties.[12] Despite this outpouring
of support and outward appearance of progress and success, by January 1835 the church was broke, and its new
symbol, the temple, would be foreclosed if sufficient funds
to make the loan payment were not acquired. Fortunately,
a believer by the name of John Tanner stopped in Kirtland
on his journey to relocate to Missouri. Tanner had recently
sold two farms and 2,200 acres of timber. When he learned
of the dire financial situation in Kirtland he immediately
loaned the temple committee $13,000 and cosigned a note
for $30,000 worth of goods needed to complete the tem-
ple. He also personally loaned Joseph Smith $2,000. Later
Smith would ask him to forgive the debt, which Tanner
gladly did. Smith often rewarded those who gave large
sums of money or extraordinary service with positions of
power within the church hierarchy, and Tanner received
his temporal reward in that manner.[13]

Smith felt particularly indebted to the soldiers of Zion's
Camp. He had seen them prove their loyalty by marching
two thousand miles and enduring disease, threat of war,
and above all disappointment at unfulfilled prophecy. In
the spring of 1835, he increased the size of the church
leadership in dramatic fashion by appointing twelve apostles and establishing a quorum of seventy men. Most, if
not all, of these appointments went to members of Zion's
Camp.[14] To this point the church had been governed only
by the First Presidency, made up of Smith, Frederick
Williams, and Sidney Rigdon. However, Smith decided it
was time to expand the leadership and created five coequal branches, the Presidency, the Apostles, the
Seventies, and the two High Councils of Missouri and
Ohio.[15] Smith also began referring to himself as the president as opposed to the prophet. It is not stated why Smith
made the title change, but perhaps he thought it better
reflected his dual mission as both head of a religious and
increasingly political organization.[16]

The Kirtland Temple was completed and dedicated in
1836. During the dedication ceremony many supernatural
events were reported. Some claimed visitations by Jesus,

Moses, Elijah, and a multitude of angels. Despite this fanfare and divine attendance, the temple still had a $13,000 mortgage to be paid, and in order to make the payments the Mormons began to speculate in real estate.[17]

Another means of paying the temple bill presented itself in an article that appeared in the August 1836 edition of the *Painesville Telegraph*. The paper recounted a story about the discovery of gold and silver buried underneath a house near Salem, Massachusetts. Believing he might have found the answer to his church's money problems Smith planned a trip to Massachusetts. His purpose was not to proselytize but to find the hidden riches.[18] The treasure Smith sought,

An 1878 etching of the Kirtland Temple. The temple was dedicated on March 27, 1838, by Joseph Smith, Jr. After Smith left Kirtland, ownership among Mormon factions shifted but it has remained a place of Mormon worship since its completion. (*Library of Congress*)

he believed, would be enough to pay off the mortgage on the temple and relieve the church of its burgeoning debt. It is unclear why Smith chose to conceal this fact from his traveling companions, but Smith decided to keep his plans to himself and told Sidney Rigdon, Oliver Cowdery, and Hyrum Smith, that they were leaving to spread the gospel. When the men arrived in Massachusetts and learned the true nature of the trip, they were disturbed and disappointed in their leader.[19]

Ultimately the money-digging trip to Massachusetts was unsuccessful and the group returned home empty-handed. In Kirtland there was general disapproval of the president's actions. Soon after their return, however, a new revelation was made that cleared Smith of any wrongdoing associated with the Massachusetts trip.[20] As a result there were no negative repercussions to Smith and the event was soon forgotten among the faithful.[21]

Despite Smith's failure to find the Massachusetts treasure he was quite successful in borrowing it when he arrived in New York City.[22] Smith obtained nearly $15,000 in cash and approximately $60,000 in household and farm goods as a result of the trip.[23] With this sort of credit even more was available to him when he returned to Kirtland.[24] Borrowing only postponed the day of reckoning, as Smith and his High Council knew. New loans paid off old ones but what he needed was a way to pay off the temple and eliminate the debts for good.

For two months the High Council debated the best way to achieve this goal. Due to the frenetic land speculation there was an enormous demand for money and banking institutions. This stemmed from President Jackson's veto on July 10, 1832, of the charter of the United States Bank. Americans were now forced to turn to private banks to supply currency. The High Council concluded that the answer to the Mormon financial woes was the Kirtland Safety Society Bank, which was formed in November 1836. The *Messenger and Advocate* announced the organization of the bank with Sidney Rigdon as president and Smith as cashier.[25] The Bank was established by revelation. The prophet said that like Aaron's rod it would swallow up all other banks "and grow and flourish, and spread from the rivers to the ends of the earth and survive when all others should be laid to ruin."[26] The plan was simple: the bank would create bank notes to pay off the Mormon debts and whenever possible would exchange the notes for hard currency.[27]

The number of state-authorized banks in Ohio had jumped from eleven to thirty-three between 1830 and 1836. In addition there were nine unauthorized banking institutions. All of these banks were issuing their own money. One particular bank sponsored by the Moribund Library Association, located in Hamilton County, Ohio, near present-day Cincinnati, issued notes with only old dog-eared books as collateral.[28] Bank note circulation rose by 75 percent between 1835 and 1836. By 1836 there were more than three hundred kinds of authorized notes in Ohio alone, not to mention the numerous illegal and counterfeit bills.[29]

The Kirtland Safety Society Bank joined the fray and began issuing its own money in January 1837. The stock in the bank was tied to land valuations. The collateral for the Kirtland Bank stock was all on land in a two-mile radius around Kirtland and each lot was valued between $1,000 and $500,000. The Mormon bank collateral lots were over-valued by five to six times their actual value. The practice of overvaluing was widespread during that time, however, and would ultimately lead to a national depression, much like most American real estate in 2007 prior to the collapse of the housing market. Smith estimated that his own land was worth $300,000.[30]

After the new bank notes arrived in Kirtland, news fol-lowed that the state had disallowed the charter for the Mormon bank. The publicity campaign asking consumers to buy stock in the bank ramped up just as the operation of the bank became unauthorized. Smith excused the con-tinued operation to his followers by stating "because we were Mormons the legislature raised some frivolous excuse on which they refused to grant us those banking privileges they so freely gave to others." In reality, it was not a prejudice against Mormons; the new year brought a change in the political makeup of the legislature. The "hard-money" wing of the Democratic Party took office with a mandate to stop wildcat bank speculation. As a result only one new bank charter was approved in 1837.[31]

So began the most prosperous two weeks in Kirtland history. Everyone's pockets were stuffed to the brim with new paper money. All local debts were paid off instantly. Joseph Smith even sent couriers back east to pay off Mormon debts with the large mercantile firms.[32] The qual-ity of the bank assets was quite suspect. Besides the over-valued real estate collateral, the bank also held "cash money" in its vault. Lining the shelves of the vault were boxes marked "$1,000." It was claimed by witnesses such as Cyrus Smalling—a convert who challenged Smith's handling of the bank, was excommunicated, and whose affidavits like those of other persons cast from the church are doubted by believers—that inside each box there was a top layer of fifty-cent silver coins, underneath which lay either sand, stone, lead, iron, or other materials to give the box added heft. Anyone suspicious of the bank's stability was encouraged to lift the lid of the boxes and feel their weight in order to confirm the assets held by the bank. "The effect of those boxes was like magic," according to C. G. Webb. "They created general confidence in the solidity of the bank and that beautiful paper money went like hot cakes. For about a month it was the best money in the country."[33] The bank secretary and subsequent cashier William Parrish wrote: "I have been astonished to hear him [Joseph Smith] declare that we had $60,000.00 in specie in our vaults and $600,000 at our command, when we had not to exceed $6,000.00 and could not command anymore; also that we had but about ten thousand dollars of our bills in circulation when he, as cashier of that institution, knew that there was at least $150,000.00."[34]

Smith and his church appeared to have gambled and won. The debt they had worried about had disappeared. In addition, Joseph could now harness the economic strength of his church and in his role as cashier he also had influence over the financial lives of his faithful. Then on January 19, 1837, the wheels fell off. A Mormon-friendly paper, the *Painesville Republican*, described the currency situation at Safety Society Bank in the following terms: "With respect to the ability of the Kirtland Society to redeem their notes we know nothing farther than the report says. It is said they have a large amount of specie on hand and have the means of obtaining much more if necessary. If these facts be so, its circulation in some shape would be beneficial to the community."[35] In other words, if the Mormon bank had as much real money as they claimed, they had better pay it to their creditors to maintain the integrity of the organization.

The news spread quickly. Soon the bills began streaming back to Kirtland. Cleveland, Ohio, merchants who had

A five dollar bank note issued by the Kirtland Safety Society Bank and signed by Joseph Smith, Jr. and Sidney Rigdon. The Safety Society Bank was one of many banks across the country that failed during the Panic of 1837. (*Currency Quest*)

already accepted around $36,000 in Kirtland bank notes instead began to refuse them.[36] In Buffalo and other parts of New York people scorned Mormon money even before the article appeared; afterward no bank would touch the Kirtland bank's notes.[37] Smith redeemed a good number of them before he realized that at this rate the continued redemption of bank notes would ruin the institution. After less than a month of operations, the *Painesville Telegraph* reported, Smith had "shut up shop . . . saying he would not redeem another dollar except with land."[38]

Smith's announcement caused a bank rush. Everyone in possession of Kirtland bank bills desperately attempted to unload them. By February 1, 1837, people were accepting twelve and a half cents on the dollar.[39] Faced with a desperate situation, Joseph Smith and Sidney Rigdon resigned their posts. Frederick G. Williams was appointed the new bank president and Warren Parrish became the cashier. The two new appointees attempted to salvage the remains of the Mormon bank.[40]

From its inception the Kirtland Safety Society Bank operated illegally. The penalty for said activity was a $1,000 fine, a share of which was given to the informer who alerted the authorities. On February 8, 1837, Samuel D. Rounds swore out a writ against Smith for operating the bank illegally. When brought before the judge, Smith's lawyers argued that because the creation of the bank had predated the creation of the law it was grandfathered and the penalty should not apply. The magistrate was unmoved by the argument and Smith received the $1,000 fine.[41] At the conclusion of the lawsuit, Warren Parrish, Smith's successor as cashier, resigned his post and left the church in the summer of 1837. He then began to openly describe the fraudulent accounting methods used by Smith.[42] Smith retorted by accusing Parrish of stealing $25,000 but could never produce any evidence to support these accusations.[43] In fact, at the time of Smith's resignation had the bank actually been possessed of such a sum, Smith would have been able to extricate the bank from the entire debacle. There was simply never any money for Parrish to steal or Smith would have already used it to pay off the bank's creditors.

Many Mormons lost their life savings as a result of the mismanagement of the bank. Eventually most believers forgave the debt. Smith's grammar school teacher said he'd personally lost $2,500. Saying of the experience, "I got for my money the blessing of the Lord and the assurance that bye and bye the notes of that bank would be the best money in the country."[44] Despite its circumstances the Kirtland bank continued to issue currency until June 29, 1837, when Sidney Rigdon, who returned to his post at the bank following the resignation of Parrish, was brought to court on charges of making "spurious money." The practice was finally stopped but it was not until August that Smith renounced the bank and warned his followers against accepting the bills.[45]

The rise and fall of the Kirtland bank brought about very little actual change in the Kirtland economy. The disaster after the bank's collapse was as much an illusion as the prosperity it had created in its first month. William Parrish noted, "Knowing the extreme poverty when they commenced in this Mormon speculation, I have been not a little surprised to hear them assert they were worth from three to four hundred thousand dollars each, and in less than 90 days after become insolvent, without any change in their business affairs."[46]

After the fall of the Kirtland bank, creditors swarmed Smith with threats and warrants. Non-Mormon creditors brought a series of lawsuits against Smith in Geauga County court. Thirteen suits were brought between June 1837 and April 1839 for principal amounts totaling $25,000 and resulting in judgments of $35,000. The nationwide financial crisis also began in May 1837 and by summer it had arrived in Kirtland. In a single month 800 banks containing $120 million in deposits suspended operations. The Mormons' Kirtland bank was just one among the many bank failures. One of the major causes of the collapse was the overvaluation of real estate practiced by the Kirtland bank. The economy could not sustain the continued inflation in real estate values and the bubble burst. Smith was arrested seven times in four months in association with the collection cases. Despite any misgivings its members had, the church raised $38,428 in total bail money to free Smith from state custody.[47]

Smith was deeply in debt; the exact amount is unclear since loyal Mormons made no claim for repayment. He and other church leaders owed non-Mormons approximately $150,000, an enormous sum.[48] The indebtedness was clearly a heavy burden on him. When he met with his followers at the annual church conference in April 1837 he explained, "large contracts have been entered into for lands on all sides, where our enemies have signed away their rights. We are indebted to them, but our brethren abroad have only to come with their money, take these contracts, relieve their brethren from the pecuniary embarrassments under which they now labor, and procure for themselves a peaceable place of rest among us." He continued exhorting his followers that, "This place [Kirtland] must be built up, and will be built up, and every brother that will take hold and help secure and discharge these contracts shall be rich."[49]

The prophecy would ring hollow as Kirtland would not be built up. Instead, dissension broke out among the

Mormons. Sylvester Smith was one of the first to turn
against Smith and his Church. He spread his message
around the church and it worked; six of the twelve apostles turned on Joseph Smith. Even Parley Pratt, the man
who had led hundreds to the church through his charisma
and eloquence threatened to sue the prophet in a letter
dated May 23, 1837. Pratt claimed that Smith had made
him pay an unfair price for certain real estate by claiming
it was God's will for Pratt to do so.[50] Excommunication
was threatened by Smith against any saint who brought
suit against another brother in the church. Smith also
ordered the trial of Pratt before the High Council on May
29, 1837. The trial eventually disintegrated when the council, which was divided, broke up in disorder.[51]

A bellicose anti-Mormon known in Mormon circles as
the "Mormon Persecutor," Grandison Newell wrote to the
Painesville Telegraph, intent on destroying any personal
prestige or respect maintained by Smith. On May 16, 1837,
and again on May 26, Newell claimed that Smith had
secretly incited two Mormons named Denton and Davis to
kill him so that Newell wouldn't try to collect debts from
Smith.[52] A suit was brought against Smith on these accu-
sations; however, it was later dismissed for lack of evidence. Smith wrote of the experience, "it seemed as
though the powers of earth and hell were combining their
influence in an especial manner to overthrow the Church
at once, and make a final end." Heber Kimball, a Mormon
church leader, later opined that at this time in the church's
history "there were probably not twenty persons on earth
that would declare that Joseph Smith was a Prophet of
God."[53]

Just when the outlook was bleakest, events took a dramatic turn. Grandison Newell's attack on Smith rallied the
few supporters Smith had inside the church, who cultivat-
ed an "us versus them" mindset. Apostles T. B. Marsh and
Orson Hyde, who had been sharply critical of the banking
failure, repented. Even Parley Pratt was reconciled,
though he asked to be sent back east on a missionary trip
so that he could repair his attitude toward God. The

prophet immediately granted the request, realizing that such mission trips could divert his followers' attention from the most recent failure and give them reason to trust and hope in his prophetic abilities once again. Smith conceived a plan where he would send out all his best and brightest followers on missions to get them out of Kirtland and away from the scene of his greatest failure to date. That summer he sent Heber Kimball, Orson Hyde, and Willard Richards to England as missionaries.[54]

As the nationwide bank failure settled into the Kirtland area, the Mormons began to reconsider their doubts concerning Smith. They soon began to view the Kirtland bank failure as simply a symptom of the overall nationwide financial problem—and perhaps it was. Other banks in Ohio and throughout the United States had failed in a similar fashion when the bubble burst on land values. Not for the last time in his career Smith took advantage of the passage of time to calm his followers' misapprehensions concerning his continued leadership of the body. Many viewed him as indiscreet but not responsible for any wrongdoing in the management of the bank.[55] In July 1837 Smith ran an apology in the *Messenger and Advocate*. The editor was quoted as follows:

> We believe that banking or financiering is as much a regular science trade or business, as those of law, physics, or divinity, and that a man may be an eminent civilian, and know nothing of consequence of the principle of medicine. He may be a celebrated divine, and be no mechanic and no financier, and be as liable to fail in the management of a bank as he would in constructing a balloon or the mechanism of a watch. ...We are not prepared in our feelings to censure any man.[56]

The apology was widely accepted among the church followers.

After the rapprochement of Smith to his followers he decided to leave Kirtland on a five-week mission trip to Canada. He hoped in his absence the enmity would continue to dissipate. Upon his return, Smith found his church split into two factions; one loyal to him and another following the prophecy of a young girl who would dance herself into a frenzy and after collapsing onto the floor would spew forth revelations while looking into a black seer stone. Among the breakaway faction's leadership were David Whitmer, Martin Harris, and Oliver Cowdery.[57]

The Mormons had not stopped believing in the use of seeing stones just because Smith had stopped using them in his ministry. Even F. G. Williams, formerly Joseph's first counselor, pledged his loyalty to the young seer and acted as her scribe.[58] Smith immediately went to work silencing the dancing seer. He was successful, and eventually Cowdery and Whitmer rejoined the church. Smith believed he could rehabilitate Cowdery and Whitmer with a mission trip as he had Pratt and others. Smith ordered them to Missouri to begin evangelism to the non-Mormon population. Martin Harris, Smith's original patron in the translating of the Book of Mormon, was actually cut off from the church, although he would later rejoin when the Mormons headed to Utah under the leadership of Brigham Young.[59]

Determined to test the loyalty of his church, Smith put his leadership up to a vote. Unanimously he was confirmed president and prophet. The triumph was short lived. The Mormon mercantile firms were bankrupt, their steam mill was closed, and the land values were in an irreversible decline. Kirtland was disintegrating and all Mormons with means were escaping to Missouri to get a fresh start. Rigdon and Smith were among those departing for Missouri, mainly to wait out the six lawsuits that were filed against Smith after his return from Canada. The total principal demanded was $6,100 in damages; Smith sent eight men out to scrounge up some money to cover the debt and decided to lie low in Missouri until the funds were acquired. He planned to return to Kirtland in three months to settle the cases. It would only take two months for the church in Kirtland to finally unravel.[60]

During Smith's eight-week absence from Ohio, a group of dissenters created their own church to the exclusion of Smith. The Mormon dissenters targeted loyal Mormons with lawsuits, and they forced the elders, including Brigham Young, to flee to Missouri to escape arrest. Joseph Smith, Sr., the prophet's father, led a group of loyalists against the dissenters which resulted in a great brawl in the Kirtland temple. The elder Smith and sixteen others were arrested on charges of rioting, but the case was later dismissed for lack of a cause of action.[61] After securing the temple, the dissenters moved to take the printing press and eight hundred copies of the Book of Mormon, which were being held by Grandison Newell.

A portrait that recenly has been claimed to be of Oliver Cowdery. Cowdery was an early convert to Mormonism and one of the "Three Witnesses." He was excommunicated from the church in 1838. (*Library of Congress*)

When Smith returned from Missouri on January 12, 1838, he learned that dissenters had gathered at the Kirtland temple and taken it for the purpose of beginning their own church. The younger Smith called for a trial in the temple. At the meeting, each side bitterly denounced the other and culminated in the profane oratory of Sidney Rigdon. He was extremely ill (possibly with malaria or some have even suggested manic depression) and had to be aided to the podium.[62] Once there, he took on new vitality. Rigdon believed the success of the church was the equivalent of his own and for that reason took the dissent personally.[63] Rigdon said that Mormonism "has puked the Campbellites effectually, no emetic could have done half so well."[64] Rigdon, who had begun his career as a Campbellite minister, was extremely harsh in his treatment of the other denomination. After his rant Rigdon was helped from the temple.

Smith took the reins but the debate spiraled out of control. Shouting above the din, Smith called for an end to debate and a vote on excommunications. One dissenter shouted back, "Yes, you would cut a man's head off and hear him after!"[65] As the meeting broke up Smith left the temple believing he had lost all he'd built over the previous seven years. A short time later, he received word that Grandison Newell had secured a warrant for the prophet Smith's arrest on charges of bank fraud. Joseph wasted no time and immediately left under cover of night headed for Missouri. Three days later the printing press, which was housed near the temple, caught fire and its building burned to the ground.

Upon Smith's flight, the dissenters took over the temple and passed resolutions proclaiming his depravity. Warren Parrish accused Smith of orchestrating the press burning as a twisted means of fulfilling his prophecy that no evil things would be printed about him and that God would destroy Kirtland for its wickedness.[66] Parrish said of Smith and Rigdon: "I believe them to be confirmed infidels who have not the fear of god before their eyes. . . . They lie by revelation, run away by revelation, and if they do not mend their ways, I fear they will at last be damned by their revelation."[67] There would be no going back to restore his church in Kirtland.

SEVEN

FAR WEST

JOSEPH SMITH QUOTED JESUS CHRIST, saying, "When they persecute you in one city flee to another."[1] He interpreted a warrant for his arrest for bank fraud as persecution and left Kirtland in the middle of the night on January 12, 1838. It did not take the sheriff and his posse long to figure out that Smith had skipped town, and they too left in hot pursuit. Smith and Rigdon fled on horseback and by late the next day had covered sixty miles before stopping to rest.[2] They had arranged to meet their families in Norton Township, Medina County, Ohio. Thirty-six hours after Smith and Rigdon had arrived in Norton their respective families had caught up with them. Smith's family was comprised of his wife, Emma, and their children: Julia, age 6; Joseph III, age 5; and Frederick Granger, age 6 months. Rigdon's family was made up of his wife, Phebe, and their children: Athalea, age 17, and her husband, George Robinson; Nancy, age 16; Phebe II, age 14; Sarah, age 12; Lacy Ann, age 10; John Wicliffe, age 8; Ephraim, age 6; and Sidney, Jr., age 4. The group departed on the thousand-mile trek for Far West, Missouri.

Far West was the seat of Caldwell County, approximately fifty miles northeast of Independence, Jackson County, Missouri, and situated in the gently rolling hills of upper

Missouri. Smith took with him the seat of government for the young church. When he arrived in Far West he planned to establish his new headquarters, more glorious in design than any previous thereto.

The group traveled through Dayton and Eaton, Ohio, without incident and finally stopped for nine days in Dublin, Indiana, to rest. The weather was bitterly cold and hard on the travelers. The group was pursued for more than two hundred miles from Kirtland by a posse led by a man named Lyons. At times Smith's party hid in their wagons to avoid being spotted by those who were looking to arrest them. On one evening both the Mormons and the Kirtland posse spent the night in the same house. Smith later claimed he could hear the group make threats against him during the night. That evening Lyons's group searched Smith's room. They had never seen Smith before and mistakenly determined that Smith and Rigdon were not the men for whom they were looking.[3]

Narrowly escaping capture, Smith and Rigdon agreed from that point on it would be safer to travel separately since their pursuers were looking for a pair. From Dublin on the two went by different routes toward Missouri. They set up a rendezvous point in Terre Haute, Indiana, where they rested for a couple of days. Running low on cash, they decided that Smith would take the remaining sums and continue the journey. Once in Far West he would send money back to Rigdon so that he could complete the crossing as well. Smith entered Missouri through Quincy, Illinois, the same point at which Smith's followers would depart Missouri later that year. Smith and his family arrived at Far West in March. After funds were sent back to Rigdon he resumed his travel and rejoined Smith on April 4, 1838.[4]

On February 5, while the supreme leadership was in the midst of its toilsome journey, the minutes of the Kirtland meetings had already arrived in Far West. The transcripts reported John Whitmer and W. W. Phelps as transgressors against the church. It instructed them to repent or face expulsion from the church.[5] This was the opening salvo in an all-out purge of dissenters. Smith was incensed about the dissenters within the church and believed that they were the reason he was ultimately run out of Kirtland. He never gave the warrant for bank fraud a second thought as being the reason but instead chose to blame the entire Kirtland debacle on enemy conspiracy and the devil. Smith determined to use any means necessary to suppress dissension among Mormons in Missouri. For Smith, "the desire for refuge from pluralism and the uncertainty of choice in a free society encouraged a quest to eliminate opposition both within and without the church through intimidation and, when necessary, violence."[6] He meant to do what he pleased, and he would accomplish it by the creation of an armed force.[7]

Smith had already attempted to use force and intimidation while still in Kirtland. Perhaps recalling the old practice of "warning out" employed in New England, Smith assembled a group of more than sixty men and delivered a signed warning to the justice of the peace, a non-Mormon, telling him to "depart forthwith out of Kirtland." The justice ignored the letter. Smith realized at that point if this sort of tactic was to work in the future it would have to include some means of backing it up.

Before leaving Kirtland, Smith had been accused of conspiring to murder his nemesis Grandison Newell, although Newell was unharmed. In June 1837 Smith was acquitted in absentia of the crime, perhaps because he had already fled from Ohio. Apostle Orson Hyde testified that "Smith . . . declared Newell should be put out of the way, or where the crows would not find him; he said destroying Newell would be justifiable in the sight of the Lord; that it was the will of God."[8] Although there was no overt nonviolence doctrine in the church, this was the first time that inflicting specific harm was approved. This new doctrine of church-sanctioned violence increased and became more intense after Smith arrived in Missouri.

Smith was received in Far West with a hero's welcome. Most Missouri Mormons saw the bank failure as an answer to their prayers. Smith could now give Zion his full attention.[9] Shortly after his arrival in Missouri, Smith began to refer to his time in Kirtland as "seven long years of servitude, persecution and affliction in the hands of our enemies."[10] In Far West Smith and his family settled into the home of George W. Harris and his family.[11]

Smith focused his energy on building the new colony. He wanted his people united and reliant on him; he decided a new temple would be the perfect vehicle to accomplish his goal. The people would be called on to give sacrificially to make the undertaking financially possible. Smith did not stop with just a temple; he laid out a new plan for the entire city of Far West. The new Mormon capital would be the ideal city, divided into neat squares separated by streets wide enough for six wagons to pass abreast.[12] Smith envisioned Caldwell County, Missouri, as a grand experiment in a new kind of frontier sanctuary.

There were approximately 1,500 Mormons in Far West when Smith arrived but by that fall the number would double to 3,000.[13] Word soon reached Smith of the growing number of converts in Canada and England.[14] News arrived that many former dissenters from Kirtland were fed up with the leaders who had replaced Smith and were planning to migrate to Far West. Non-Mormons believed the Mormons had breached their agreement to restrict their settlements to only Caldwell County. The influx of new converts from Canada and the East at the behest of Smith made it necessary to find new lands for Mormon settlements or risk overcrowding. There was no written agreement by the Mormons agreeing to such restrictions, however there is evidence to suggest that Mormons requested prior written consent of Ray County residents before a settlement was started near Crooked River, twelve miles due south of Far West. This seems to indicate that an oral agreement concerning Mormon settlement restrictions may have existed.[15] Thus a combination of new unapproved settlements outside Caldwell as well as the continued influx of Northern and foreign immigrants to the area threatened the peace between Mormons and non-Mormons and set the stage for all-out civil war.

Six hundred Mormons left Kirtland, reducing the size of the town to what it had been when Smith had arrived in 1831.[16] They would not arrive in Missouri until October, but in doing so made Far West the second most populous city in western Missouri, after Liberty.

When Rigdon rejoined Smith they immediately set plans in motion to renew the communal economic approach like the one previously used in the "United Order" in Kirtland.[17] They would need the people to give their land to the church and also donate large amounts of money. Each follower was to receive a home and his food simply by virtue of working. The church would allocate the labor and the resources so that each person would have exactly what he or she needed. As a result, Smith would have absolute sway over the lives of every one of his followers.[18] The only roadblocks were his persistent dissenters.

Smith's continued practice of mixing the church with politics led to further dissension. Oliver Cowdery accused Smith of trying to "set up a kind of petty government, controlled and dictated by ecclesiastical influence, in the midst of this national and state government."[19] Additionally, John Whitmer and his brother David as well as Cowdery opposed giving their lands to the church, as they had seen the results of the old "United Order" and they felt they could manage their assets more effectively than the church. David Whitmer and Oliver Cowdery went as far as to threaten legal action to defend their property rights should Smith feel inclined to usurp their land rights. Smith was not about to stand for this insubordination from his longtime allies. Instead he determined to root out the dissension and Smith turned to Rigdon for assistance.[20]

The stage was now set for a showdown between Smith and some of his earliest followers: Oliver Cowdery, John Whitmer, David Whitmer, W. W. Phelps, and Apostle Lyman E. Johnson.[21] On April 6, 1838, the church held a general conference. Smith spoke briefly concerning the Kirtland bank failure. Smith's focus then shifted to dissenters. He used the occasion to begin clearing dissenters from leadership positions. John Corrill was appointed to replace John Whitmer as the church historian. Calling him incompetent, Rigdon drafted a written demand on John Whitmer to hand over his church history notes, which both he and Smith signed. In it they insulted Whitmer, saying he was capable of producing only unpublishable work. Nonetheless they demanded the transcript.[22] Whitmer offered no response to the insults and shortly thereafter was excommunicated from the church.

Smith next excommunicated Oliver Cowdery. Cowdery attempted a defense but eventually the church approved his excommunication. The purging of the church was now in full swing, Smith turned his attention to David Whitmer. On April 13, Smith leveled five counts of insubordination against Whitmer. The same day Whitmer sent the church leadership a letter that said he would spare them further trouble and withdraw his membership.[23] Also that day Apostle Lyman E. Johnson had three charges filed against him. They were sustained without any response by Johnson and he too was cut off from the church.

The reason for the excommunications was economic: Smith—and in extension, the church—required land to start the new United Order. If members refused to contribute to the wealth of the church as divinely dictated according to believers, then they could no longer remain. Even ostracized, former church members remained a threat. In order to protect the church from the destructive force of dissension, Smith authorized the creation of a secret Mormon armed force.[24]

A former Kirtland business associate of Sidney Rigdon, Sampson Avard, proposed calling the newly organized secret army the "Danites." Officially it would be called the

Daughters of Zion, but it would take its nickname from the prophecy in Daniel 2:44-45:

> And in the days of these kings the God of heaven will set up a kingdom which shall never be destroyed; and the kingdom shall not be left to other people; it shall break in pieces and consume all these kingdoms, and it shall stand forever. Inasmuch as you saw that the stone was cut out of the mountain without hands, and that it broke in pieces the iron, the bronze, the clay, the silver, and the gold—the great God has made known to the king what will come to pass after this. The dream is certain, and its interpretation is sure.[25]

Smith described the purpose of the group: to intimidate and remove dissenters and to make war on the non-Mormon enemies of the church.[26] Smith would later deny involvement with the group; however, one of its tenets was complete devotion to the instructions of Smith. Members took an oath to defend all actions of the church leadership. Danites also employed secret handshakes to help identify their members.[27] Smith enjoyed the power the Danites afforded him.[28]

Sampson Avard was appointed the group's initial leader. Born in Great Britain, he immigrated to the United States in the early 1830s and initially worked as a doctor. In Pennsylvania in 1835 he became a Campbellite minister, after the same fashion as Sidney Rigdon. In that year he was converted to Mormonism by Orson Pratt. He rose in the church quickly and in 1837 he was ordained a high priest, though he would be stripped of the office in the same year.[29] His first act as the Danite commander was to make heresy against Smith the most heinous crime of treason. Avard said, "If I meet one damning and cursing the presidency, I can curse them too." According to Danite member Ebenezer Robinson, he then described in detail how he would get such an offender drunk, kill him, and hide the body.[30] Avard was clear; his instructions were to kill anyone insulting the church leadership. Smith was aware of the instructions; Robinson noted, "Joseph Smith,

Jr. . . . sanctioned and favored the . . . organization of 'Danites.'"[31] Even the newly appointed church historian, John Corrill, who attended the organizational meetings of the Danites, said: "The first presidency [Smith, F. G. Williams, and S. Rigdon] . . . would . . . go into their [Danite] meetings . . . and sanction their doings."[32]

The violent rhetoric Avard spouted at the Danite meetings began to worry Corrill and Danite member Reed Peck.[33] Corrill decided that he should discuss the matter with the other church leaders. After bringing up the subject of Avard's disturbing instructions, Sidney Rigdon simply warned Corrill to stay away from future Danite meetings.[34] At a later meeting Avard instructed his captains as follows:

> Take to yourselves spoils of the goods of the ungodly Gentiles [non-believers]. The riches of the Gentiles shall be consecrated to my people, the House of Israel, and thus you will waste away the Gentiles by robbing and plundering them; and this way we will build up the Kingdom of God, and roll forth the little stone Daniel saw cut out of the mountain without hands and roll forth until it filled the whole earth. For this very way God destines to build up his Kingdom in the last days. . . . I would swear to a lie to clear any of you; and if this would not do, I would put them under the sand as Moses did the Egyptian; and in this way we will consecrate much unto the Lord . . . and if one of this Danite society reveals any of these things, I will put him where the dogs cannot bite him.[35]

Smith both was aware of and approved of Avard's teaching and message. In fact, during his own speech at a Danite meeting, Smith proclaimed a blessing on Sampson Avard, who became one of the most powerful men in the Mormon church.[36]

The persecution of dissenters had begun by simply ostracizing them from Mormon society. Smith had hoped such treatment would be enough to make Cowdery, John and David Whitmer, and Lyman Johnson abandon their property and move elsewhere. When they all decided to remain in Far West, Smith decided that stronger measures were necessary. Smith encouraged Rigdon to signal the Danite forces of his desire to be rid of the group. The result on June 17, 1838, was the "Salty Sermon."[37]

It began, "Ye are the salt of the earth, but if the salt hath lost its savor, where with shall the earth be salted? It is henceforth good for nothing but to be cast out and trodden under foot of men." For more than an hour Rigdon spewed forth a hateful message from the pulpit. He threatened, "If the county cannot be freed of these men [dissenters and specifically Cowdery and the Whitmers] any other way, I will assist to trample them down." As a final warning Rigdon bellowed he would "erect a gallows on the square in Far West" to hang any such men who remained in their midst. Rather than treat these acts as a crime, he taught instead "it would be an act at which the angels would smile with approbation."[38]

Sidney Rigdon was a Campbellite preacher who converted his entire Kirtland, Ohio, congregation to Mormonism in 1830. He became a counselor in the church's First Presidency. He did not support church-sanctioned polygamy and following the death of Joseph Smith, Jr., in 1844, he believed that he was the rightful heir to the control of the church, ultimately leading him to form an independent faction of Mormonism. (*Public Domain*)

The speech lightly referenced Matthew 5:13: "You are the salt of the earth. But if the salt loses its saltiness, how can it be made salty again? It is no longer good for anything, except to be thrown out and trampled underfoot." Rigdon contorts the passage to say that murder of opponents of Smith was approved gospel. In order to back up his interpretation of the passage Rigdon referred to a revelation given by Smith in February 1834 wherein he authorized the first presidency to take drastic steps against Mormons who "hearken not to observe all my words."[39]

Rigdon's anger galvanized the Mormon crowd in attendance and a murmur of retribution could be heard.[40]
Smith immediately rose. Assuming a role as mediator he
added, "I don't want the brethren to act unlawfully." Smith
then added oddly, "I will tell you one thing. Judas was a
traitor and instead of hanging himself was hung by
Peter."[41] The church historian John Corrill believed that
Rigdon's sermon and Smith's follow-up message signaled
to the Danites to kill Cowdery, the Whitmers, and
Johnson.[42] Corrill immediately went to the men's homes
and warned them their lives were in danger from Danite
attack. Corrill recommended they flee Far West before it
was too late.

Upon hearing this news John Whitmer approached
Smith and asked what could be done to reconcile their
differences. Smith responded coldly, "The excitement is
very high and I don't know what can be done to allay it."
In other words, Smith was not going to lift a finger to calm
the anger Rigdon had stirred up against Whitmer and his
cohorts. Smith then revealed: "I will give you a frank opinion—if you will put your property into the hands of the
bishop and the high council and let it be disposed of
according to the laws of the church, perhaps after a little
while the church might have confidence in you." Whitmer
refused: "I wish to control my own property. I want to be
governed by the laws of the land and not the law of the
church." It made little difference to Smith whether his
opponents surrendered voluntarily or not; in the end, he
would have their property. Showing his disdain for any
rule but his own, he concluded the conversation by saying,
"Now you wish to pin me down to the law."[43] Smith's message was that any authority other than his own would not
be tolerated in Caldwell County. Whitmer left his meeting
with Smith, discouraged and concerned about what he
and the other dissenters should do in response to the
growing anger directed at them.

A day after the "Salty Sermon" and Smith's meeting
with John Whitmer, the dissenters received a bombastic
letter signed by Rigdon and eighty-three leading

Mormons, including Hyrum Smith and the High Council, the majority of whom were Danites.[44] Smith's name is absent from the letter. After his many scrapes with the legal system, Smith carefully avoided the potential for civil or criminal liability and directed all activities orally and through middlemen. The letter, ironically similar to the manifesto given to Mormons in 1833 by settlers in Jackson County, stated the following:

> Whereas the citizens of Caldwell County have borne with the abuse received from you at different times, and on different occasions, until it is no longer to be endured . . . out of the county you shall go, and no power shall save you. And you shall have three days after you receive this communication including twenty-four hours in each day; for you to depart with your families peaceably, which you may do undisturbed by any person; but in that time, if you do not depart, we will use the means in our power to cause you to depart for go you shall.

The letter then detailed the specific complaints against Cowdery, the Whitmers, and Lyman Johnson:

> Prosecuting cases to pick flaws in the title to certain real estate;
>
> Counterfeiting money . . .;
>
> Threatening to raise a mob from Clay and Ray counties to run the Mormons out of Caldwell;
>
> Threatening to shoot the senders of the letter if the senders try to molest the dissenters.[45]

Rigdon warned those Danites who signed the letter: "It was the imperative duty of the church to obey the word of Joseph Smith, or the presidency, without question or inquiry, and that if they would not, they should have their throats cut from ear to ear."[46]

There is an old saying that "only a fool is his own attorney." Lawyer Oliver Cowdery must have been aware of it because upon receipt of Rigdon's letter he encouraged the men to leave for Liberty, Clay County, where they hired a non-Mormon attorney to protect their interests.[47] When Cowdery, Johnson, and the Whitmers returned home they were met on the road by their families, who had hastily packed a portion of their belongings into some wagons and were fleeing for their lives. The wives told their husbands that an armed contingent of Danites surrounded their homes and ordered the women to pack the blankets and leave immediately. They were told if anyone in their family returned it would mean their death. The Danites then proceeded to steal everything but the families' bedding and clothing.[48] Considering themselves fortunate to all be alive and unharmed, the dissenters left Caldwell and headed back to Clay County. (Throughout this ordeal Smith left William W. Phelps alone. He was the U.S. Postmaster and lived on a small lot in town. It is likely he was untouched because he was postmaster, a federal office, and Smith feared repercussions from the federal government; in addition, Phelps's landholdings were small enough that Smith may not have wished to seize them.)

Joseph Smith described the scene in his diary: "These men took warning, and soon they were seen bounding over the prairie like the scape goat to carry off their own sins." John Whitmer described the experience quite differently, "While we were gone Joe [Joseph Smith] and Rigdon and their band of gadiantons [Danites] kept up a guard and watched our houses and abused our families and threatened them if they were not gone by morning they would be driven out and threatened our lives if they [Danites] ever saw us in Far West." David Whitmer simply stated, "The voice of God from heaven spake to me, separate myself from among the Latter Day Saints, for as they sought to do unto me, so should it be done unto them."[49] Whitmer's desire would soon prove only too true.

EIGHT

THE ELECTION
BRAWL

JUST WEEKS AFTER THE EXPULSION, the church took the dissenters' land. The expanse of acreage was the last prerequisite for Joseph Smith to unveil his new United Order.[1] With it Smith would be able to employ and feed all residents of the county. He explained that all church members were required to give their land and one tenth of their annual income to the church. In return they would receive an "everlasting inheritance."[2] The bishop was instructed to use the "surplus property" to build the temple and support the church presidency.[3] Sidney Rigdon followed up Smith's speech with a heated warning to anyone considering not following the prophet's revelation. He prophesied that anyone who failed to consecrate their property to the Lord would eventually lose it to "Gentile" marauders. Rigdon followed that statement up with the threat that anyone who disobeyed would be turned over to the Danites for retribution.[4] He then called for a vote on the acceptance of the United Order among the faithful.

The official vote was unanimous acceptance. In reality, the United Order was unpopular among Smith's followers.[5] The Danites made it clear that anyone who refused to go along with the concept would suffer the same fate as

Cowdery, Johnson, and the Whitmers. Whether the Mormon people remembered the first United Order's disastrous outcome, Smith's mismanagement of funds on the Zion's Camp adventure, or even the failure of the Kirtland Safety Society Bank, it was a generally held opinion that their money was safer in their own hands than it was in the church coffers.[6] Regardless of the vote, most Mormons followed the example of Ananias and Sapphira, who according to the Acts of the Apostles in the New Testament, secretly held back some of their monies from the church.[7] One Mormon, Reed Peck, described the situation in Far West at the time. Most had been "violently opposed to the new church order but that after much argument, preaching, teaching and explaining by Sampson Avard all but a few gave up their property" to the church.[8]

Soon, Smith revised the new United Order by allowing everyone to retain title to their land but forcing them to agree to a long-term lease to the church at no cost for periods of time ranging from one to ninety-nine years.[9]

Under the United Order, the church was divided into four corporations: Farmers, Mechanics, Shopkeepers, and Laborers. Each was assigned tasks by the leadership and given church land to use for the common good.[10] In theory the corporations employed members at a wage of one dollar a day, and the church surplus was paid out as the people had need. Under the program each person was entitled to a comfortable home in just a few days. All a person had to do to pay for his home was provide labor to the cooperative.[11] Only the farming corporation was ever fully organized. It operated on 7,000 acres and had a centralized allotment of workers, horses, and machinery.[12] The system was not fully developed when the Mormons were run out of Missouri and was never reestablished during Smith's lifetime.

In 1836, the Missouri legislature created Caldwell County as a sanctuary for displaced Mormons in the hope no further Mormon expansion would occur. With the growing number of converts moving in from Ohio, Canada, and other locations it was soon apparent that Caldwell County was not going to provide sufficient space for all Mormons to thrive. By early 1838, the population had swelled to approximately 4,000. There was already a settlement of Mormons along the Crooked River in the disputed six-mile strip of land originally set aside as part of Caldwell County but later reapportioned to Ray County. Also, near Haun's Mill there was a settlement of Mormons that had stretched into Livingston County.[13] Shortly after Smith's arrival in Missouri he took a boat trip up the Grand River in southern Daviess County. On that trip he declared he had discovered where Adam had moved his family after the fall described in the book of Genesis; Smith called it Adam-ondi-Ahman.

This was not the first time Smith had created a holy land to encourage migration. Smith had previously instructed his followers that Independence, Missouri, was not only Zion (where Christ's second coming would occur) but also the original site of the Garden of Eden. The new announcement worked as planned and soon multitudes of Mormon families were pouring into Daviess County.[14] New residents included Danite Colonel Lyman Wight, who established a band of faithful Danites in the new settlement.

To spread the church's message, Wight favored an extremist brand of evangelism that was growing in popularity among mainstream believers. One witness to events, William Swartzell, described Wight in his journal in June 1838: "I cannot listen with ease to the preaching of Lyman Wight—his exhorting a war upon the peaceful citizens of Missouri. . . . In one of his sermons he denounced them because they would not embrace the Mormon faith as 'hypocrites, long-faced dupes, devils, infernal hobgoblins and ghosts, and they ought to be damned and sent to hell where they properly belonged.'"[15]

The Danites were organized into bands of ten and fifty men, the latter known as "fifties."[16] These heavily armed bands were getting bored with drilling and maneuvers. According to John Corrill, relations had been improving between Mormons and non-Mormons after the Mormon resettlement from Clay to Caldwell County until the summer of 1838.[17] Even with Mormon settlement in Daviess County the Mormons continued to get along well with their neighbors. Corrill reported that non-Mormon attitudes changed and old prejudices began to arise when suspicions of Mormons' domination in Daviess County emerged. "Many of the Church became elated with the idea of settling in and round about the new town [Adam-ondi-Ahman], especially those who had come from Kirtland, as it was designed more particularly for them. This stirred up the people of Davies[s] in some degree; they saw that if this town was built up rapidly it would injure Gallatin, their county seat, and also that the Mormons would soon overrun Davies[s], and rule the county, and they did not like to live under the laws and administration of 'Joe Smith.'" [18] No mobs were formed, but non-Mormoms began to insult the Mormons and their leaders. This reaction caused the Danites to increase their hostility toward the settlers of Daviess County.[19]

Back in Caldwell County, the first task assigned by the presidency was to address the upcoming local vote. Sampson Avard received a list of church-approved candidates and organized his army to canvass the entire county, drumming up the vote. As a result of his intimidation tactics, all but fifteen or twenty votes went to church-approved candidates. However, Smith recorded the results in his diary as being unanimous. No church leaders ran for office except Rigdon, who was elected postmaster, replacing dissenter William W. Phelps.[20]

Joseph Smith had determined July 4, 1838, as the day the cornerstone of the new Mormon temple would be dedicated in Far West.[21] The event was heralded in the community and a great parade was organized. Thousands of Mormons attended what Smith styled his church's

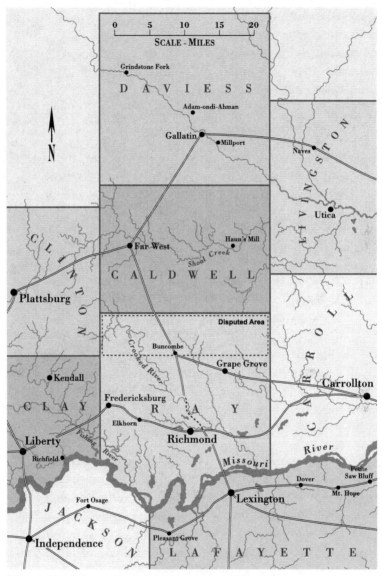

Western Missouri counties and settlements in 1838.

"declaration of independence from all mobs and persecutions."[22] News of the planned Mormon festivities were so widespread that many non-Mormons from surrounding counties traveled to see the event.[23] The parade began promptly at 10 A.M. and was led by a Danite infantry unit.

Second in line was the First Presidency leadership, which included Joseph Smith, Hyrum Smith, and Sidney Rigdon. The procession closed with a troop of cavalry bringing up the rear.[24]

The parade went through the town of Far West to the sound of music and the cheers of the crowd. The group marched to the site which was excavated for the new temple and formed a circle around it. A group of Mormon men then proceeded to lay the southeast cornerstone in place and a dedication was given by Sidney Rigdon.[25]

Rigdon began: "Better far better, to sleep with the dead than be oppressed among the living." The speech started out as any typical Fourth of July address might. He then began to stir up the crowd saying, "Our cheeks have been given to smiters, and our heads to those who have plucked off our hair. We have not only, when smitten on our cheek, turned the other, but we have done it again, and again, until we are wearied of being smitten, and tired of being trampled upon." Once he had warmed up the crowd's emotions he concluded with a great exhortation, "But from this day and hour, we will suffer it no more. . . . And that mob that comes on us to disturb us, it shall be between us and them a war of extermination; for we will follow them till the last drop of their blood is spilled, or else they will have to exterminate us; for we will carry the seat of war to their own houses and their own families, and one party or the other shall be utterly destroyed."[26]

The Mormons present broke into wild cheering and shouted, "Hosanna, hosanna to God and the Lamb!" By contrast the non-Mormons in the crowd took the opportunity to quietly slip out of town in fear for their safety.[27] Smith was so taken with the speech that he had it printed into pamphlets for easy dissemination.[28] He stated his support of the speech, calling it, "the fixed determination of saints, in relation to the persecutors . . . for to be mobbed any more without taking vengeance we will not."[29] The retribution Smith approved for use against non-Mormons is consistent with the measures he had ordered against dissenters. The speech set the tone for future Mormon and non-Mormons interaction by giving non-Mormons physical proof of Mormon hostile intentions. The brand of extremism promoted in the speech would affect the governor's decision on the appropriate response to the growing conflict between Mormons and other citizens of Missouri.

Leading up to election day Smith travelled to Adam-ondi-Ahman to further scout areas for his ever increasing number of converts to settle. Smith and Rigdon returned to Daviess County with a new group of Canadians and settled them in their new homes.[30] Meanwhile back in Far West the First Presidency leadership and Bishop Partridge assembled to determine what was to be done with the property seized from the dissenters. They determined to use proceeds from its sale to cover the expenses of the First Presidency and specifically Smith's.[31] Days later Smith again returned to Daviess County to settle even more Canadian converts. During this time elders from England came to Far West to share the progress the Mormon message was achieving in England. All in all there was much to celebrate in Far West. Smith's influence was spreading throughout the English-speaking world, a cancerous dissension had been cut out of the Far West fellowship, and the numbers of Mormons in Caldwell, Daviess, and Carroll counties were swelling so that soon Smith's followers would outnumber the other Missourians in the region.

In mid-July Judge Josiah Morin, a non-Mormon from Millport, Daviess County, paid a visit to Far West to warn the Mormon leaders of trouble brewing in the county. After Rigdon's fiery speech, particularly the threats of extermination, Colonel William P. Penniston and his supporters intended to prohibit Mormons from voting in Daviess County in August.[32] Penniston gained notoriety from his outspoken support for the expulsion of Mormons from Clay County in 1836. Judge Morin's warning was ignored and the Mormon leadership insisted that all Mormons should vote in the August election.

In Gallatin, the Daviess County seat, on August 6, 1838, Mormons and "Old Settlers" squared off at the polls. The election was expected to be close. Colonel Penniston took the opportunity to give a speech to stir up the non-Mormon vote and spoke for over an hour. He shouted, "the Mormon leaders were a set of horse thieves, liars, counterfeiters, and you know they profess to heal the sick and cast out devils, and you know all that is a lie." His tirade continued, "the members of the Church were dupes, and not too good to take a false oath on any common occasion; that they would steal, and he [Penniston] did not consider property safe where they were; that he was opposed to their settling in Daviess County; and that if they suffered the 'Mormons' the vote, the people would soon lose their sufferage." Penniston concluded by reminding those Mormons in the audience, "I headed a mob to drive you out of Clay County, and would not prevent your being mobbed now."[33]

As he concluded, a Mormon living in Daviess, Samuel Brown, arose and marched over to the polls to cast his vote in defiance of Penniston's remarks. A large brutish man by the name of Richard "Dick" Welding quickly moved to bar Brown's way. He informed Brown, "the Mormons were not allowed to vote in Clay County no more than negroes." Brown started to argue the point and Welding took a swing at him. Brown blocked the blow with his umbrella and fell back a few paces. Welding had been drinking and was inebriated enough to make his assault unsuccessful. Another Mormon, Perry Durphy, tried to break up the fight by grabbing Welding and holding him back. As soon as Durphy put his hands on Welding a group of five or six non-Mormons rushed over to attack Durphy. They began beating him with boards shouting, "Kill him, kill him."[34]

John L. Butler, a lifelong Mormon, later reflecting on the events of that day said, "The first thing that came to my mind was the covenants entered into by the Danites."

Seeing Durphy's distress, Butler immediately signaled the Danites in Gallatin to the defense of their brothers. He shouted, "O yes, you Danites here is a job for us."[35] John D. Lee, another Mormon present in Gallatin that day, said, "I was a stranger to all who were engaged in the affray, but I had seen the sign, and like Samson when leaning against the pillar, I felt the power of God nerve my arm for the fray."[36] Butler spoke of the event later and said, "There was a power rested upon me such as one I never felt before... I never struck a man a second time, and while knocking them down, I really felt that they would soon embrace the gospel."[37] The Mormons had positioned themselves next to a stack of oak hearts, which were the center portion of a log about the size of a baseball bat. The hearts made excellent weapons, and the Mormons began beating back the crowd of non-Mormons with them. (No one was armed at the polls, as it was uncommon to carry weapons at a public event.)

During the exchange one Mormon, Abraham Nelson, was knocked down and had his clothing stripped off by his attackers. He tried to get up but the mob continued to attack him. Finally his brother Hyrum beat back Abraham's attackers with a horse whip and saved him. Dick Welding did not fare as well during the brawl. He was dropped to the ground when Riley Stewart struck him in the head with a club. Seeing Welding fall, the settlers screamed out "Dick Welding's dead; who killed Dick?" The Missourians near Welding immediately grabbed Stewart, intent on harming him. Their plans were foiled when John L. Butler came to Stewart's rescue. Butler drove the pack of Missourians back swinging a great oak heart. The struggle lasted only five minutes. The Daviess County residents outnumbered the Mormons but could not defeat the club-armed men.[38] The residents slipped away in search of their own weapons.

Afterward Butler gave a rousing speech. "We are American citizens; our fathers fought for liberty, and we will maintain the same principles." He continued, "My ancestors served in the War of the Revolution to establish a free and independent government—a government where all men have equal rights." Then defiantly marching toward the poll he said, "I aim to have my rights as a free-born citizen, even if I have to fight for them. As for my religion, that's a matter between my God and me, and no man's business but my own. This day I'm going to have my vote, and I'll die fighting before I'm driven from these polls without it."[39] Each Mormon then proceeded to the polls and cast his ballot. Afterward the county officials asked the Mormons to disperse. The officials confirmed the existence of a plot to keep the Mormons from voting.[40]

The Mormons left Gallatin and began their trip back to Adam-ondi-Ahman. They paused a quarter of a mile outside the Gallatin city limits to confer about what had just happened and determine whether they were in danger from pursuers. As they spoke, some men noticed a large group of armed non-Mormon riders approaching from Gallatin. They feared the group would be after them and so they hurried home to their families and to prepare a common defense against an expected raid.[41] No attack would come that night, but the settlers now had the fodder they needed. Penniston would stoke the embers of Mormon distrust into full flame. Likewise, the brawl reinforced the Mormons' suspicions from the settlers and county officials that lawlessness in Missouri was rampant. Subsequent events would push the Mormons and non-Mormons toward open, premeditated hostilities.

NINE

CONFLICT

I T TOOK A DAY FOR NEWS OF THE election brawl to reach Joseph Smith in Far West. Non-Mormon riders reported that three Mormons were killed and their bodies left in the street and that Daviess County settlers would not allow them to be buried.[1] Sampson Avard, the Danite general, and Joseph Smith immediately ordered an armed force to ride up to Gallatin to help the Daviess County Mormons. Sidney Rigdon spurred them on, shouting, "Now we as the people of God do declare and decree," waving his sword, "by the Great Jehovah, the eternal and omnipotent God, that sits upon his vast and everlasting throne, beyond that ethereal blue, we will bathe our swords in the vital blood of the Missourians or die in the attempt!" Twenty armed men left that same day.[2]

Along the way to Daviess County, the call to arms spread throughout Caldwell County, and many more armed Mormons joined the force. The group headed first to Adam-ondi-Ahman and the home of Danite colonel Lyman Wight to organize their group and rest their horses. At Wight's house, the force met with Mormons who had been attacked in Gallatin the day before and learned to their great relief that no Mormons had actually been killed. According to Mormon witnesses, 150 settlers attacked twelve to thirty Mormons, who fought them fiercely with some sturdy oak hearts. Participants recorded that several settlers had their skulls cracked during the skirmish; nine settlers had been knocked out cold. Smith commended the men for their valor in fighting for their rights.[3]

With no dead in Gallatin, Smith and Wight halted the advance, regrouping for a new objective. Smith, eager to avoid expulsion from yet another Mormon city, devised a plan forcing Daviess County leaders into peace negotiations. Smith had an affidavit prepared effectively prohibiting the residents from forcefully removing Mormons from Daviess County. If he could have every citizen of Daviess County sign it, the Mormons could, in his theory, never be run out against their will. To execute the hastily contrived plan, a force of approximately 150 armed men rode out under the pretense of surveying the defenses of Adam-ondi-Ahman. The Mormons had torn down cabins and constructed block houses, built a breastwork to prevent penetration of mounted troops into the city, and gathered food and supplies for a siege. Once satisfied with the defenses against any settler incursions, the army sought to obtain signatures on their affidavit of peace. By good will or by force they were bent on establishing peace for continued Mormon expansion.

During their mission Smith and his armed men rode to the home of Daviess County judge Adam Black. Elected to the county bench in the August 6 election, Black was already a justice of the peace, which allowed him the authority to hear disputes and issue warrants within Daviess County. Black was rumored, along with Colonel William Penniston, to harbor anti-Mormon sentiment. In order to stop the violence, Smith would proceed directly to the source of authority in order to extract a promise of peace and equal treatment of Mormons in Daviess County.[4]

Smith's doubt about Black's neutrality had a basis in fact. Black had sold some land to a Mormon named Vinson Knight. He accepted the down payment but now was reportedly acting in concert with the anti-Mormon faction to have Knight and all the other Mormons run out of the county.[5] If Knight failed to make the payments he would forfeit the sums already paid to the judge. Black would repossess the land and be free to sell it to another buyer. It would be a financial windfall for the official if the Mormons were removed. Rumors surfaced that Black began organizing the anti-Mormon settlers in the county, and that he may also have had a part in the Gallatin election day brawl.[6] Smith decided to confront Black face to face about the rumors.

With armed Mormons surrounding the house, Joseph Smith and his leaders obtained entry into Black's home. Whether because of the intimidating men surrounding his house or because of actual involvement, Black admitted to the connection. Smith then asked Black to sign an agreement pledging that he would fairly administer justice in Daviess County as the new judge.[7] Black would not sign, and would later report to the governor that upon his refusal, Mormons threatened his life unless he changed his mind.[8] Black persisted in his defiance regarding the Mormon-prepared statement, though he conceded to sign a statement he wrote himself.[9] Black declared, in the document, not to be attached to any mob either present or future. Black concluded by stating that he would not "molest" the Mormons if the Mormons did not "molest" him. The signed statement pacified the Mormons. The next day Smith and the main body of his army returned to Far West.[10]

The majority of Daviess County officials were unaware of Smith's August 8 visit to the home of Adam Black. Intent on reestablishing the peace between Mormons and non-Mormons, Daviess County dispatched a group of officials to negotiate a way to diffuse the tension. Upon Smith's return to Far West, the Daviess County delegates were already waiting to broker a peace deal with the Mormons over the Gallatin election brawl. Among the Daviess

County group were senator-elect and former judge Joseph Morin, representative-elect John Williams, and James B. Turner, circuit clerk. The Mormon representatives for this meeting were Smith, Wight, Vinson Knight, John Smith, and Reynolds Cahoon. After a couple days of discussion, both sides agreed to live in peace, not withholding wrong-doers from justice.[11]

Back in Daviess County, the Mormon visit to Judge Black's residence set off a chain reaction. Daviess County militia Colonel William Penniston, a Whig, was sore from losing his bid for state senate to the Democrat candidate Judge Josiah Morin in the August election, the same judge who had earlier warned Smith of the potential for anti-Mormon violence in the county. Penniston realized the Mormons had supported his opponent, and when he got wind of the Mormon intrusion upon Black, two days after the incident he had Ray County Circuit Judge Austin King swear out an affidavit regarding the matter. Judge King presided over the entire 5th Circuit, which comprised most of northern Missouri at the time. King, a tall slender man three years Joseph Smith's senior, presided over actions in multiple counties and would hear all the most difficult cases that were not appropriate for the justices of the peace or the county judges. The affidavit said, "A body of armed men who had unlawful intent or insurrectionary intent of 500 men and they or at least 120 of them went to Adam Black's house and forced him under threat of death to sign a writing of a very disgraceful character." Penniston continued, "The same group threatened immediate death on sight to William Penniston." He claimed, "Joseph Smith, Jr. and Lyman Wight are the leaders. The group's object is to take vengeance for injuries or imagined injuries done to some of their friends and to intimidate and drive from the county all the old citizens or to put them under their dominion."[12]

A later, separate affidavit by Judge Black confirms the same facts, so they are most likely both from this source. The larger issue is whether or not Penniston had any first-hand knowledge upon which he could base his affidavit. It is quite clear that Penniston was not present at Adam Black's house on the 8th, and therefore all the statements made in his affidavit would be secondary in nature; his report contained statements he had only heard to be true. In legal terms, the document was hearsay and without some mention of Penniston's independent knowledge would be inadmissible in a court of law based on its unreliable nature. As head of a circuit court, Judge King would certainly have known and understood the hearsay rule, as it was an established rule of evidence for many years before he took the bench. It was as inappropriate for Penniston to swear out an affidavit as it was for King to certify it as a

Judge Austin King presided over the 5th Circuit Court of the United States which encompassed northern Missouri. He certified an affidavit against Joseph Smith, Jr. and other Mormon leaders. (*Library of Congress*)

sworn document. Notwithstanding the hearsay deficiency, Penniston immediately dispatched the affidavit to Governor Lilburn Boggs—who had succeeded Daniel Dunklin to the post in 1836—in hopes of stirring him to action.[13]

Joseph Smith now believed all issues in Daviess County to be resolved. Unaware of any developing problems, he returned to Daviess County to visit his newly arrived and settled Canadian Mormon converts. He warned them not to settle beyond the safety of Adam-ondi-Ahman, except at their own risk. The warning went unheeded; the Canadian Mormons continued to pour into Daviess County, further angering the original settlers. On August 11, 1838, while Smith was away in Daviess County, a delegation of officials from Ray County arrived in Far West to barter a peace deal. They had come after receiving copies of Penniston's affidavit and were concerned about Smith's intimidating visit to Adam Black's house. A meeting was organized with Bishop Edward Partridge and George Robinson in lieu of Smith and his group of presidential leaders. No resolution was reported from the meeting and the Ray County delegation had returned to Richmond by the time Smith returned to Far West on August 13. Smith reported that on his way back to Far West he had been chased by a group of angry residents. Smith received word, just eight miles from Far West, of a warrant for his own arrest based on Penniston's affidavit.[14]

Judge King probably acted prematurely by issuing a warrant for Smith's arrest without corroboration of Penniston's statements by an actual eyewitness. Adam Black would not issue his own affidavit until August 28, nearly two weeks after the warrant. Perhaps a twenty-first-century review of King's decision is overly critical in that modern rules for the issuance of a warrant require probable cause, a concept that had yet to be established in Judge King's time.[15]

Nonetheless, even by nineteenth-century standards, testimony of a witness with actual knowledge of the alleged crime should have been required prior to issuing a warrant for an individual's arrest. It is not enough to say that perhaps King just acted hastily and made a mistake. King would later become governor of the state and could only achieve such an office if he was respected for his ability and intellect. Perhaps Judge King's decision was driven by his passion or emotion. His brother-in-law had been killed in Jackson County during the Mormon-settler riot in 1833. Or maybe King realized that without swift action this seemingly small problem could grow into a larger conflict. As the circuit judge, King probably conferenced with Judge Black during his travels and prior to the warrant's issuance. Both the Penniston and Black affidavits corroborated the same version of events and with verified firsthand knowledge in the latter. Based on the alleged Mormon threat to Black's life, a warrant was justified.[16]

On August 16, 1838, the Daviess County sheriff, in the company of senator-elect Judge Morin, appeared in Far West intent on executing the arrest warrant for Smith.[17] The two men did not come with an army and were aware that Smith would not be taken from Far West by force. The sheriff asked Smith to submit to the Daviess County warrant and accompany him to Gallatin to stand trial. Smith responded that he would submit to be tried but not in Daviess County, because the people there were "exasperated with him." In actuality he was fearful that he would be lynched if he submitted to the jurisdiction.[18] He would only consent to be tried in Caldwell County.[19] There, of course, he was insulated from criminal liability; he would be tried by Elias Higbee, justice of the peace, who was one of his followers and a member of the Danites.[20]

The sheriff had no power to alter the warrant to list Caldwell County as the venue for Smith's case, so he was unsure what his next step should be. He wisely or perhaps pragmatically decided to wait to make an arrest and first consult with Judge King regarding Smith's request for a change of venue. Smith informed the sheriff he would await his return and the judge's answer in Far West. The sheriff returned to Far West on August 19 and informed Smith that he, the sheriff, was outside his jurisdiction period. He could not execute the writ in Caldwell County. The sheriff did inform Smith that if he would voluntarily submit to Daviess County jurisdiction he could then request his change of venue to Caldwell County.[21]

The affidavits and warrant achieved their desired goal for those opposed to the Mormons. On August 30, 1838, Adjutant General B. M. Lisle in Jefferson City ordered the militia called up to immediate "readiness." The order went out to Major Generals John B. Clark, Samuel D. Lucas, David Willock, David R. Atchison, Lewis Bolton, Henry W. Crawther, and Thomas D. Grant. Each was ordered to call up four hundred mounted men, armed and equipped as

infantry or riflemen. General Lisle suggested that each
commander use propriety and a manner calculated to produce as little excitement as possible. There was alarm in
Jefferson City, but not to the point that martial law would
be required. General Lisle described the reason for mustering the troops: "indications of Indian disturbances on
our immediate frontier, and the recent civil disturbances
in the counties of Caldwell, Daviess and Carroll." He continued that such actions rendered "it necessary, as a pre-
cautionary measure, that an effective force of the militia be
held in readiness to meet either contingency."[22]

Judge Austin King was thoroughly frustrated with the
state of affairs in Caldwell and Daviess counties and the
governor's less than reactionary orders. Smith's offer to be
tried only in Caldwell galled him; he deemed Smith's
actions disrespectful to the court. King contended that the
law should not be compromised for Smith.[23] The wanted
men must first submit to the law and then a venue transfer
could be considered. If the Mormons refused to submit
and were so numerous and well armed that Daviess
County officials could not bring them in, then the task
would require some help from an armed force.

Governor Boggs continued to be inundated with
reports and requests for the next two months. After Adam
Black issued his affidavit corroborating all the facts previously provided, affidavits from other parts of the state hit
the governor's desk. On September 1 an affidavit from
Carroll County was sent claiming Mormons were conspiring with Indians to overrun the whole of upper Missouri.
The authors, Senator Daniel Ashby, James Keyte, and
future Confederate general Sterling Price, were writing
from Brunswick, a town miles from any Mormon settlements. To their credit they admit as much, saying, "Being
remote from the immediate vicinity of the Mormon troubles, we can give but a little of authentic data on which to
act but we are strongly of the opinion, that there is a deeply
laid scheme existing among these fanatics, that will be
highly destructive in character and at once subversive to
the rights and liberties of the people."[24] They continued,

"We have the best authority for believing that in their public teachings, their people are taught to believe and expect that immense numbers of Indians of various tribes are only waiting the signal for a general rise, when, as they state it, the flying or destroying Angel will go through the land, and work the general destruction of all that are not Mormons." The source of the affidavit's information was provided by a man named Nathan March, a Chariton County settler turned Mormon. March was reputed to be an honest man and after five months among the Mormons had this to say regarding his time there: "I distinctly recollect hearing Joseph Smith, the prophet, state . . . he had fourteen thousand men, not belonging to the Church, ready, at a moment's warning (which was generally understood to be Indians)." It was common knowledge that "Indians would be the principal means by which [they would] protect one another against the Civil officers of the County [and] accomplish the work of destruction" of the county.[25] When Smith had given an interview some months before for the local Mormon paper, he was asked whether the Mormons were inciting the Indians to rise up against the Missouri government with the promise of being restored to their lands. Smith denied it at that time and would also deny the veracity of the affidavit's contents. The only evidence to support the assertions are the affidavit's sources and the knowledge that one of the first missionary works of Oliver Cowdery in Missouri was attempting to convert the Indians to Mormonism. In 1831 he did encourage them to join by assuring them that as God's people from the Book of Mormon they would be restored to their lands.[26]

Another former Mormon turned dissenter, this time from Daviess County, added his report to the growing number of alarms being sent to Governor Boggs. His name was John N. Sapp and he reported the Mormons were "building . . . fortifications for the protection of themselves and families in time of war." He further explained that their plan was to make provision for enough food for their families by their labor, but should they fall short of their need, they "are to take the balance from the Missourians." Sapp also mentioned the Mormon paramilitary group to the governor. He described the Danite band as a group between "eight and ten hundred men well armed and equipped who have taken an oath to support Joseph Smith and Lyman Wight in opposition to the State of Missouri." Sapp claimed that "Sidney Rigdon and Lyman Wight say . . . their object was to induce the Indians to join them [Mormons] in making war upon the Missourians this fall or next spring at farthest."[27]

Citizens of Daviess and Livingston counties added their voices to the furor by dispatching letters to the governor. They were fearful of the alleged Mormon war preparations and requested state-supplied firearms and powder for their county militia units. The state honored their request and issued forty-five rifles, two hundred pounds of lead, and several kegs of powder. As the supplies passed through Caldwell County they were intercepted by Mormon troops and confiscated. The couriers were taken prisoner by the Mormons acting through the Caldwell County sheriff, also a Mormon, and were held in custody for several weeks without being charged with a crime.

Justice of the peace William Dryden issued an affidavit to the governor, confirming the Mormons were holding prisoners. Dryden had issued the warrant for the Mormons listed in Adam Black's affidavit other than Joseph Smith, namely Andrew Ripley, George Smith, Ephraim Owens, Harvey Umstead, Hiram Nelson, A. Brown, John L. Butler, Cornelius Lott, John Woods, H. Redfield, Riley Stewart, James Whiteacre, Andrew Thon, Amos Tubbs, Dr. Gourge, and Abram Nelson. In his affidavit Dryden also explained that the persons named in his Daviess County arrest warrant were being withheld from justice by means of a large armed force. He calculated the Mormon numbers in Daviess County to be 1,500, now outnumbering other county residents. Dryden had appointed deputy Nathaniel H. Blakely and authorized ten guards to execute the writ, but they had been driven from Mormon settlements in Daviess County by force. Concluding his

plea for help, the beleaguered justice of the peace observed that
Daviess County was without
power to enforce civil or criminal
process against the Mormons and
asked the governor to send a sufficient number of troops to execute the laws of the land.[28]

A few days later a Mormon
troop of fifty armed men raided
the home of James Weldon, a
leading man in Livingston
County, to seize some of his property. The Mormons made the family their hostages and collected all
their property, as well as taking
three men and two women back
to Far West. The incident caused a
general alarm in Daviess and
Livingston counties. Nearly two
thirds of the Daviess County pop-

David Rice Atchison became
a U.S. senator for the state
of Missouri in 1844.
Staunchly pro-slavery, he led
a paramilitary group against
free-soilers during the
"Bleeding Kansas" crisis in
the 1850s. (*Library of
Congress*)

ulation—all non-Mormons—left their homes to seek pro-
tection in other counties.[29] Mormon converts freshly
arrived from Canada continued to flood into the Daviess
County region and were immediately plugged into the
Mormon armed force that patrolled the area.[30] All duly
elected officials had been driven from the county and the
Mormons had achieved de facto control of Daviess
County, accomplishing their goal of making it the second
Mormon-run county in Missouri.

Judge Austin King in an act of desperation pleaded his
case directly to Major General David R. Atchison, one of
the militia generals called up to readiness at the end of
August by the governor. King wrote, "since my letter to
you . . . yesterday I have received divers and sundry com-
munications from Grand River, [which runs southeast
directly through the middle of Daviess and Livingston
Counties and joins the Missouri River at DeWitt, the lone
Mormon settlement in Carroll County] all going to show

that the people in that quarter on both sides need protection, nothing but an armed force can do it." King continued, "The Mormons named in the warrant issued by
Esquire Dryden, will not be taken, and I send you a letter
from Smith and Rigdon [from which] you can learn somewhat of the state of affairs."[31]

Judge King then blatantly solicited Atchison's forces,
giving him an option to act without direct orders from the
Governor. "I do not know of any authority I have to direct
your movements in the matter, but I will advise you and
hope you may deem it your duty to act in the matter to
send a force of say 200 men, or more if necessary." Hoping
Atchison would continue to read, King issued the following order, "Dispel the force in Daviess and all the assembled forces in Caldwell and while there to cause those
Mormons who refused to give up, to surrender and be recognized." Judge King concluded saying, "I shall inform the
Governor of what I have done advised, and I have no
doubt but he will approve of it to take time beforehand to
send to him will be useless, for the mischief will be done
before he could act."[32]

Atchison, who had, in 1833, represented the Mormons
in their lawsuit against Jackson County, would later
become the Missouri senator largely responsible for the
passage of the Kansas-Nebraska Act of 1854, which many
view as the opening salvo of the Civil War period. Perhaps,
Atchison was eager to make a name for himself and if so
King further added fuel to the fire with his statement
regarding the slowness with which Boggs would act if the
matter was left to him. In his letter, King listed the three
prisoners being held by the Mormons in Far West as John
Comer, William McHaney, and Adam Miller. King hoped
that they could be identified and released by General
Atchison.

King's letter had an immediate effect. On September
12, 1838, Atchison confirmed to Governor Boggs that an
"insurrection does actually exist." He explained himself to
the governor by stating, "upon the urgent solicitations of
Citizens of both counties [Daviess and Caldwell] and also

upon the petitions of Citizens of the adjoining counties I have deemed it my duty to order out an armed force to put down such insurrection and to assist the civil officers in the execution of the laws also to prevent as far as possible the effusion of blood and to restore quiet if possible to the community." Atchison explained to the governor, "this I have done by the advice of the Judge of this Circuit."[33] General Atchison ordered four companies of fifty men each from the militia of Clay County and a like number from the militia of Ray County. He reasoned with Governor Boggs that "the citizens of Daviess County and Caldwell County are under arms so that it is deemed dangerous for peaceable citizens to pass through said counties."[34] The state had another problem on its hands: "Citizens of other counties were flocking in to the Citizens of Daviess County and the Mormons were flocking to the assistance of the Mormons in those counties so that . . . there cannot be less than 2,000 men in arms without any legal authority." Atchison concluded, "It is very much feared that if once a blow is . . . struck there will be a general conflict the termination of which God only knows."

By September 15 the governor, convinced of the threat from an insurrection, determined Atchison's preemptive use of militia troops should be approved and continued. Accordingly he sent Adjutant-General Lisle the following order: "You will issue an order directed to Major Genl. Atchison Commanding the 3rd Division of the Militia of the State, and direct him to cause a sufficient force of the Troops under his Command to aid the Civil officers within the County of Daviess in executing such writs or process as may be legally within the province of their respective duties."[35]

Boggs made special mention of Dryden's affidavit and ensuring that the troops aided in making the arrest of Smith on the Daviess County warrant. The wheels of power in Jefferson City had finally begun to turn. Contrary to Judge King's prediction, the governor reacted quickly to quell the Mormon troubles.

* TEN *

MILITIA ON THE MOVE

GOVERNOR LILBURN BOGGS HAD TAKEN NOTICE of the issues and probably recalled the Mormon trouble in Jackson County when he was lieutenant governor. He planned to visit the site of the new disturbances and see if his presence would ameliorate the situation. On September 18 the governor had General Lisle send orders to the captain of the Boonville Guard that "you will cause your company to be held in readiness and mounted, each man with ten days provision and the necessary arms and ammunition to proceed immediately upon the order of the Governor with him to the scene of difficulty in the counties of Daviess and Caldwell."[1] Simultaneously the governor had orders issued for the remaining generals to prepare their troops to march to Daviess County some 130 miles away. Lisle's dispatch read as follows: "On the 30th ultimo an order was directed to you to cause three hundred mounted men to be raised and held in readiness." Lisle continued, "an insurrection now actually exists in the Counties of Caldwell and Daviess. You will therefore . . . immediately march to the scene of the difficulty, and cooperate with General Atchison . . . in restoring quiet to the Country." He instructed the generals to make all necessary preparations: "In suppressing the insurrection, each man will furnish himself with at least ten days provision, and the necessary arms and ammunition."[2]

Meanwhile, the non-Mormon residents of Daviess County were running out of options. The situation they described to Governor Boggs on September 12 was bleak. "For several weeks . . . the Mormons have been making formidable preparation for a civil war—and one which they are pleased to call a 'war of extermination.'" The beleaguered citizens continued, "The Mormons keep a lawless armed force stationed in our county, and are constantly throwing out menaces, threats and challenges to our citizens." Fearful of what might happen if they failed to act, "we sent an express to Richmond last week for arms and ammunition and on their return with their loads of guns, say forty-five, and several kegs powder and 200 lbs. lead they were intercepted." The ammunition caravan had been taken in Caldwell "by a banditti of those fanatical enthusiasts." (Enthusiast here is an archaic use, meaning religious zealot or one made excitable at being possessed or inspired by God.) The Daviess County citizens were "made prisoners . . . and taken to Far West—where they . . . are still held in custody." The affidavit went on to confirm that a band of fifty armed Mormons had raided a town in Livingston County to remove property and had taken prisoners during the exchange. As a result, the letter concluded, "two thirds of the families of Daviess County have left and gone to seek protection among the neighboring counties while a few old settlers are still here and are determined only to surrender their houses with their lives." The group admitted that "for about four weeks we have humbly and unceasingly been petitioning our neighboring counties for aid but are yet . . . helpless and defenceless. Believing our lives and our liberties our property and our all are in the most eminent danger." The letter concludes with a specific plea, "help us get rid of the Canadian emigrants."[3] Such a request begs the question as to whether their complaint was less about religion and more about the influx of northern sympathizers regarding

the issue of slavery. The southern Missouri settlers regarded the Canadian Mormons as both foreigners and as a
threat to their way of life because of their abolitionist sympathies. It may also reflect that an inordinate number of
new Canadian converts were pressed into armed service
for the church. Regardless of any ulterior objective, the
major issue on the minds of Daviess County citizens was
defending their homes from the Mormon army, which at
this time numbered between 300 and 500 soldiers.[4]

Another of the Mormons' former attorneys and the legislator behind the creation of Caldwell County as a
Mormon homeland, General Alexander Doniphan, also
recognized the dire situation developing in upper
Missouri. Without orders to do anything other than make
ready for further instruction, Doniphan ordered his unit
on September 12, 1838, to the Ray–Caldwell county line.
He stationed them in the timber on the Crooked River.
Then, accompanied by only his aide, Doniphan rode to Far
West to confront the Mormons directly. There he was
allowed to see the prisoners Comer, Miller, and McHaney
as well as the store of munitions seized from the prisoners.[5]

Doniphan reported, "I demanded of the Guard, who
had them in confinement, to deliver them over to me,
which was promptly done. I also found that the guns that
had been captured by the Sheriff and Citizens of
Caldwell, had been distributed and placed in the hands of
the soldiery and scattered over the County." Doniphan
ordered that the guns and ammunition be "immediately
collected and delivered up to me." He then sent for his
regiment to come to Far West and collect up the guns and
ammunition, and reported with pride that his troop
"arrived about 7 am making 40 miles since 10 am on the
previous day." When his troops arrived, the guns and
ammunition were delivered by the Mormons. Joseph
Smith, present in Far West, communicated to General
Doniphan that the prisoners had been detained and
weapons seized for fear that they were being supplied to a
mob of Daviess County citizens to drive the Mormons out.
Smith further explained that the prisoners were being held

and tried for the alleged crime and that if Judge King wanted the prisoners to be turned over to the general, then the Mormons would comply.[6] Doniphan did report with dismay that only "42 stand" (a measure of firearms) were produced. "Three stand could not be produced, as they had probably gone to Daviess County." The guns and Comer were transported under guard to Ray County. The other two prisoners, who were from Daviess County, remained with Doniphan's troops for protection until they could be returned safely to their homes in the north. As soon as they arrived in Daviess County, Doniphan "release[d] them on parol of honor, as I conceived their detention was illegal."[7]

Alexander Doniphan, a slave-owner, advocated the gradual elimination of slavery. He led Missouri volunteers in both the Mormon War and the war with Mexico. He disobeyed orders to execute Joseph Smith, Jr., and other Mormon leaders. (*Library of Congress*)

General Doniphan's troops were encouraged by their success in Caldwell County. They received orders to disperse all nonauthorized armed forces roaming about the countryside, marching thirty-seven miles to Millport in Daviess County. There they arrived at the encampment of the Daviess County non-Mormon volunteers. The group amounted to between 200 and 300 men, all under the command of Carroll County resident Dr. William Austin. Doniphan informed Austin of General Atchison's order that all unauthorized forces were to disperse. Austin protested that his unit was there purely for defense and should be allowed to remain. Despite Austin's claim, Doniphan noted, "Myself and others who approached the camp were taken to task and required to wait the approach of the sergeant of the guard." Doniphan, clearly suspicious of Austin's motives, noted that the Carroll County "volunteers'" movements were not defensive, as the doctor claimed. That fact combined with the lack of official state authority to muster the Carroll County force led Doniphan to conclude that Austin's intentions were ignoble. He also described Austin's troops' movements: "His professions were all pacific—but they still continue in arms, marching and counter-marching."[8]

General Doniphan then proceeded from Millport to Adam-ondi-Ahman to the Mormon encampment commanded by Colonel Lyman Wight. During a conference of the two leaders Doniphan recorded that Wight "professed entire willingness to disband and surrender up to me every one of the Mormons, accused of a crime, and required in return that the hostile force, collected by the other citizens of the county should also disband."[9] After the meeting, Doniphan moved his regiment two and a half miles east of Colonel Wight's encampment and directly between the two hostile factions. Doniphan reported that "some times the other camp [Dr. Austin's settlers] is nearer and some times further from me—I intend to occupy this position" until General Atchison arrived with more troops. Doniphan concluded his report, "I deem it best to preserve peace and prevent an engagement between the parties and if so for a few days they will doubtless disband without coercion."[10]

By September 17 General Atchison had moved his troops into position on the Grand River by Adam-ondi-Ahman. Before reconnoitering with General Doniphan, Atchison estimated the size of the Mormon troops at approximately two hundred and fifty men, between fifty and one hundred of whom were Mormons from Caldwell County. In his report to Governor Boggs, Atchison described the situation in Daviess: "Both parties [Mormons and settlers] have been scouting through the country and occasionally taking prisoners, threatening and insulting each other, but as of yet no blood has been shed." Atchison had "ordered all armed men from adjoining counties to repair to their homes—the Livingston County men and others to the amount of 100 men, have returned, and there remains now about one hundred and fifty, who will . . . return in a few days." Atchison was informed by the Mormons that all those charged with a violation of the law would be put on trial that same day. Atchison pointed out, "When that is done, the troops under my command, will no longer be required in this County, if the citizens of other counties will return to their respective homes." Despite his optimism, Atchison had still made arrangements to leave "two companies" of fifty men each "for the preservation of order, until peace and confidence are restored."[11]

Joseph Smith and Lyman Wight retained generals Alexander Doniphan and David Atchison to negotiate a surrender and trial on terms favorable to the Mormons.[12] According to the terms, Smith and Wight surrendered on the warrant with a hearing to be held before Judge King in Daviess County only a half mile north of the Caldwell County line.[13] Smith, who had remained in Caldwell County since the visit of Judge Morin and the Daviess County sheriff, also arranged for an armed force of Mormons stationed on the Caldwell–Daviess County border to come to his rescue in the event of a lynch mob. On September 7 all Mormons charged with a violation of the law were arraigned before local justice of the peace Dryden. The prosecuting attorney, Thomas C. Burch, conducted the hearing under a grove of trees near the southern Daviess County border as a concession to the Mormons who were concerned about reprisals.[14] The hearing was uneventful, resulting in Smith being bound over to circuit court on a $500 bond to keep the peace. After the payment of the same he was free to return to Caldwell County. His next court appearance was scheduled before Circuit Judge Austin King.

Writing from Liberty, Missouri, on September 20 General Atchison reported to Governor Boggs, "The troops ordered out for the purposes of putting down the insurrection supposed to exist in the counties of Daviess and

Caldwell, were discharged [today] with the exception of
two companies of the Ray Militia, now stationed in the
county of Daviess under the command of Brigadier
General [Hiram G.] Parks." At this point, orders from the
governor appear optional; Atchison took the liberty of
ordering the citizens and his troops at will. Governor
Boggs seemed to have taken little interest in the transpir-
ing events. Atchison provided his customary justification
for his actions explaining, "It was deemed necessary in the
State of excitement in that county [Daviess] that those
companies should remain there for a short period longer.
Say some 20 days, until confidence and tranquility should
be restored." Atchison explained his choice, and inciden-
tal imposition, on so highly ranked an officer, as follows:
"the reason that an officer of General Park's rank was left
in command were: 1st that if necessary he might call to his
assistance upon the shortest notice the whole force of his
Brigade, 2nd the moral influence of an officer of his rank
would be greater than an officer of less grade," and perhaps the most important reason, "3rd I could not find an
officer of less grade in my Division to manage affairs of so
much delicacy and importance."[15]

Atchison justified his decision to move his command: "I
deemed it my duty to order out the military forces. And I
have no doubt of the propriety of the measure." The militia's action "has convinced the Mormons that the law will
be enforced, and other citizens that it can be enforced and
is ample to redress all grievances." With those milestones
accomplished Atchison was convinced he had "prevented
blood from being shed for the present, and I am in hopes
for the future."[16]

Atchison's dispatch included some encouraging news.
He reported to Boggs that all unauthorized settler troops
from Daviess and adjoining counties had been dispersed.
Additionally, all unauthorized Mormon forces had
returned to their homes. He described Lyman Wight,
leader of the Daviess County Mormons, to the governor as
"bold, brave, skillful, and . . . desperate." Atchison confirmed that the Mormons "appeared to be acting on the

defensive, and I must further add, gave up the offenders with a great deal of promptness." On the issue of the missing munitions the general stated, "The arms taken by the Mormons and prisoners were also given up on demand with seeming cheerfulness." One can only presume they sensed that their cooperation would calm the disturbances. "I consider," remarked Atchison, "the insurrection for the present at least to be at an end." He went on to warn, "from the state of feeling in the county of Daviess and adjoining counties it is very much to be feared, that it [violence] will break out again, and if so, without the interposition of the commander-in-chief the consequences will be awful."[17] Atchison felt that only the governor's appearance and authority would settle everyone down. Mormons from the town of DeWitt had desperately sent the governor a similar request. The guns had been holstered, but the spirit of insurrection was still alive. Despite the pleas, the governor cancelled his plans to visit the region. His decision might have been based on the overly optimistic dispatch from General Parks that was sent without Atchison's knowledge or approval. "I am happy to inform you that there is not any necessity to use a larger force here at present [100 men]—than now under my command."[18]

Parks also detailed the attitude of the Mormons. "Whatever may have been the disposition of the people, called Mormons, before our arrival here, since we have made our appearance, they have shown no disposition to resist the laws, or of hostile intentions." Parks explained he had visited the Mormon towns to verify reports and noted, "As soon as they saw the militia interpose between them and the people of this and some of the adjoining counties, who had assembled in arms, they went to work, and abandoned their hostile attitude." Parks genuinely believed that the Mormons were not a threat as long as the settlers remained in check. "At this time peace and tranquility have every appearance of being restored. How long things may maintain their present attitude I know not." Just to be sure the governor did not mistake his report of saying there had never been an insurrection, he was quick to add that upon his arrival, "We found a large body of men from the counties adjoining; armed and in the field, for the purpose . . . of assisting the people of this county against the Mormons." All this "without being called out by the proper authorities . . . Major General Atchison very promptly prevailed on [them] to return to their homes." Parks also praised Atchison's initiative, saying that "if the Major General had not taken the field with a sufficient force as promptly as he did there is every reason to fear a dreadful conflict would have ensued."[19]

Wanting to convey to the governor that the full letter of his orders had been accomplished, Parks continued, "On next Saturday the 29th there will be brought to trial some fifteen to twenty individuals of the Mormons before a Justice of the Peace." Parks confirmed he had the personal pledge of Lyman Wight that the Mormons would appear in court to face the charges. These were the individuals named in the William Dryden warrant and the men specifically mentioned by the governor in his order. Progress was also being made to finally resolve the land dispute between Mormons and non-Mormons. Parks noted, "A committee has been appointed on behalf of the citizens of Daviess County to meet the Mormons tomorrow for the purposes of proposing to buy or sell them out. They will meet in Adam-ondi-Ahman, where I will attend with a force to ensure tranquility." Parks was truly surprised that things were not as bad off in the area as he had heard and reported as much to the governor: "There has been so much prejudice and exaggeration concerned in this matter, that I have found things on my arrival here, totally different from what I was prepared to expect."[20] Parks may have contributed to future problems in Carroll County by convincing the governor to reduce the number of militia troops in the field, but from Parks's limited perspective he was conveying the fullest and fairest assessment of the situation.

General Parks forwarded the governor's orders to General Atchison with a note explaining the news he had conveyed to Jefferson City. Parks also mentioned that he had only just received word of a threat from the citizens with regard to the buy out or sell out negotiations taking place in Adam-ondi-Ahman. "I have this moment heard a threat thrown out by the men of this county that should the . . . measure fail[,] their intention is to drive the Mormons with powder and lead from the county."[21]

Despite the foreshadowing of a return to violence, Atchison reported to Governor Boggs, "Things are not so bad in that county as they have been represented by rumor—and in fact from affidavits, I have no doubt your Excellency has been deceived by the exaggerated statements of designing and half crazy men. I have found no cause for alarm on account of the Mormons—they are not to be feared—they are very much alarmed."[22]

The news of the end of hostilities in upper Missouri was well received in Jefferson City. On September 22 Secretary of State Glover sent word to the governor: "From the tenor of the papers it would appear that there is no necessity for the troops that have been raised from this Division to march. The commanding officer, however does not consider that he would be justifiable in disbanding them, or suspending for a few days, operations without express orders to that effect from the Commander-in-Chief."[23] Taking Glover's hint, Governor Boggs ordered Adjutant General Lisle on the 24th to order the disbanding of the militia. "The commander-in-chief having this morning received information by express that the civil disturbance in the counties of Daviess and Caldwell have been quieted and order restored to the country. He therefore orders that the troops under your command destined for that service be immediately discharged."[24] The order was sent out to Generals Bolton, Lucas, Clark, and Atchison, thereby disbanding any and all forces called up in the mustering order of August 30. This reaction would turn out to be premature.

ELEVEN

THE DeWITT
STAND-OFF

NEARLY HALF OF THE DAVIESS COUNTY population in 1838 was comprised of Mormons. The Daviess County non-Mormon populace was aware of the odds and realized that if they directly attacked the Mormons they would be driven from the county. In addition to their sizable numbers the Mormons were also well equipped to fight. Atchison described the Mormons' arms and attitude: "Most of them [are] equipped with a good rifle or musket, a brace of large belt pistols, and broadsword; so that from their position, their fanaticism and their unalterable determination not to be driven, much blood will be spilt, and much suffering endured, if a blow is once struck."[1] Given the daunting conditions reported by General Atchison, the settlers realized it was foolish to fight the Mormons. As the militia had dispersed friendly forces from surrounding counties, it was in their best interest to work for a lasting peace.

Though the legalities had been dealt with, daily life was about to become extremely hard for the Mormons outside Caldwell County, however. The miller in Millport, the only mill in Daviess County, refused to grind Mormon grain into flour. Caldwell County had only one mill on the east side of the county, called Haun's Mill, but it could not keep up with the demand for flour in both Caldwell and Daviess counties. Bread became scarce in Adam-ondi-Ahman and Far West. Women began boiling unmilled wheat and grating corn crudely in order to have enough food. They found that corn proved edible when baked with pumpkin, but the wheat was sodden and indigestible.[2] To make matters more complicated, there was insufficient housing for the nearly 1,500 Canadian and English Mormons recently arrived in the Caldwell County area.[3] Many were still living out of their covered wagons or in bark tents, and the prospect of a fast-approaching winter brought with it the dangers of exposure and starvation.[4]

The Mormons living beyond the borders of Caldwell County were also soon confronted by armed bands of Missouri settlers that had begun prowling about. They would set fire to haystacks and granaries and steal horses and cattle. They even whipped Mormon farmers who attempted to put up a fight. As time progressed it was no longer safe for Mormons to live outside the larger settlements of Adam-ondi-Ahman in Daviess County and DeWitt in Carroll County.[5] As their provisions ran out, each city received word from the land agents from whom the Mormons had originally bought their land that they were willing to buy it back so that the Mormons could leave peaceably. The very thought of selling their land was unbearable to the Mormons, who remembered their exit from Jackson County only six years before.

Smith's first reaction to the increased violence was to expand the Danite organization. He dubbed it the "Armies of Israel" and conscripted every able-bodied man into the force. General Atchison had estimated that the total force of men between Daviess and Caldwell counties capable of bearing arms between 1,300 and 1,500 men.[6] One convert described his duties as "guarding, spying, foraging [and] arms manufacturing."[7] In addition, the Mormons once again turned to Alexander Doniphan for aid. His services were retained to negotiate a settlement with Daviess County settlers to sell their land to the Mormons. He immediately took the Mormon offer to Gallatin and started his work to convince the Daviess County settlers to move out and make room for the Mormons. His powers of persuasion nearly succeeded. Doniphan and the settlers were about to hammer out the terms of an agreement when dramatic events in Carroll County halted his progress and again turned the tide against the Mormons.[8]

In late August Joseph Smith learned of renewed dissension among his faithful. Word was spreading that the actions condoned and taken by the prophet were not in the best interests of the church and that it was driving them toward war with the Missourians. The source was John Corrill, the new church historian and newly elected state representative for Caldwell County. Corrill felt an obligation to both the state and the Mormons and walked a fine line between the two loyalties. This conscientious approach won him the respect of many non-Mormons such as Alexander Doniphan but would cause him great turmoil with the church leadership. On August 30 Sidney Rigdon and Joseph Smith paid Corrill a friendly visit to confirm their information and to put a stop to the talk undermining the church leadership.[9] Specifically, Corrill was vehemently opposed to violent measure against non-Mormons.

Corrill confirmed that he had been critical but also that he felt it was his right to speak his mind. He told them he was a Republican (a believer in the Republic, not a member of a political party) and therefore would make up his own mind about the propriety of any course of action proposed by the church leadership. He asserted his right to question the leadership of the church or even God if the instruction came through Joseph Smith's revelation.[10]

Smith admonished Corrill for his attitude, saying, "The foolishness of God is wiser than a man; and the weakness of God is stronger, than a man." With that knowledge, Smith wondered how Corrill could trust his own judgment over that of the church doctrine. When he received no response Smith turned the floor over to Rigdon, who spewed his angry threats against Corrill. Afterward Smith records that Corrill acknowledged he understood things differently after the interview than he did before it.[11] Smith, focused on keeping up the appearance of unity in the Mormon ranks, wanted it to appear as though historian and state representative John Corrill was reconciled to his leadership. Corrill would play along temporarily but only months later he would publish his *Brief History of the Church* and thoroughly distance himself from the church and its leaders.[12]

As Doniphan was working the Daviess County settlers toward a resolution of selling out to the Mormons, the people of Carroll County had different plans in mind. The lone Mormon settlement in the county, DeWitt, was near the confluence of the Missouri and Grand rivers and was strategically important as the Mormons' only port city. Church leaders had acquired the land earlier that spring and planned to use it to aid importing and exporting supplies and to make the transfer of new converts by steamboat much simpler.[13] After the Rigdon extermination sermon on July 4, 1838, Carroll County settlers put the issue of the Mormon settlement of DeWitt on the ballot.

In August the settlers made a formal demand on the Mormons of DeWitt to leave and return to Caldwell County shortly after the election with an October 1 deadline. Mormon leaders George Hinkle and John Murdock informed the Carroll County Committee, a group of non-Mormon leaders from that county, that the Mormons, as American citizens, would settle where they liked and refused to leave. On August 7 the settlers met and voted to remove the Mormons by force of arms.[14]

Acting without orders, the Carroll County militia lay siege to DeWitt. A Mormon witness, Smith Humphrey, remembered the events: "On the morning of the 19th of August 1838 I being in DeWitt I was returning home and was met by an armed force of men I supposed nearly one hundred commanded by Colonel [William Claud] Jones and by force took and kept me prisoner about two hours during which time they made many threats against the

people called Mormons such as that they were determined
to drive them from that County."[15] On and off for the next
two months Carroll County vigilantes attacked Mormons,
burning their homes and stables, until the only refuge was
behind a barricade around DeWitt. Smith decided, in
reaction, to send 200 newly arrived Canadian converts to
reinforce the Mormon defenders.[16] Mormons in DeWitt
also sent a petition to Governor Boggs on September 22
pleading for state assistance to stay in their homes and
stop the lawless acts of the Carroll County settlers. They
described the situation in the following terms:

> That whereas your petitioners have on the 20th inst.
> been sorely aggrieved by being beset by a lawless mob
> certain inhabitants of this and other counties to the
> injury of the good citizens of this and the adjacent
> places, that on the afore said day came from one hun-
> dred to one hundred and fifty armed men & threat-
> ened with force & violence to drive certain peaceable
> citizens from their homes in defiance of all law &
> threatened them to drive said citizens out of the
> county. But on deliberation concluded to give them
> said citizens till the first of October next to leave said
> County, & threatened if not gone by that time to
> exterminate them without regard to age or sex and
> destroy their chattels [livestock], by throwing them in
> the river-We therefore pray you to take such steps as
> shall put a stop to all lawless proceedings.[17]

The governor took no acts to stop the Carroll County
settlers from expelling the Mormons and left them to
defend themselves. In fact by the time he received the
request the governor had already declared the insurrection at an end and issued orders to disband the militia that
had been called up at the end of August.

After October 1 the settlers laid the siege in earnest, firing on all who approached the city. Henry Root, a Mormon
there on that day, recalled: "There was collected in the
vicinity of DeWitt; an armed force consisting of from thirty to fifty persons, and on the morning of the 2nd of

October, came into the town of DeWitt and fired on the civil inhabitants of that place." Root was an eyewitness to the activities of thirteen attackers, and he requested the authorities' help, saying, "I believed there is an insurrection in that place."[18] When General Parks received news of the events on October 5 he immediately dispatched his remaining one hundred men under the command of Captains Samuel Bogart and Houston. Each man took six days' provisions and fifty rounds of powder and ball. Parks expected his men to see some action in Carroll County.

Despite having been given his orders to disband, General Samuel Lucas had proceeded down the Missouri River into Carroll County to investigate the rumored disturbance. Lucas reported to the governor that his men had seen a large armed force of Mormons at DeWitt. Colonel Hinkle, the commander of those forces, reported he had two hundred men under arms. The Mormons were hourly expecting an attack from the citizens of Carroll County.[19] An armed force of Carroll County citizens were encamped six miles outside DeWitt. That group was awaiting reinforcements from Saline County, and it was anticipated thereupon that the settlers would mount an attack on DeWitt to drive the Mormons out. Colonel Hinkle informed General Lucas the Mormons were determined to put up a fight if attacked.

Lucas reported to the governor that on October 3, "a fight took place . . . and several persons were killed." (This observation was incorrect; no one was actually killed in the DeWitt standoff, although both sides occasionally exchanged gunfire.) He continued, "If a fight has actually taken place, of which I have no doubt, it will cause a great excitement in the whole of upper Missouri and those base and degraded beings will be exterminated from the face of the earth." Convinced the trigger of chaos had just been fired, Lucas painted a grim picture to the governor. "If one of the citizens of Carroll should be killed, before 5 days I believe that there will be from four to five thousand volunteers in the field against the Mormons and nothing but their blood will satisfy them." After his morose assessment, the general's next statement is the epitome of understatement: "It is an unpleasant state of affairs — the remedy I do not pretend to suggest to your Excellency." Lucas concluded his report by reminding the governor that his troops of the 4th Division of militia were only just dismissed and could be recalled at an hour's notice.[20]

General Atchison sent a dispatch to Governor Boggs on October 5 confirming the events in Carroll County as reported by General Lucas. "I have just received by express from Brigadier General Parks. It seems the Mormon difficulties are not brought to a close." Atchison continued, "In Carroll County the citizens are in arms for the purpose of driving the Mormons from the county." Again deeming it his duty, General Atchison ordered General Parks's brigade to move in and quell the uprising. He assured the governor that things remained quiet in Daviess County and that troops were no longer required there to maintain the peace.[21]

The militia was not the only group to report the Carroll County disturbance. On October 4 a group of concerned citizens from adjacent Chariton County infiltrated the area and met with both sides. They reported "a large portion of citizens of Carroll and the adjoining counties assembled near DeWitt, well armed." The number was approximately two hundred armed citizens, intent on driving the Mormons from the county.[22] Among their chief complaints was that the Mormons came from other parts of the world. The Carroll County citizens informed the Chariton County citizens they were "waging a war of extermination," using Sidney Rigdon's own well-circulated words, and that they would succeed in removing the Mormons by force. The Chariton citizens then proceeded to visit the Mormons and reported their condition. "We found them in the act of defence, beging for peace, and wishing for the civil authorities to repare there as early as possible to settle the difficulties between the parties." The Chariton County committee sent the governor the same message: "Hostilities have commenced and will continue until they are stopt by the civil authorities."[23]

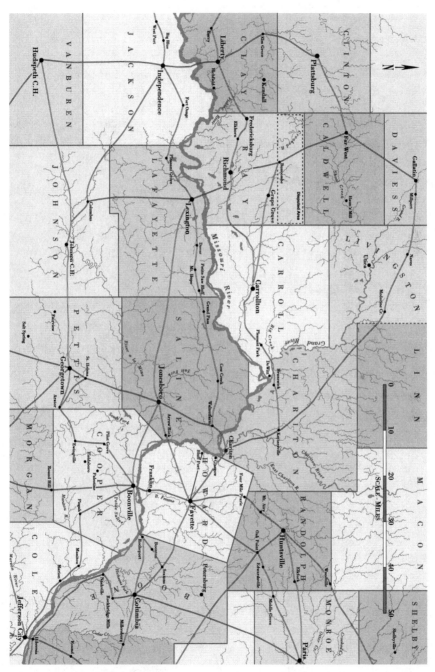

Western Missouri in 1838, showing the relative positions of Jefferson City (the capital), Liberty, Far West, Richmond, Carrollton, DeWitt, and Gallatin.

Forces hostile to the Mormons saw the situation in a different light entirely. The citizens of Howard County, a county southeast of Carroll, were in the area of DeWitt on October 7: "This county is the theatre of a civil war and will soon be one of desolation, unless the citizens of the adjoining counties lend immediate assistance." They viewed the Mormons as the problem: "The infatuated Mormons have assembled in large numbers in DeWitt, prepared for War, and are continually pouring in from all quarters where these detestable fanatics reside." The Howard County citizens sent word to the governor claiming the Mormons were the first malefactors. "The war is commenced: blood has been shed they shed it; they waylaid and fired upon a body of the citizens of Carroll County and wounded some. They are the aggressors. They have violated the laws, and shed the blood of our citizens, and we think this one of the cases of emergency in which the people ought to take the execution of justice into their own hands." The report is silent as to why a group of Carroll County citizens was assembled or what they might be doing which would incite the Mormons to fire on them. Nonetheless, the citizens continued in their plea to the governor: "Speedy action is necessary, the progress of their imposition, insult and oppression ought to be checked . . . the people must act together. They must act energetically."[24]

The commander of the Howard County citizens sought to get the support of the militia. "Mormons are lurking around our camp and making preparations to attack us before day. Our number is much less than theirs, and we have to act on the defensive until we procure more assistance." They also reported the reinforcement of Mormons from Far West. On the 5th one hundred mounted Mormons had arrived from Far West. Again on the 6th a band of sixty-two armed riders arrived, and it was reported that each night thereafter more troops continued to pour into DeWitt. The commander concluded to the governor, "you cannot fail to come forward immediately, can you not be here by Sunday or Monday at the farthest."

Fearing the governor would ignore the plea, he continued, "This is no false excitement, or idle rumor; it is the cold reality, too real." His brazen tone was born out of a sense of desperation: "We will anticipate you immediately, and shall expect your cooperation and assistance in expelling the fanatics, who are mostly aliens by birth and aliens in principle from the country. We must be enemies to the common enemies of our law, religion and country."[25]

Even Captain Bogart of the Missouri militia, who was not engaged in the action at DeWitt, observed that each time they met a Mormon, "he is armed in best manner and continually throwing out his threats." Bogart described his company's next movements. "We were ordered to DeWitt in Carroll County. When we arrived at Carrollton we were informed that the people of Carroll and the Mormons, who were mostly Canadians, were assembled within a mile of each other, ready for battle." In a later report, Bogart explained, "Mormons from Caldwell were on their way to DeWitt." Captain Bogart requested his company be allowed to move across the road between Far West and DeWitt and intercept the Mormon reinforcements, forcing them back to Caldwell. General Parks, writing from Daviess County, denied his request and Mormon reinforcements were allowed to freely pass into DeWitt, swelling the number of defenders. General Parks did order his troops to move closer to DeWitt after the reinforcements arrived but made no efforts to disperse the combatants; Bogart was infuriated. After two days of encamping his force outside DeWitt, Parks ordered his troops home. He left over two hundred well-armed Mormons in DeWitt that had come from Caldwell, disobeying the express orders of General Atchison to quell the uprising.

The conditions in DeWitt were dire. The Mormons had no food to eat or kindling to build fires. Attempts to forage for food and firewood resulted in vigilantes beating any Mormons who ventured out of the town. The women and children were even harried within their homes by volunteer gunmen who rode up within two hundred yards of the town, spraying the buildings with gunfire.[26]

On October 6 General Parks finally arrived at DeWitt
from Daviess County with his two companies totaling one
hundred mounted men. Colonel James, under Parks's
command, was ordered to raise three additional companies from Carroll County and meet up with General Parks
in Carrollton before proceeding to DeWitt. When the
troops failed to materialize, the general suspected it was
because they were sympathetic to the non-Mormons'
cause and therefore did not want to interfere with their
activities, or they were themselves participating in attacks
on the Mormons. Parks had ordered two companies from
Livingston County but did not expect them to report
given the current state of agitation directed toward
Mormons in Livingston and Daviess counties.[27]

Upon his arrival at DeWitt, General Parks found a body
of armed men under the command of Dr. William Austin,
who had previously been encamped around Millport in
Daviess County. Dr. Austin's troops besieged DeWitt with
a force of two hundred to three hundred armed men and
one piece of field artillery. The citizen troops were poised
to launch an attack on the Mormons in DeWitt. The
Mormon defenders under Colonel Hinkle numbered
three hundred to four hundred and were intent on holding their ground to the death. Parks reported to General
Atchison that on October 4 the sides exchanged fire, and
no more than sixty guns on each side were discharged.
One Saline County citizen was wounded but no other
injuries were reported. The firefight did convince Dr.
Austin to delay his attack on DeWitt until he received
additional troops. He anticipated his force would reach
five hundred within the week and afterward he would
order a second attempt to take the town by force. With the
militia forces under General Parks at only one hundred,
he was hardly in a position to disband either side and
decided instead to play the role of mediator in order to
forestall any bloodshed.[28]

Parks was pleased to receive a dispatch from General
Atchison instructing him to call on General Doniphan's
five companies for reinforcements. Atchison believed

these troops would show, and with a sufficient force he would be able to bring the standoff to an end. General Parks reported that the Carroll County men were blood-thirsty, "nothing seems so much in demand here as Mormon scalps." Despite the outward aggressiveness, General Parks reported that the Carroll citizens "are scared, I believe Hinkle with his present force and position will beat Austin with 500 of his troops." In addition to the superior position, General Parks also noted Colonel Hinkle's determination: "The Mormons say they will die before they will be drove out . . . as yet they have acted on the defensive." General Parks opined that "the Mormons will have no rest until they leave; whether they will or not, time only can tell." Parks was certain that if the governor would make an appearance, "he need not order out any forces. His Excellency would have power to quell this affair than [an entire] regiment; should he come which I hope he will for this is no little affair."[29]

When he learned of the developments in Carroll County on October 9, General Atchison instructed General Parks to disarm all armed Mormons and citizens from adjoining counties as soon as his reinforcements arrived. He further instructed Parks to urge the Mormons to sell out to the Carroll County citizens and remove themselves from the county in order to prevent further bloodshed. Atchison sent a dispatch to the governor requesting he make an appearance in Carroll County to restore the peace.[30]

Joseph Smith, riding from Far West, had snuck into DeWitt under cover of darkness with one of the reinforcement brigades of two hundred mounted men. He was determined to rally his beleaguered troops and hold DeWitt. Once there, Smith learned that men sent out to forage were beaten with hickory hearts by the vigilantes and returned empty-handed.[31] Carroll County citizens fired on all persons attempting to enter or exit the city, and supplies were dwindling. The strength to resist was quickly wasting away. The governor had not responded to the pleas for help, and militia troops were not intervening to stop the blockade of the Mormon city. Smith was faced with the prospect of encouraging his force to launch an all-out assault on an armed force of unknown size, or surrendering to regroup in Caldwell County and fight another day. Looking around, Smith could see the people were starving and appeared grossly outnumbered. Finally, on October 10 Smith ordered the surrender of the city to the Carroll County settlers.[32] The adversaries met to discuss the surrender that day with compensation being made to the Mormons for their surrendered holdings, and with the terms concluded, all Mormon settlers departed Carroll County.

The citizens of Carroll County suspected that the Mormons' true intentions were to consolidate forces and push the citizens out of Daviess and Livingston counties. Bogart independently reached the same conclusion; however, he was also aware of the resolve of Carroll County citizens to prevent further Mormon intrusions outside Caldwell and feared the conflict was not over. Captain Bogart urged the governor to action: "If not some effective means are taken to settle this difficulty much blood will be spilt soon."[33]

Bogart further suggested that "too many of our officers are seeking popularity with the Mormons supposing their votes in time will be of some service to them." Taking into account his service as an attorney for the Mormons and his efforts as a legislator to create Caldwell County as a Mormon safe haven, Bogart is probably referring to Atchison. This report among others caused Governor Boggs to distrust Atchison. Bogart concluded his missive to the governor with a scolding: "You may rest assured times grow worse and worse here; Mormons embolden themselves, keep out guards, and refuse to let any person see their forces, had you proceeded to Daviess Co. you could have easily viewed for yourself the state of things which are desperate in the extreme. . . . I hope you will take steps to make a final settlement of this matter, if it is not done soon our country is ruined."[34]

When the DeWitt Mormon wagons arrived in Far West, the seasoned converts chalked up the defeat to their continued martyrdom, but the younger members were bent on revenge.[35] The news of the Mormon expulsion from Carroll County spread like wildfire. Daviess County soon rejected Alexander Doniphan's overtures of settlement with the Mormons. Residents in Daviess reasoned that if Carroll County could successfully drive out the Mormons, so could they. The Daviess settlers spread the word, "To Hell with compromise! To Hell with Doniphan's peace settlement!"[36]

On October 14 Smith called a meeting of all able-bodied men in Far West. "We are an injured people," Smith began. "From county to county we have been driven by unscrupulous mobs eager to seize the land we have cleared and improved with such love and toil. We have appealed to magistrates, judges, the Governor, and even to the President of the United States, but there has been no redress for us." He continued defiantly, "The latest reply of Boggs to our Petitions is to tell us to fight our own battles. And that brethren, is exactly what we intend to do."[37] Smith continued, "I have a great [reverence] for the Constitution, but for the laws of this state I have no regard whatsoever, for they were made by a parcel of blacklegs."[38]

Smith announced, "General Doniphan has authorized this body to act as a regiment of the state militia under the command of Col. Hinkle." Doniphan had procured a militia unit for Caldwell County; however, its use was subject to the orders of the governor just as it was in all other Missouri counties. Smith did not have authority to call up the Caldwell militia to readiness and Governor Boggs never issued an order asking them to deploy. Despite his disdain for Missouri law Smith quickly confirmed: "We are therefore acting within the law. All who are with me will meet tomorrow to march to the defense of Adam-ondi - Ahman." He reminded his followers, "Greater love hath no man than this, that he lay down his life for his brethren."[39]

Smith's tone darkened as he noted missing dissenters from the meeting, "Brother Rigdon likes to call them 'Oh don't men!' In this time of war we have no need for such. A man must declare himself friend or enemy. I move a resolution that the property of all 'Oh don't men' be taken over to maintain the war." The crowd burst into shouting and adulation. Sidney Rigdon, eyes blazing, jumped up and shouted, "I move that the blood of the backward be spilled in the streets of the Far West!" Smith silenced him saying, "No, I move a better resolution. We'll take them along with us to Daviess County, and if it comes to battle, we'll sit them on their horses with bayonets and pitchforks and make them ride in front!"[40]

In closing Smith declared, "If the people will let us alone, we will preach the gospel in peace. But if they come on us to molest us we will establish our religion by the sword. We will trample down our enemies and make it one of gore and blood from the Rocky Mountains to the Atlantic Ocean." He prophesied, "I will be to this generation a second Mohammed, whose motto in treating for peace was 'the Alcoran [Qur'an] or the Sword.' So shall it eventually be with us—Joseph Smith or the Sword!"[41]

TWELVE

THE RAID ON GALLATIN

MAJOR GENERAL DAVID ATCHISON reported to Governor Boggs on October 16, 1838 that "the Mormons in Carroll County . . . sold out and left" voluntarily. Atchison glowingly observed that now "everything is quiet there."[1] As Atchison certainly knew that Missouri volunteer troops had surrounded the town and were firing on the Mormons, this report misrepresented the facts to the governor. Perhaps the Mormons had ultimately left under their own power and on negotiated terms, but had the decision been left to them they would have remained in DeWitt.

Perhaps Carroll County was now relatively calm, but things were far from quiet overall. General Lucas's comments to the governor a few days earlier were much more in line with reality. The whole of upper Missouri was about to come to blows over the Carroll County affair. Fresh from their victory in driving the Mormons out of their county, the Carroll County Missourians took their cannon and headed for Daviess County to help citizens there drive away the Mormon population. Even in his letter to the governor, Atchison acknowledged that if the Carroll County vigilantes arrived in Daviess, "the same lawless game is to be played over, and the Mormons will be driven from that county as well." If no intervention was made by the militia, Atchison anticipated that the Missourians would not stop at Daviess but would then proceed to the Mormon stronghold of Caldwell County and force out the Mormons to the last man. He reasoned the citizens would continue to take matters into their own hands and make the Mormons leave until they were made to realize that the laws of the state were going to be enforced. "Nothing," in Atchison's opinion, "but the strongest measures within the power of the Executive will put down this spirit of Mobocracy."[2]

The troops under General Parks's command in the field were susceptible to the mob spirit themselves, as they sympathized with the non-Mormon citizens. Atchison stated to Governor Boggs, "I believe Parks to be mistaken"; however, he again pleads, "I would respectfully suggest to your Excellency . . . a visit to the scene of excitement in person, or at all events a strong proclamation." He goes on to point out, "the state of things which have existed in the counties of Daviess and Carroll for the last two months, has been . . . ruinous to the people and disgraceful to the State." "Strong measures," Atchison continued, were necessary "to put down this spirit of mob, and misrule." In the alternative he suggested: "Permit them to fight it out, if your Excellency should conclude the latter expedient [and] best calculated to produce quiet and restore order." This suggestion dripped with sarcasm; obviously letting the two sides fight it out would produce no quiet. No doubt frustrated with the governor's silence, General Atchison baited Boggs to "issue an order . . . to discharge the troops now engaged in that service." He would follow it immediately.[3]

General John B. Clark, whom the governor would later designate as the overall field commander of the militia forces to replace Atchison, sent a dispatch voicing his disappointment over the governor's decision to disband the militia on October 9. "I regret exceedingly that your Excellency received information making it necessary to discharge the troops you had on the march. Nothing but such step, in my opinion, will ever settle the affair."[4]

Perhaps it was his discerning opinion that caused the governor to select him, but whatever the reason, Clark's intuitions proved correct.

Reports of Mormon atrocities in Daviess County began to pour into Jefferson City. On the 13th Captain Bogart, who had recently returned to Daviess County from his deployment around DeWitt, sent a dispatch directly to the governor. He stated that "Our country is in a deplorable condition. I just arrived home from a second tour of duty putting down the insurrection." He explained: "The citizens who lived in Daviess and adjoining counties knew and expressed themselves that the Mormons were determined to drive the citizens from Daviess County. The Mormons have since expressed [the same intent]. The lives of the people of Daviess have been threatened . . . and have fled for safety to the adjoining counties."[5]

The Missouri citizens were not the only ones interested in taking the law into their own hands. When the governor ignored their request for help in DeWitt, Mormons lost faith that the laws of the state would be enforced equally. Smith convinced a majority of Mormons that the state would not intervene to protect Mormons from Missourians. They allowed themselves to imagine the events of 1833 in Jackson County played out again in Caldwell County.[6]

After Smith's speech on October 14 in Far West, he and one hundred armed and mounted Mormons left Caldwell and rode to Adam-ondi-Ahman, in Daviess County, swelling Lyman Wight's troops there to three hundred fifty men.[7] Upon arriving in the Mormon stronghold Smith met in conference with Wight and made plans to drive the residents from the county by force. Wight gathered his men together. He was dressed for a fight, wearing a red handkerchief around his head with the knot tied in front, Indian-style. His fine brown horse was also covered in a bearskin blanket in Wight's signature style.[8] He sat upon his horse and drew his cutlass. "The sword has been drawn, and shall not be sheathed until we have won back everything the mobs have wrenched from us," shouted Wight. "Our cause is just . . . the Lord is on our side." He encouraged the men: "It makes no difference if our enemies number 50 or 50,000."[9] The speech worked its desired effect. John D. Lee, a Danite soldier present, felt bulletproof. He remarked, "I thought one Danite would chase a thousand gentiles and 2 could put 10,000 to flight."[10] The Mormon leadership had determined to split their force into three units and attack the three largest non-Mormon cities in Daviess County. Once the invasion of Daviess was complete, Smith left his options open to take the fight elsewhere.[11]

Fear of death was a reality in Daviess County for non-Mormon citizens. A post rider sounded the alert, stating he had seen the citizens of Caldwell paraded in Far West for the purpose of driving out of Daviess all of the citizens who were not friendly to them. It was estimated that the Mormons could raise a force between one thousand and two thousand men strong.[12] On October 16 those Mormon troops marched to Adam-ondi-Ahman. On the 17th a snowstorm hit upper Missouri and the Mormons had to wait to execute their plan to assault the three cities until the following day. Not wanting to lose momentum on the 17th, small parties of Mormons began to disarm the non-Mormon Daviess County population near Adam-ondi-Ahman. Henry Lee, a citizen from Daviess living in the countryside, was visited by a group of Mormons who told him to get out of his house. The Mormons informed him they were going to take his property and that he had better get away. He left his home immediately.[13]

The next day the Mormons raided Gallatin, Millport, and Grindstone Fork. One company of approximately one hundred men was ordered to attack Gallatin under the command of David Patten, code-named Captain Fearnought. At the same time another company of one hundred men under the command of Col. Lyman Wight was given the task of attacking Millport. A third company of

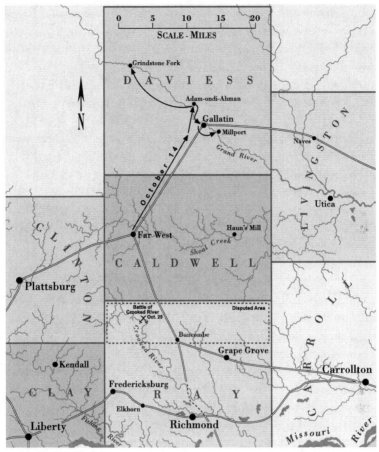

The Mormons mounted a three-prong attack on Daviess County, raiding the communities of Gallatin, Millport, and Grindstone Fork. Displaced settlers and Mormons opposed to the attacks fled to Richmond in southern Ray County and other western Missouri towns. Emboldened by their success in Daviess, the Mormon army raided parts of Livingston County to the east.

one hundred men under the command of Seymour Brunson attacked Grindstone Fork. The first objective was to take provisions for the winter and compensation for Mormon losses in Jackson and Carroll counties. The second objective was to drive all non-Mormons from the county. The Mormons rounded up all horses, cattle, and hogs they could find and brought them back to Adam-ondi-Ahman.[14] A young Mormon by the name of Oliver Huntington, who was not allowed to participate in the raids because of his age, had climbed up to Adam's altar, the highest point in Adam-ondi-Ahman, to see what he could of the fighting. He recollected of the day: "I saw the smoke rising toward heaven, which filled me with ambition." The following day the youth reported, "I went to Bishop Knight's house and saw the plunder . . . and heard them tell in what order they took the place."[15]

When news and evidence of the Mormon exploits in Daviess reached Far West, Sidney Rigdon spread the news of the victory and clapped when the first wagon of stolen, or as the Mormons called it, "consecrated," property pulled into the square. For many Mormons in Far West the scene evoked horror rather than joy.

The Gallatin postmaster G. W. Thornton reported being driven from his office and house. Both buildings were robbed and ultimately burned to the ground. The Mormon attackers ordered Thornton and the other citizens of Gallatin to leave the county by the 19th or pay for their disobedience with their lives. Over the next few days a group of three hundred armed Mormons marched back through Daviess County loading up all the property left behind by the fleeing citizens. As they cleaned the houses out they would set fire to them to ensure that the citizens could not return. Among the houses destroyed was that of justice of the peace Adam Black, who would be an important source of information. Joseph Smith had threatened Black in the same house in August 1838, in response to the voting brawl in Gallatin.[16]

On October 18 the sheriff, William Morgan, was riding to Gallatin. When he arrived he saw five men ride off from the direction of Jacob Stallings's general store. One hundred Mormons had already come to the town en masse. They took all the valuables and set the buildings on fire. The sheriff found both the general store and post office buildings burning and deserted. Property that would not fit on the Mormon wagons was strewn and scattered about the streets. When the sheriff finally found Stallings's store clerk he confirmed that the Mormons were responsible. Captain Fearnought [David Patten] had issued a warning that all non-Mormon citizens of Daviess County must leave the county or face death.[17] Heeding the warning, nearly all citizens were moving their families to Livingston County, including the sheriff and several justices of the peace. The sheriff wrote to the governor expressing the citizens' urgent need for assistance: "Our country is in a desperate situation [the Mormons are] burning and driving as they go."[18] Daviess County justice of the peace Phillip Covington confirmed Sheriff Morgan's statement of the facts. He further described an armed band of twenty-five Mormons who had come to his house giving orders to leave or they "would be upon me and my family." Justice Covington confirmed after he moved his family from the county the Mormons had robbed and burned his home and those others nearby.[19]

According to Adam Black, a troop of four hundred armed Mormons visited the home of William Osbern. Finding only his wife at home, they ordered her out of the house at gunpoint and pushed and shoved her to the ground. They left no option but for her to leave immediately or be shot. They then began looting her home and preparing to set fire to it. The Mormons seized forty-two head of Osbern's cattle. Finishing with the Osberns, the Mormons crossed Grand River to the north side and set upon justice of the peace William Dryden.[20]

Justice Dryden had, no doubt, raised the Mormons' ire when he notarized the first of Adam Black's affidavits in August. The Mormons took Dryden's son, Jonathan L. Dryden, and nephew as prisoners. They also confiscated two saddles and a pair of saddlebags.[21] Young Dryden was sick in bed with fever but was nonetheless removed from his home and transported a mile away by his captors. At that point the Mormons left the boy and transported him no further due to his poor health. Perhaps they assumed he would die if abandoned to the elements or simply thought he was too sick to continue on; more likely, they were afraid he would spread infection. Regardless, Dryden survived and was able to convey what the Mormons described to him as their reason for the raid. "They had applied to the Governor diverse of times for protection and he had never sent them any assistance, and now they believed the Governor to be as big a mob man as any of them, and the plunder which they were now taking was to pay them back for property, which they . . . lost in Jackson County [in 1833]."[22] From there the Mormons proceeded to Livingston County.

A Daviess County doctor named Samuel Venable delivered a baby born of a woman who had been driven from her home by Mormon marauders. She was in labor when she was forced to abandon her home to the Mormons who proceeded to rob and plunder it. She traveled eight miles to locate the doctor prior to giving birth. The doctor and patient had met at an ad hoc campground assembled by a Mr. and Mrs. White of Livingston County for the Daviess County refugees. While the doctor was attending to patients another woman arrived at the campground with a four-day-old child. Dr. Venable described the situation: "I saw a good deal of mischief . . . done [by the Mormons]. They had plundered the house, taken clothes and other articles, destroyed all their bee stands taken off drawing chains, log chains [and a] quantity of oats fodder and corn." This was the Whites' property, used to feed the two hundred horses of the Mormons.[23] Finally the Mormons threatened Mrs. White that if her husband "was at home they would take his life." Afterward the Mormons threw down the fences and rode their horses through the Whites' field of corn, destroying much of the crop. They attacked two other houses in Livingston County before retiring with their prisoners and booty to Adam-ondi-Ahman.[24]

The same day as the raid on Gallatin, Lyman Wight took his band of armed men into Millport. When he returned Wight reported they "saw no one to fight" and that the unarmed citizens abandoned their homes and property upon his command.[25]

The belligerent actions of the Mormons in Daviess County brought forth a new group of internal dissenters who did not condone the use of violence. They left the church and emigrated out of Caldwell County under cover of darkness. Every time a new defection was discovered in Far West it prompted Sidney Rigdon to respond with further threats. The events in Gallatin and Millport caused Thomas B. Marsh, the president of the twelve Mormon apostles, a distinguished position in the church, along with Orson Hyde, one of the twelve Mormon apostles, to disappear with their families and escape to Richmond, Ray County, Missouri. Their defection signaled to Rigdon that he must do something to address the situation. In rare form, Rigdon delivered a speech he hoped would strike fear into the hearts of any other would-be deserters.[26]

"The last man has run away from Far West that is going to. The next man who starts shall be pursued and brought back, dead or alive," Rigdon threatened. He continued, "I move a resolution that if any man attempts to move out of this county or even packs his things for that purpose, then any man in this house who sees it shall without saying anything to any other person, kill him and haul him aside into the brush." Rigdon described leaving his victims' bodies to be eaten by buzzards and refusing them a Christian burial. The level of rhetoric is astonishing but also reflective that the Mormons were now playing for keeps and the stakes were high. As if his inflammatory statements were not enough to drive fear into the hearts of all who heard it, Rigdon concluded his speech saying, "Yesterday one man in Far West slipped his wind and was dragged into a hazel bush for the buzzards to pick at. But the man who lisps it shall die!"[27] ("Lisps it" was Rigdon's emphatic way to describe even the smallest whisper or murmur.) It is not known if any Mormon had actually been killed, but Rigdon's point was that he wanted Mormons to police their neighbors for fear of death.

The dissenters who fled to Richmond were not silent. In his affidavit, Henry Marks, the son of Mormon parents, was eighteen when he had moved to Far West on April 17,

1838. He and his family lived in the home of Sidney
Rigdon and he had the opportunity to hear Joseph Smith
speak on several occasions. He quoted Smith on Election
Day that August, saying he would like "to have a play of the
whole U.S.," in a fight if necessary. Marks also confirmed
that he had often "heard the Mormons say they would as
soon shoot the dissenters . . . as shoot anything else."
Marks heard several Mormons take credit for burning Mr.
Stallings's (also spelled Stollings) store in Gallatin. David
Patten, or Captain Fearnought as he preferred to be
called, was the commander of the company that raided the
store. When on the mission, he had ordered the Mormons
not burn the goods but take them to repay Mormon losses
in Jackson County. Among the property confiscated were
twenty-four horses and thirty-two guns. When news of the
raids reached Far West, Marks said Rigdon shouted
"Hosannah to the victors" and also gave a speech encouraging all Mormons to remain brave.[28]

Shortly upon arriving in Richmond, dissenter Thomas
B. Marsh made a detailed report to the Ray County
Committee, a group of Ray County's leading citizens. The
committee had been called to investigate the problems in
Daviess and Caldwell counties. Marsh conveyed all he had
seen and heard concerning the Mormon disturbance to
the committee. "Shortly after the settlement of the difficulties at DeWitt . . . a call was made by the Mormons at
Far West, for volunteers to go to Daviess County, to disperse the mob." Joseph Smith had incited the Caldwell
County Mormons by saying, "all the Mormons who
refused to take up arms . . . in difficulties with the citizens,
should be shot; or otherwise put to death." Based on that
instruction, Marsh had thought it prudent to go with the
troops to Daviess County. Once there Mormon scouts
went in search of mob troops, but they found none.
"Scouting parties frequently went out and brought in
intelligence that they had seen from three to five men,"
hardly a mob. With no one to oppose them, Marsh reported seeing a company of approximately eighty Mormons
under Captain David Patten march off toward Gallatin.

Upon their return Patten reported they had run off about thirty men from Gallatin. Marsh later learned the same company had burned the town. Property the Mormons took from Gallatin was deposited in the bishop's storehouses in Adam-ondi-Ahman.

That evening Marsh saw a group of Mormon soldiers returning to the camp from the direction of Millport with wagons laden with beds, clocks, and other household furnishings. The next day Marsh witnessed honeycombs being harvested from the property seized in the raids and a group of Mormons taking the fattest animals and slaughtering them in preparation for the expected retaliatory siege on Adam-ondi-Ahman.[29]

Marsh explained that the Danites "considered [themselves] true Mormons . . . who have taken an oath to support the leaders of the church in all things, that they say or do, whether right or wrong. Many are dissatisfied with this oath, as being against moral and religious principles." At a meeting in Far West a secondary group called "the destruction company" was formed for the purpose of burning and destroying. According to the Mormons in Far West, if the people of Buncombe, in northern Ray County, came to do mischief upon the people of Caldwell and committed depredations on the Mormons, the destroyers would retaliate by burning their city. Furthermore, if the people of Ray and Clay counties moved against the Mormons, these destroyers had orders to burn Liberty and Richmond. Adopting partisan techniques, the burning would be done in secret by individual arsonists as opposed to by a large armed force. Sampson Avard proposed and Sidney Rigdon conveyed the intention to start a "pestilence among the gentiles" by poisoning their corn, fruit, etc. This would be, according to Avard, "the work of the Lord."[30]

Ultimately all proposals fell under Smith's jurisdiction. It is not clear the extent of Smith's ambition—some claimed he intended to take Missouri by force, if necessary, and once that was accomplished he would take the United States and finally the world. At this time it was taught by Smith and believed by every true Mormon that the prophecies of Joseph Smith were superior to the law of the land.[31] According to Marsh, Smith taught his followers that they would "tread down his enemies and walk over their dead bodies."[32]

Mormon dissenters in Far West would no longer be tolerated. If any tried to leave, orders were given that they "should be shot down and sent to tell their tale in eternity."[33] Learning the extent to which Smith's faithful would go to enforce these orders, Marsh decided to escape to Richmond with his family. When he left Daviess County there were between three hundred and four hundred armed men in Adam-ondi-Ahman.[34]

Livingston County resident Thomas I. Martin was one of the prisoners taken that day. He relates his captivity: "I was intercepted and taken prisoner, by the body of people called Mormons, which presented their guns, and told me that I had one of two things to do, that was: relate to them all I knew concerning their munitions, etc. or to be laid on the sod and let birds eat me." The Mormons took him twelve miles and along the way Martin witnessed the looting of the Whites' house. While he was a prisoner the Mormons told Martin they had no intention of allowing any man to remain in Daviess County that was not friendly to the Mormons. They were taking the law into their own hands to redress the injuries previously sustained in Jackson County.[35]

A mounted Mormon force came to the house of James Stone in Daviess County and informed him if he "did not leave Daviess County by sunrise the next morning they would take his head with their sword." To accentuate the threat the riders then drew their swords and waved them at Stone. As the marauders prepared to ride off, they issued a final threat to "take his heart blood if he did not leave the county." Taking the ruffians at their word Stone left his home by 10:00 P.M. The next day Stone and two other men returned and confirmed his home had been robbed but spared from fire. He did report seeing a group of Mormons later that day herding stolen cattle toward Caldwell County.[36] Justice of the peace Adam Black informed the governor on the 24th that there was "not a single officer left in [Daviess] County, to execute the laws of our land. And in behalf of the citizens of said county, and in my own behalf ask the Executive of the State to be reinstated in our homes."[37]

Colonel William P. Penniston, the anti-Mormon agitator, reported to the governor, "It's unheard of and unprecedented the conduct and high-handed proceedings of the Mormons." On October 15 they had learned "the Mormons were collecting in Far West, for the purpose of driving, what they term the mob, from this county." The Mormons used that term to include all the citizens of Daviess County who were not Mormons. Colonel Penniston went on to describe the actions of the Mormons: "They have plundered and robbed and burned every house in Gallatin," including the county treasury office. The Mormons "have driven almost every individual from the county, who are now flying before them with their families, many of whom have been forced out without necessary clothing–their wives and children wading, in many instances, through the snow without shoes." Penniston continued to describe the ghastly conditions the Daviess County settlers suffered at the hand of the Mormons. "When the miserable families are then forced out, their houses are plundered and then burned." The Mormons "are making this universal throughout the county." The colonel reminded the governor, "these facts are being made known to you . . . hoping that your authority will be used to stop . . . this banditti of Canadian refugees and restore us to our lost homes."[38] Penniston concludes his letter to the governor by discrediting the reports of Mormon sympathizing leaders. "Can such proceedings be submitted to in a government of laws? I think not— notwithstanding the political juggling of such men as David R. Atchison and some others, whose reports and circulations setting the conduct and character of the

Mormons more favorably before the community, are
believed by the people of this county to be prompted by
the hope of interest." Here was yet another report discrediting Atchison to the governor, hastening his replacement
as field commander-in-chief.

On the 22nd General Atchison, writing from his headquarters in Liberty, Clay County, Missouri, changed his
tone regarding the Mormons. Perhaps he was also hearing
reports that both his own officers and leading Daviess
County residents were criticizing his friendly posture
toward the Mormons. He records, "almost every hour I
receive information of outrage and violence; of burning,
and plundering in the County of Daviess. It seems the
Mormons have become desperate and act like mad-men."
He recounts the reports of the burning of Gallatin but
breaks the news of the burning of Millport. "They have it
is said plundered several houses and have taken away the
arms from diverse citizens." This included the cannon
"employed in the siege of DeWitt." Careful to keep the
news balanced Atchison also reported "the anti-Mormons,
have when opportunity offered, disarmed the Mormons
and burnt several of their houses." Rather than take blame
for the premature dismissal of troops he placed the blame
on his subordinates, "the great difficulty in settling this
matter seems to be in not being able to identify the
offenders." Atchison continued trying to further outline
the opposing sides to the governor: "I am convinced that
nothing short of driving the Mormons from Daviess
County will satisfy the party opposed to them, and this I
have not the power to do . . . legally." Atchison boldly
asserted, "There are no troops . . . in Daviess County; nor
do I deem it expedient to send any there for I am well convinced that it would make matters worse, for sir I do not
feel disposed to disgrace myself, or permit the troops
under my command to disgrace the State and themselves,
by acting the part of a mob." Atchison believed that state
militia troops thus far had stood by and watched as
Missouri irregulars forced out the Carroll County
Mormons. The general was not going to do it again in

Daviess. "If the Mormons are to be driven from their homes let it be done without any color of law, and in the open defiance thereof; let it be done by volunteers acting upon their own responsibilities." Atchison was not about to stand by and have his name tarnished by the acts of the residents. He had worked hard and staked his career on establishing a Mormon homeland in response to earlier Missourian intolerance of the sect. If the volunteers, as he called them, were to do anything illegal at least later they could be prosecuted and held accountable for their actions. Not so if the militia supported them in their efforts. Atchison concluded his letter to the governor with a request he make some order. Given Atchison's strict sense of formality and propriety, his reply was a scathing rebuttal: "It will be my greatest pleasure to execute any order your Excellency should think proper to give in this matter with promptness and to the very letter."[39]

Interestingly, the remaining troops under Atchison's command were already on their way to Daviess County under the orders of Brigadier General Hiram Parks. On the 16th two companies of mounted men made it as far as Crooked River, which flowed near the border of Ray and Caldwell counties. He was intent on suppressing what he suspected as malfeasance brewing in Adam-ondi-Ahman. Parks intended to meet up with General Doniphan and join forces in Far West, the Caldwell County seat. The snowstorm that hit in Daviess County and delayed the raid on Gallatin also struck Parks's men. The effort to reach Daviess County would be abandoned and the troops would be sent home pending further orders and an improvement in the weather. Parks, accompanied only by his aide, proceeded on to Far West where he learned that General Doniphan had already disbanded his force, so that no Clay County troops remained. Believing it wise to explore the situation in Daviess County, Parks went on without his soldiers. When he reached the town of Adair in Daviess County, Parks confirmed the previous intelligence reports that Mormons had moved on Gallatin and committed various and numerous "outrages."[40]

Concerned about the size of the Mormon force, Parks proceeded to Adam-ondi-Ahman where he found five hundred Mormon troops under arms. They were well armed and about two hundred of them mounted. When he inquired as to why the Mormons were armed he was informed, "They intended to defend that place—they had been driven from DeWitt and other places, and here they were determined to stand and die rather than be driven from that place."[41] Not entirely believing these statements, Parks proceeded to Millport and on his way discovered the inhabitants of the county had all fled their homes. Parks's report to General Atchison describes the situation in Daviess as bleak: "That county is in a worse state than at any former period, and I believe that the Mormons are now the aggressors, as I have seen depredations, which they have committed." Parks warned Atchison, "I would not be surprised, if some signal act of vengeance would be taken on these fanaticks—Wednesday next is fixed for a full and general meeting of all citizens of this county." Parks admits, "I do not know what to do. I will remain passive until I hear from you." Despite his indecision, the general makes abundantly clear: "I do not believe calling out the militia would avail anything towards restoring peace, unless they were called out in such force as to fight the Mormons and drive them from the County. This would satisfy the people—but I cannot agree to it." In conclusion Parks declares, "I hold myself ready to execute . . . any order from you." Again he requested Atchison to relay the need for the governor to visit the county and finally quiet the situation.[42]

Emboldened by the lack of resistance by Daviess County residents and the militia, Mormons had sacked the entirety of Daviess County and had made incursions into Livingston County at will. Daviess County was all but abandoned by everyone but the Mormons, and the residents of Livingston County were fearful that they might be next. To this point Governor Boggs had issued no order to stop the Mormon aggression. Even Generals Atchison and Parks thought they should let everyone fight it out as opposed to using the state militia as an extension of mob justice. If the Mormons had stopped their aggressive behavior at this point they may have been able to consolidate their Daviess County gains and restore the peace. Perhaps with better communication within the Mormon leadership and a genuine opportunity for frank discussion, this course might have been pursued. However by that point Smith was unquestionably in charge of all decisions and the course of the church was not open to debate. In his view the governor was just another mobocrat. Smith's solution was to challenge anyone not supporting his church.[43]

On October 18, after the weather had calmed and his men had had a chance to resupply at their homes, Captain Bogart recalled his company. He settled his command in a clearing twelve miles north of Elkhorn, which lay near the line dividing Caldwell and Ray counties. Mormon troops had been spotted patrolling the area in force. Bogart informed General Atchison that the Mormons had turned their threatening posture toward Ray County. "They have threatened to burn Buncombe and Elkhorn." Captain Bogart had, on his own direction, ordered his company, which numbered fifty men, to prevent any such outrage from occurring. The militia troops were going to be grossly outnumbered. Realizing his precarious situation the captain earnestly sought additional assistance from General Atchison. He warned the general, "the people of Ray are going to take the law into their own hands and put an end to the Mormon War."[44]

Bogart was correct; on the 23rd, the same day he sent his dispatch to Atchison, the citizens of Ray County held a committee meeting in Richmond for the purpose of deciding what should be done about the recent threats and events. They determined that a final demand for assistance must be sent to the governor. The fallback measure would be for Ray County citizens to volunteer and defeat the Mormons before they were allowed to sack and pillage the county. In their petition to the governor the committee confirmed that they received confirmation of the fact

Gallatin and Millport had been burned and sacked, that all non-Mormon residents of Daviess had fled for either Livingston or Ray counties, that the Mormons had taken the firearms of all the Daviess County residents, including a cannon. Summing up, the committee reported, "the news . . . reaches us hourly that they are destroying the property of the citizens that they cannot carry away, all that they can carry away they take; blood and plunder appears to be their object. All those who do not join with them . . . are banished from Caldwell and all those from other counties who are opposed to them are threatened."[45]

The committee made it clear that the governor's presence was required. In addition, "it is the desire of the citizens that his Excellency . . . call out a sufficient number of troops to put a stop to the further ravages of these fanatics." They warned the governor, "if some such measures are not taken shortly, the whole country will be overrun, but we now firmly believe they are the aggressors, and say they will indemnify themselves for the losses in Jackson and Carroll." The Ray County citizens' report also included the following: "We are not alarmists, and have had no fears until lately these fanatics would have dared to behave as they have." The report concludes with a strong call to action: "Unless a military force is brought to act against them . . . shortly, they will destroy as far as they are able."[46]

The following day Fifth Circuit prosecuting attorney, Thomas C. Burch in Richmond, also sent a report to the governor. He confirmed the Gallatin and Millport incidents and included information that several prisoners had been taken by the Mormons. In addition he reported that "Mormon dissenters are daily flying to Ray County for refuge from the ferocity of the prophet Jo. Smith, who they say threatens the lives of all Mormons who refuse to take up arms at his bidding, or to do his commands." The numerous dissenters confirmed reports Burch and others had heard concerning the Danite band. "Jo Smith infuses into the minds of his followers a spirit of insubordination to the Laws of the Land, telling them that the Kingdom of the Lord is come, which is superior to the institutions of the earth, and encourages them to fight and promises them the spoils of the battles."[47] The dissenters among the Ray County populace reported, "the Danite band . . . bind themselves to support the high council of the Mormon Church, and one another in all things whether right or wrong, and that by false swearing." Burch concluded by saying, "I have no doubt but that Jo Smith is as lawless and consummate a scoundrel as ever was the Veiled Prophet of Khorassan [an eighth-century Islamic imposter in Persia].[48] I believe the criminal law in Caldwell County cannot be enforced upon a Mormon. Jo declares in his public addresses that he can revolutionize the United States and that if provoked he will do it. The evil is alarming beyond all doubt."[49]

THIRTEEN

MASSACRE AND
CAPITULATION

Returning to Richmond on October 24, 1838, were three Ray County men sent to investigate the situation in Daviess County. Charles Morehead, William Thornton, and Jacob Gudgel had traveled to see Millport and Gallatin after Mormon threats against Buncombe were reported. The leadership saw no point in allowing rumors and threats to cause anxiety. Once they had first-hand knowledge, they could determine how to react to the menace on Buncombe.

The trio headed first to Millport, which they found deserted. They then proceeded a quarter of a mile outside Millport to the home of Judge Morin, who was in and startled to see the men. He began to speak in hushed tones and ushered them into his house as if scared that anyone should see them conversing. The Ray County men explained that they had heard that Gallatin and Millport had been burned and robbed and that Daviess County had been evacuated by all but Mormons.

The judge confirmed what they heard was substantially true and that the Mormons had done much more to the Daviess County citizens than had been reported. In order to show them the extent of the degradation and destruction, the judge rode with the men to Millport. There they found all the houses in ashes, except the grocery store of Mr. Slade and the house of Wilson McKinney, both of which had visible signs of having been robbed. Colonel Penniston's properties had been especially targeted by the Mormons. His house and horse-mill were completely destroyed. Judge Morin said he "saw Mormons . . . taking off beds and other things belonging to Wilson McKinney."[1]

Morin expected the Mormons to return that very day to pick up the remaining property which littered the streets of Millport and to burn the remaining houses.[2] The judge was himself in a precarious situation. Mormons had permitted him to stay, but only long enough to hire a wagon, collect his belongings, and leave the county. The judge received this special treatment because he had always treated the Mormons kindly and had warned them of the election interference planned in Daviess County. His wagons were scheduled to arrive that day and he intended to move to Richmond immediately. He did not want any Mormons to know he was speaking with residents or that he was giving any unfavorable reports concerning the Mormons' activities.

The men found the rest of Daviess to be utterly deserted. The Mormons had taken the opportunity of the farmers' flight from the county to harvest all the corn still in the field. The judge reported to the men that he had been to Adam-ondi-Ahman just a few days before their arrival and there he had seen a company of Mormons drive a herd of one hundred head of plundered cattle into the town. Judge Morin had also seen a slave belonging to a Mr. Morgan whom the judge knew was in the Mormon stronghold. The strength of the Mormon force was approximated by the judge at six hundred men. He advised the Ray County men not to risk a trip there, as he felt the Mormons were nothing but a band of robbers and desperadoes. Upon this advice the trio returned by the way they came to deliver their information.[3]

After the Ray County committee heard the report of Morehead and company, they sent a new dispatch to the governor more urgent than the last. "It is the imperious duty of the executive, by armed force, to quell the insurrection put on the foot by the Mormons. We view with the utmost concern the conduct of the Mormons in . . . Daviess and Livingston, and that immediate action is necessary for the protection of our property and homes from this lawless banditti." The committee felt, under normal circumstances, the correct procedure was simply to allow the civil authorities such as the sheriff, prosecutor, and judge to deal with the matter. However, in this situation, those authorities were not adequate. "In the opinion of this meeting . . . a resort to the laws will be worse than useless, and wholly insufficient to afford the country protection to which it is entitled. . . . Give the people of upper Missouri protection from this fearful body of thieves and robbers." The committee was quick to address the issue of dissenting Mormons: "All who have in good faith renounced the Mormon religion should be protected." They concluded their resolution stating, "Men should be raised to go to the most northern border of this county and guard it from intrusion by the Mormons; and that General Parks be requested to raise three companies for that purpose, or that they be raised by volunteers."[4]

Judge Austin King had attended the Ray County committee meetings and detailed the facts he learned there to the governor. "Our relations with the Mormons are such that I am perfectly satisfied that the arm of the civil authority is too weak to give peace to the country." He explained his opinion had only just recently changed. "I thought the Mormons were disposed to act only on the defensive but their recent conduct shows that they are the aggressors and that they intend to take the law into their own hands—Jo Smith made known his views to the people and declared the time had come when they would avenge their own wrongs and that all who were not for them, and take up arms with them, should be considered as against them." He explained that Smith intended to finance his operations by confiscating the property of dissenters.[5]

King believed that Smith was intentionally inciting the Mormons to outrages and degradations, citing as an example "300 to 400 men, with Smith at their head marched to Daviess County [and after the snowstorm] they commenced their ravages upon the citizens driving them from their houses and taking their property." The judge also described the raid on Gallatin and Millport, reporting that the spoils were now kept in Smith's church storehouses.

The judge confirmed that siege preparations were under way in Mormon-held areas. Livestock was slaughtered and salted and fifty to one hundred wagons were being employed to harvest the entire corn crop of the county. "They look for a force against them, and are consequently preparing for a siege, building block houses." The judge described the Mormon paramilitary group called the destructives as "a band of twelve . . . whose duty it is to watch the movements of men and of communities and to avenge themselves for supposed wrongful movements against them by privately burning houses property and even laying in ashes towns." He continued, "the Mormons expect to settle the affair at the point of the sword, and I am well warranted in saying to you that the people in this quarter of the State look to you for protection, which they believe you will afford when you learn the facts." King concluded with an ominous warning to the governor, "the country is in great commotions and I can assure you that either with or without authority, something will shortly have to be done."[6]

Just after dawn on the 25th the conflict took an ominous turn. Joseph Smith, in the guise of rescuing "three prisoners" taken by "a mob" in Ray County, ordered sixty men under the command of David Patten to rescue the prisoners. Fearing these alleged prisoners would be shot just after daybreak, Patten and his men raced from Far West under cover of darkness. In their path was Captain Samuel Bogart's company, which had made their camp twelve miles north of Elkhorn along the Crooked River on the Ray County side of the border between Caldwell and Ray counties to prevent anticipated Mormon attacks into

Ray County. The militia forces were entrenched behind a slough bank on the north side of the river, in a thicket of oak trees and flanked on the east by hickory trees. In order to cross the Crooked River from the north and make their way toward Elkhorn, the Mormons would have to cross Bogart's path from the east. From Bogart's position, enemy forces approaching from the east would be unaware of Bogart until they were marching among the troops. As the Mormon patrol unwittingly approached the position of the militia, the picket guard located their approach and sent word to Captain Bogart. The remaining picket forces took aim at the Mormon riders.[7]

As the Mormon company crested the hill in the early light, their bodies were perfectly silhouetted against the sky. The guards took aim and fired a volley and then began to return to the main militia position. One Mormon soldier instantly fell dead. Captain Patten, seeing the militia position, gave the order to charge, "Go ahead, boys; rake them down."[8] The men drew their weapons and rushed down the hill toward the state troops, shouting, "God and Liberty!" Patten led the charge, his brilliant white blanket coat shining in the early light, no doubt making a rally point for his troops but also a conspicuous target for their adversaries.[9]

The Mormons made easy targets from the entrenched position of Bogart's men, who in the first volley hit three riders, unseating them from their horses. The Mormons rushed into the oak grove with swords drawn and fury growing from the continued casualties. They charged over the slough bank and drove all but one of Bogart's men from their position and into retreat. As the militia fell back, one man took careful aim at Patten's white jacket and fired. "Captain Fearnought" was shot in the stomach and dropped to the ground in agony. He was unable to participate in the remainder of the battle and would die from his wound later that night.[10]

Parley Pratt, enraged at the loss of their leader, killed one man and wounded a second. A group then gathered around the wounded militiaman, Samuel Tarwater, and began to mutilate him. "With their swords, striking him lengthwise in the mouth, cutting off his under teeth, and breaking his lower jaw; cutting off his cheeks," and finally leaving him for dead. The man would miraculously survive and press charges against Pratt for attempted murder.[11] Despite the Mormon success in driving out the militia, the loss of Patten shook their spirits. John D. Lee, a Mormon soldier, expressed the growing sentiment: "My dream of security was over. One of our mighty had fallen, and by Gentile hands." The Mormons were coming to understand that Smith's statement of their near invincibility was not to be.[12]

Captain Bogart fell back after the Mormon attack but held fast the northern half of Ray County. The initial express messenger to Richmond reported all but three of the fifty to sixty militiamen had been massacred in the attack.[13] In fact only one militia soldier had been killed. It was also reported that Bogart had been overrun by three hundred Mormons and that most if not all of the unit was captured. Ray County's citizen committee, despairing the imminent raid on Richmond, immdediately sent dispatches to the governor and the surrounding counties asking for immediate assistance in repelling the Mormon invasion. Major Amos Rees and Colonel Wiley Williams sent a dispatch to General John B. Clark at midnight on the 25th reporting the attack and other Mormon atrocities in Daviess County, lamenting the prospect that all of the men of Bogart's command taken prisoner would be killed by the "wretched desperadoes" of Caldwell.[14]

The Mormons were reportedly planning an attack on Richmond the following night and the city was in a panic. The women and children were being shipped down to Lexington and other surrounding cities. Lafayette County Judge E. M. Ryland sent Rees and Williams instructions to alert the governor of the situation and all the counties along the way. Richmond "is expected to be sacked and

burned [by Mormons but that] we sent one hundred well-
armed and daring men." Ryland was confident the
Lafayette County men would "give the Mormons a warm
reception in Richmond, tonight."[15] He concluded with
urgency, "haste must be made in order to stop the devastation menaced by these infuriated fanatics. The volunteers must be prepared to expel or exterminate the
Mormons from the State. Nothing but this can give tranquility to the Public . . . and reestablish the law." Once
again the extermination wording first coined by Sidney
Rigdon in his July 4th address and distributed by Smith
all over northern Missouri would come back to haunt
them.

When Governor Lilburn Boggs received this report he
was appalled. If the Mormons were going to declare war
then he was finally going to have something to say about
it. After weeks of little response to the conflict in upper
Missouri, Governor Boggs issued Order No. 44 to General
Clark.

> Sir: Since the order of this morning to you directing
> you to cause 400 mounted men to be raised within
> your division I have received by Amos Rees Esqr of
> Ray & Wiley C. Williams Esqr. one of my Aids infor-
> mation of the most *appal[l]ing character which entirely
> changes the face of things and places the Mormons in the
> attitude of an open and armed defiance of the laws And of
> having made war upon the people of this State.* Your
> orders are therefore to hasten your operation with all
> possible speed. *The Mormons must be treated as enemies
> and must be exterminated or driven from the State* if nec-
> essary *for the public peace their outrages are beyond all
> description.* If you can increase your force you are
> authorized to do so to any extent you may consider
> necessary I have just issued orders to Majr Genl
> Willock of Marion Co to raise 500 men and to march
> them to the Northern part of Daviess and there unite
> with Genl Donphaon of Clay who has been ordered
> with 500 men to proceed to the Same front for the
> purpose of intercepting the retreat of the Mormons to

the North they have been directed to communicate with you by express. You can also communicate with them if you find it necessary. Instead therefore of proceeding as at first directed to reinstate the Citizens of Davis in their homes you will proceed immediately to Richmond and there operate against the Mormons. Brig Genl Parks of Ray has been ordered to have four hundred of his Brigade in readiness to join you at Richmond. The whole force will be placed under your Command. I am very respectfully Yr Obt St

Lilburn W Boggs Com in Chief.[16]

These words marked the first and only time in the history of the United States that a government official ordered the extermination of American citizens. Here, the Mormons as an entire group, with no distinction made between those active in the fighting and those who were opposed to it, were to be punished with banishment or death. It is clear that there was precedent for quelling with force any threat to the government of the United States, even at the state level, such as Shays's Rebellion or the Whiskey Rebellion, and such insurrection could not be protected by religious practice, but without due process those Americans who chose not to participate in their church's aggression were to be deprived of their First Amendment rights, as well as other Constitutional protections and guarantees. The attack on Missouri militia which automatically signaled an attack on the state was a line the Mormons should not have crossed; however, based on the circumstances it is far from certain the Mormons knew whom they were attacking, although that my not have mattered to them. Nonetheless, the damage was severely done; there were no longer shades of gray, all was black and white. All Mormons became the enemy. Violent behavior may have achieved temporary gains but now the sleeping giant, the Missouri state government and its militia, which had previously been content to watch from the sidelines, was in the fight. They were determined to eliminate the Mormons. While many Americans gave little thought to the war being waged against the American Indians by the

U.S. Government, the Mormon War now pitted citizen against citizen with the government entering the fray. It would be another twenty-three years before such conflict would erupt again during the Civil War.

Skipping over Atchison, the governor appointed Major General John B. Clark as the commander of militia forces against the Mormons. He ordered Clark to gather his men and proceed immediately from his location east of Caldwell County to Richmond and drive the Mormons back from Ray County. The governor's previous orders had authorized a force of four hundred men, but Clark could now muster any number he thought necessary to accomplish the governor's request. Orders were also issued to Brigadier General Parks to raise the strength of his command to four hundred men. They were to be ready to join General Clark in Richmond but to act defensively until he arrived. Boggs also issued orders to Major General Willock to raise five hundred men to approach Caldwell County from the north so as not to allow any Mormons to escape. After the Mormons were removed, the generals could then focus on reinstating the Daviess County citizens to their homes.[17]

Underestimating the eagerness with which volunteers and regular militia would respond to the muster call, Adjutant General Lisle issued orders to the 1st, 4th, 5th, 6th, and 12th divisions to raise four hundred men each. It is worth noting that Governor Boggs issued no orders to General Atchison to specifically sideline him during the conclusion of the conflict. The combined militia force would number nearly five thousand troops. During territorial days and presumably moving forward into statehood, militia officers were directed to wear the same uniform as United States federal soldiers, and the enlisted men wore uniforms as their officers directed. More than likely the enlisted men would wear the same uniforms as their commanding officers or no uniform at all.[18]

The 4th Division under Major General Lucas would be coming from Independence, Missouri, to the west of Caldwell; they were to proceed directly to Richmond. The other four divisions were coming from the east and were expected to rendezvous in Howard County by November 3 before proceeding to Richmond. The conflict would be over before that day had even arrived. General Lisle warned the generals of the expulsion of Daviess County residents from their homes and the burning of Gallatin and Millport. Lisle also ordered General Parks and General Doniphan to raise five hundred men each and to await the arrival of the main force in Richmond.[19] The orders were designed to prevent the scorched-earth tactics used in Daviess County against Ray County citizens.

Learning that his men had fired upon state troops, Joseph Smith earnestly prepared Far West for a siege. He ordered many of the cabins torn down to construct breastworks around the town. This would prevent the Missouri cavalry from charging into Far West. Food supplies continued to be gathered and blacksmiths were ordered to make as many broadswords and pikes as possible.[20] Smith patrolled the city, inspecting the siege preparations and trying to lift the spirits of the Mormon defenders. One Mormon soldier wrote to his father: "Come to Zion and fight for the religion of Jesus. Many a hoary head is engaged here, the prophet goes out to the battle as in the days of old . . . is this not marvelous?"[21]

There were eight hundred Mormon troops mustered. Many had already participated in the offensive operations in Daviess and were well armed. The additional munitions taken from the residents of Daviess and the Far West blacksmiths equipped the rest. Still believing their army to be invincible, the Mormons' morale was high. Despite the outward optimism the women received instructions to pack their things into bags and prepare for flight northward in the event of disaster.

A call was sent out to all outlying Mormon settlements that everyone should gather in Far West for safety. By the 29th all outlying Mormon settlements had been emptied, except one. On Shoal Creek on the east side of Caldwell County a man by the name of Jacob Haun had just finished building his flour mill, which he was not about to abandon to a Gentile arsonist. Smith responded that it was better "to lose your property than your life." Haun ignored the warning and determined to remain and defend against any attackers. As he left, Smith turned to Lyman Wight and John D. Lee and said, "I wish they were [here] for their own safety. I am confident they will be butchered in the most fearful manner."[22]

The next day the Mormon scouts and pickets were driven back into Far West by a large body of Missouri militia approaching from the southeast. The militia halted just outside the range of Mormon guns and the two forces faced off. General Doniphan sent a messenger to Far West with a copy of the governor's extermination order and word that General Lucas and General Clark were on their way to Far West with a command of six thousand men to execute the order. Just then news arrived that there had been trouble at Haun's Mill.[23]

On October 30, three days after Governor Boggs issued the order legalizing the killing or armed removal of all Mormons within Missouri, a force of two hundred militia troops approached the Haun's Mill settlement. Jacob Haun had founded the settlement in 1835 and it was occupied by ten to fifteen families in 1838. Approximately thirty-five Mormon men defended the group as they prepared for an assault from the militia forces.[24] Missouri State Senator Daniel Ashby was among the troops and described the attack. The Mormons opened fire on the approaching militia. The militia dismounted and returned fire. The Mormons set up their two main defenses, the first in the blacksmith shop which they thought would make a strong fort. The second was along Shoal Creek under the bank of the creek. They laid down a constant barrage of fire on the advancing militia troops.[25]

The blacksmith shop turned out to be poorly constructed for use as a fort, with wide cracks between the logs, and the militia troops were able to get effective fire into the

Carl C. A. Christensen's painting of the attack on Haun's Mill. The militia are shooting through the gaps in the log walls of the blacksmith shop in the center while women and children are seen fleeing in the background. The original is at the Brigham Young University Museum of Art.

building from the cover of a grove of nearby trees. The order to charge the shop was given and promptly obeyed. As the men ran toward the blacksmith shop, some of the militia provided covering fire to stop the Mormons along the creek from cutting down the advance. When the militia arrived at the side of the shop, one man shoved his gun through the cracks in the walls and fired on the Mormons inside. The other militiamen saw this and repeated it. Soon they kept up such a constant fire through the cracks that the Mormons could not get their guns out to shoot. The interior quickly resembled a slaughterhouse.[26]

The surviving Mormons broke out of the blacksmith shop and ran toward the creek and the second Mormon defensive position. Many fell as they fled, including an older man named Thomas McBride. As he lay wounded he surrendered his gun to a militia man who immediately pulled out a corn cutter and hacked McBride to pieces. When his body was recovered, he was mangled from head to foot. Seeing the atrocities the women fled from the battle toward the brush on the opposite side of the creek.

Militia troops fired at them but none was hit.[27] Senator
Ashby heard the call for quarter by militia forces. He
echoed the call until all firing had ceased on the part of
the militia. The Mormons mistook the call for quarter as
the militia giving up and sent a volley of fire toward the
Missouri troops. Once fired upon, the militia renewed
their fire upon the Mormon position along the creek. They
continued the attack until every Mormon had been driven
from the settlement or shot. Near the end of the battle
Ashby saw some Mormons escaping: "I saw some of the
Mormons that had reached the top of the hill south of the
creek about 300 yards from us. They stopped turned
around and shot at us and then ran off." From what he
could see outside Ashby denied that any maltreatment was
directed toward the wounded Mormons. "After the battle
subsided I saw some of our men carry one wounded man
into a house and laid him on a bed and I talked with
him."[28]

Despite Ashby's assurances, inside the blacksmith shop
the shooting continued when some militia troops entered
to finish off the wounded. Among the wounded they
found the nine-year-old Sardius Smith, the nephew of
Sylvester Smith, hiding beneath the bellows. His younger
brother, who had been shot through the hip and was pretending to be dead, heard the soldiers oust Sardius from
his hiding place. "Don't shoot, it's just a boy," one militiaman said. His companion replied, "It's best to hive them
when we can. Nits become lice." The man then placed the
barrel of his rifle against the boy's temple and fired.[29]
Once they obtained a wagon for their wounded the militia
pulled out.[30] Officially, thirty-one Mormons were killed
and seven militia men wounded. After dark the women
and survivors crept back into the settlement to bury the
dead and care for the wounded. They counted only seven-
teen slain and fifteen wounded. The dead were heaped
into an unfinished well and the wounded were hidden in
the brush for fear that the militia troops might return.
Those that could walk then made their way toward Far
West.[31]

When the news of the massacre at Haun's Mill reached
Mormon troops they cursed the militia and the obstinacy
of Jacob Haun. They all believed that if Haun had moved
his family and settlement into Far West as requested by
Joseph Smith the tragedy could have been avoided. The
news also had a devastating effect on the morale of the
troops. Now not only had the beloved Captain Fearnought
fallen at the hands of the Gentile enemy, but an entire settlement had been wiped out. Smith had trouble sleeping
that night. He felt responsible for the tragedy and he
could imagine the same events played out a hundred times
more in Far West.[32] Reports continued to pour in from his
scouts that the Mormons in Far West were now outnumbered by five to one. In each report the number of militia
forces doubled and then tripled. It was suspected that if
the numbers continued to grow at the same rate they
would soon be facing a force of ten thousand.[33]

Smith knew the strength and perseverance of his force.
Many were stalwart and as determined as Jacob Haun.
Others, however, he could only count on to destroy what
little morale remained after news of the Haun's Mill
defeat. He feared his army would surrender in the event of
a prolonged siege or heavy fighting. Not wanting to
demoralize his men by any outward act of capitulation,
Smith secretly sent for Reed Peck and state representative
and church historian John Corrill. Smith knew that
General Doniphan respected the two men and he told the
pair, "Find General Doniphan, and beg like a dog for
peace."[34] After sending out the two messengers Smith
went about encouraging his troops and making a show of
defiant resistance.

Smith gave a speech to the assembled combatants. "I
care not a fig for the coming of the troops. We've tried
long enough to please the Gentiles," he reminded them.
"If we live among them [like in Jackson County] they don't
like it. If we scatter [referencing Haun's Mill] they massacre us for it. The only law they know is 'might makes
right.' They are a damned set, and God will blast them to

hell!" Smith continued, "If they want to attack us we will play hell with their applecarts . . . and for everyone we lack in number to match the mob, the Lord will send an angel to fight alongside."[35] Smith was trying to reestablish that sense of invincibility that was crumbling after the loss of Captain Patten and the Jacob Haun tragedy. Having given his troops a sense of security, Smith settled in to await word on peace terms. He would not have to wait long.

General Lucas and General Atchison, who had earlier marched from their respective headquarters in Independence and Liberty, combined forces to make up an army of approximately 1,800 men.[36] During the process the governor's extermination order had arrived. Without direct orders from the governor, General Atchison determined not to participate and returned to Liberty, leaving Lucas in sole command of the assemblage.[37] Rather than march to Richmond as ordered, General Lucas determined to proceed against Far West instead. One hour before sundown on the 30th, Lucas established his headquarters at Goose Creek, approximately one mile south of Far West and an excellent point from which to stage an attack on the city. There were open fields on all sides of the city, across which Lucas could order the attack on Far West and cut off the retreat of any fleeing Mormons. He then began to make preparations for an attack the following day.[38]

General Doniphan reported to Lucas that he had located mounted Mormons making their approach to Far West from the east. He requested permission to intercept them, which was granted. Doniphan's men rode off at top speed to capture the riders but they were too late; all Mormon forces reached the fort. Doniphan approached within two hundred yards of their outer defenses and estimated their troop strength at eight hundred men. That evening General Lucas received a message from Colonel Hinkle, the commander of the Mormon military force, requesting a meeting at a point between the enemy lines the next day. Busy receiving new troops hourly and finding room to encamp them, Lucas postponed the meeting until 2 o'clock on the 31st.

For the militia, General Lucas, his staff officers, Brigadier Generals Wilson, Doniphan, Graham, and Parks attended the parley on an eminence situated between the two factions.[39] On the Mormons' behalf appeared Colonel Hinkle, John Corrill, Reed Peck, W. W. Phelps, and John Cleminson. Smith's instructions to the contingent had been that "a compromise must be made on some terms."[40] Hinkle addressed the Missouri officers to determine if there could be a compromise or settlement without the resort to arms. Lucas then informed the Mormons of his terms.

First, give up their leaders to be tried and punished; Second, make an appropriation of their property, all who had taken up arms for the repayment of any debts caused by their destructive behavior; Third, immediately leave the state, under militia escort; and finally, surrender all arms of every description, for which they would receive a receipt.

The Mormons had not expected the terms of surrender to be so one-sided. However Hinkle, not wanting to lose the chance for a negotiated peace, agreed to the proposal readily. It was reported to Joseph Smith that General Hinkle had allegedly sent signals to the militia of his intentions to betray the Mormons. According to Mormon sources, Smith became aware of Hinkle's intentions prior to the commencement of the siege and nonetheless sent him to negotiate the surrender.[41] Despite this outward acceptance of the terms, Hinkle asked that the Mormons be given until the next morning to formally respond to the offer. General Lucas agreed but with a catch. The Mormons could have until the following day to decide but they would have to purchase that right by surrendering Joseph Smith, Jr., Sidney Rigdon, Lyman Wight, Parley Pratt, and George Robinson to militia custody. The leaders would be held overnight as a pledge of good faith. Lucas promised Hinkle that if in the morning the Mormons determined to fight, the prisoners would be returned to their custody. If, however, they agreed to the terms then the Mormon prisoners would be held for trial under the

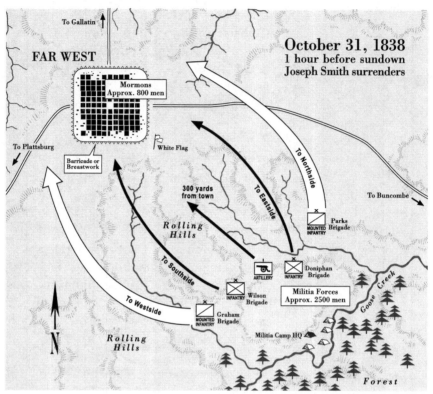

The disposition of Missouri militia around the Mormon stronghold of Far West.
In order to avoid further bloodshed, Joseph Smith, Jr., and other Mormon
leaders gave themselves up to the militia commanders.

first stipulation of the peace accords. They had until an
hour before sunset to make up their minds.[42] Both sides
then retired to their camps.

   Lucas busied himself and his troops planning the
potential attack on Far West. The orders were that an hour
and a half before dark his men should assemble for the
assault. General Parks's troops were to be mounted and
form on the right flank of the army. They were to make all
speed to pass entirely around the town and establish a line
of attack on the north side of Far West, thereby cutting off
a potential Mormon escape route. At one hour before sunset he was to sally forth and once in position on the northern front await the report of the cannon as the signal to
begin the attack.

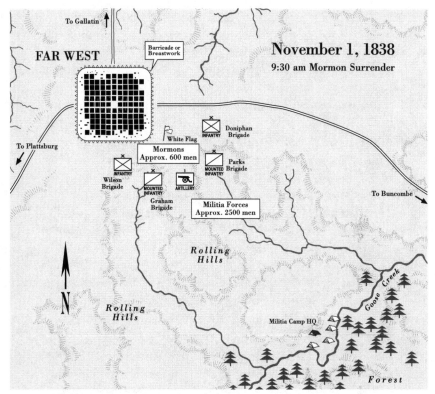

On the morning of November, 1, 1838, the town of Far West surrendered. The Mormon leaders were held under arrest while the town was taken over by the militia.

General Graham's brigade was also to be mounted but would form on the left flank of the army. Graham's troops would act as left side flankers and make all speed to pass entirely around the town and establish a line of attack on the west side of Far West. This position would cut off a Mormon escape route to the west. The timing of movement and commencement of battle was the same for both brigades.

General Doniphan's brigade was ordered to parade on foot to the left of General Parks's position. His orders were to form a line of battle on the east side of Far West. General Wilson's brigade was ordered to parade on foot to the left of General Doniphan with instructions to form the line of battle on the south side of Far West. The artillery company, which would have been equipped with canons capable of firing either 6, 12, or 18 pound shot, would be placed at the head of both Doniphan's and Wilson's brigades, with instructions to occupy a prominent place within three hundred yards of the town. Using his now swollen force of 2,500 men with this encircling strategy, Lucas intended to overrun Far West before the close of day.[43]

Inside Far West there was a state of panic. With only an hour to decide what course to take, Smith's first act was to call in his leaders most in danger of being prosecuted. These were the leaders in the battle with Captain Bogart's men. He instructed them to flee immediately to the north and get out of Missouri. Next Smith ordered all plunder taken from citizens of Daviess County be assembled in one central location. He feared that if any Mormon were later found with stolen property on his person, he would immediately be hung for stealing. Once these wheels were put in motion Smith called for an assembly of this troops.[44]

Smith began, "You are good and brave men, but there are 10,000 men approaching Far West, and unless you were angels themselves you could not withstand so formidable a host" — despite his earlier teachings that they would be supplemented by angel warriors. Smith continued, "You have stood by me to the last; you have been willing to die for me for the sake of the Kingdom of God." Then shifting the focus Smith continued, "the bloodthirsty Lucas has demanded my surrender. I shall offer myself up as a sacrifice to save your lives and to save the Church." Having broken the bad news, Smith concluded, "Be of good cheer, my brethren. Pray earnestly to the Lord to deliver your leaders from their enemies. I bless you all in the name of the Christ." Now his army and his church would accept the surrender gracefully and with great admiration for Smith.[45]

At the appointed time no hostages could be seen and so General Lucas ordered the assault to begin. General Parks's and General Graham's mounted troops raced toward their appointed positions. General Doniphan's and

Wilson's commands began their march accompanied by the cannon. When the troops were approximately six hundred yards from the outer defenses of the city, a white flag was seen exiting the Mormon lines. With it rode the hostages Lucas had demanded. General Lucas ordered the halt of his advancing army and rode out to meet the Mormon contingent. He was greatly pleased to discover the hostages were being delivered and immediately put them under armed guard. The militia withdrew to its encampment for the night and Colonel Hinkle was given until the following morning to surrender his troops.

General Lucas praised his troops' determination and deliberateness. "They marched . . . like old veterans. No noise or confusion—nothing but eager anxiety upon the countenance of every man to get at the work." Such morale boded well in the event of a conflict the following morning. Lucas described the taking of the prisoners, "when the hostages were received, the troops with slight exception marched back to camp in profound silence." Parley Pratt, one of the hostages, described the scene, "if a vision of the infernal regions could come suddenly to mind with thousands of malicious fiends, all clamoring, exulting, deriding, blaspheming, mocking, railing, raging and foaming like a troubled sea, then could some idea be formed of hell which we had entered."[46]

That night the hostages slept on the open ground. The ground was wet from the recent snow; the prisoners were taunted by their guards and during the night it began to rain. At midnight General Lucas appeared to the men and called on Lyman Wight. "I regret to inform you your die is cast, your doom is fixed, you are sentenced to be shot tomorrow on the public square," implying that a court-martial had concluded.[47] Wight spat on the ground. "Shoot and be damned," he replied. Lucas looked at him with a mixture of regret and disdain: "We were in hopes you would come out against Joe Smith, but as you have not, you will share his fate." Wight told him, "You can thank Joe Smith that you are not in hell tonight, for had it not been for him, by God I would have put you there!"[48] The

approach used by Lucas here seems more focused on coax-
ing evidence for use against Smith and therefore indicative
that no court-martial had yet occurred. Even if it had,
Governor Boggs makes it quite clear from later orders that
Lucas had no authority to conduct a court-martial and
should leave the trial of the Mormons to the civil authorities.[49] It is uncertain whether a court-martial ever occurred
and there are no militia or state records of Lucas ever
holding one.

On November 1 General Lucas ordered his force to
parade at 9 o'clock in the morning and take up a line of
march for Far West. The general was obviously expecting
a capitulation because he formed his army 200 yards
southeast of the Mormon defenses without any concern of
receiving fire. General Wilson's brigade formed the west
line, General Doniphan's brigade formed the east line,
General Parks's and General Graham's brigades formed
the south line with the artillery company in their middle.
They left the north side of the square open.

At 9:30 A.M. Colonel Hinkle and his army emerged from
Far West. Their number had been reduced by desertions
and flights to six hundred men. Hinkle marched the
Mormons through the space on the north end of the militia's square into the center of the troop. They formed a
hollow square and grounded their arms. Hinkle then rode
up to General Lucas and delivered his sword and his pistols, thereby surrendering his army. Lucas ordered a company from each brigade to flank the Mormon prisoners on
all sides and march them back into Far West and to protect them and take charge of them until they could be
dealt with the following day. One additional company was
called on from Doniphan's brigade to take charge and
inventory the abandoned Mormon arms. General Lucas
allowed his army to take some pleasure in the victory by
ordering them to parade through the streets of Far West,
intending to show the Mormons what they were up against
if they changed their minds about the terms of the truce.[50]

Considering the war at an end, General Lucas began to
disband his army. First he issued orders for General

Doniphan's brigade, with the exception of the company inventorying weapons, and General Graham's brigade to go to their home headquarters and be dismissed. General Wilson was ordered to take charge of the prisoners demanded for trial and the surrendered Mormon arms. Wilson was to direct them to Lucas's headquarters in Independence to await his further orders.

On November 2 General Lucas relieved the Far West guard with four companies from General Parks's brigade. The new guard was under the command of Colonel Thompson, who was instructed to wait and take his orders from General Clark once he arrived. Thompson was also ordered to hold the Mormons in Far West to prevent their escape and also to offer them protection. To execute this order one might imagine his forces would surround the town, but no such step was taken and many Mormons who feared reprisal for their acts fled the city. The remainder of General Parks's brigade was ordered to Adam-ondi-Ahman with instructions to disarm the Mormon forces there. All prisoners and arms taken there were to be directed to General Clark for further instruction. Lucas's final act was to commandeer the governor's aide-de-camp, Colonel Wiley Williams, Major Amos Rees, together with Colonel Thomas Burch, to draw up a formal legal document which would summarize the terms of the peace accord.[51] With just the details remaining, Lucas prepared to retire to Independence, satisfied with his and his troops' accomplishments. The Mormons were defeated.

FOURTEEN

Exodus

I T IS CLAIMED THAT JOSEPH SMITH NARROWLY escaped the firing squad in Far West at the order of General Lucas. When the appointed time came on November 2, 1838, General Doniphan refused to execute the order. "By God you have been sentenced by a court martial to be shot . . . but I will be damned if I will have any of the honor of it or any disgrace of it. I have ordered my Brigade . . . to leave camp, for I consider it . . . cold blooded murder!"[1] General Lucas called a second court-martial that same day to address Doniphan's insubordination. There is, however, no military record of either court-martial. During the second court-martial, if it did occur, Doniphan again defied General Lucas: "If you execute these men, I will hold you responsible before . . . a tribunal." Lucas decided against execution and sent the prisoners, arms, and ordinance to his permanent headquarters in Independence.[2] Encouraged that he had not been shot on the spot Smith began to hope for his survival. "Be of good cheer, brethren," he extolled them. "The word of the Lord came to me last night that our lives should be given us." Not so sure of his own prophetic revelation, he also wrote to his wife Emma just before reaching

Independence: "Oh Emma for God's sake do not forsake me . . . if I do not meet you again in this life may God grant that we meet in heaven."[3]

As it turns out, General Lucas was guilty of his own brand of insubordination. Governor Boggs, in his final orders concerning the state's response to the insurrection, had appointed General John B. Clark as the field commander in charge of all troops in this action, and as such General Lucas was not to have participated unless it was as a subordinate of General Clark.[4] Not able to submit to what he perceived to be a junior officer to his grade, although they were both major generals, Lucas simply ignored the orders to hold fast at Far West until Clark arrived.[5] After Clark got word of Lucas's disobedience and the surrender of Far West, he instructed the rogue general to remain on the scene, or if that was not practicable, to take the prisoners and arms to Richmond. Under no circumstances was he to finalize a peace treaty with the Mormons.[6] Lucas not only finalized the treaty with the Mormons, but he also took the prisoners and arms to Independence and refused to return them to Richmond. General Clark was finally forced to send one of his officers with a contingent of troops to Independence to collect the prisoners and arms.[7]

General Atchison was not asked to participate in any fashion. The governor's reasons for the exclusion of Atchison were twofold. First, he was a member of the legislature and would be busy preparing for the next session slated to begin in November. Second, many citizens had complained about his pro-Mormon sentiments.[8] It is doubtful that Atchison would have participated even upon orders from the governor since he had left Lucas in command of his troops upon learning of the extermination order. His final dispatch to Boggs expressed the opinion that expulsion of the Mormons would only injure the state's reputation because both sides were guilty of aggression one against the other. The unspoken reason the governor left General Atchison on the sidelines was a growing animosity between the two men. Atchison did not approve of the way the governor was handling the Mormon conflict and the governor knew that.

General Clark brought this point up while offering encouragement to the governor. He admitted that he did not understand the background on the struggle between the Mormons and the citizens, but he felt confident the country would back up the governor's actions because they were right. "I regret exceedingly to learn that any acts of yours should create any heart burnings, or collision with your Excellency and any General Officer . . . which I understand exists between you and General Atchison."[9] It would be cold comfort to the governor. Boggs hoped that once all the facts were examined by men with a full understanding of the struggle, like Atchison, his actions or lack thereof would be approved.

The Mormons who remained in Far West were to be confined to the city under orders of General Lucas.[10] However, Lucas's main body of militia was allowed to disband, leaving the general with only a small detachment to guard Far West for four days before General Clark arrived with his army. During that time no watch was kept around the town to prevent the Mormons from escaping.[11] Those Mormons who did remain were subjected to horrid conditions. Provisions were scarce because over the course of a week nearly five thousand Missouri militiamen had replenished their supplies from the Mormon storehouses. Many families went without food. Worse still, the remaining soldiers left behind by Lucas, essentially without command, abused and reportedly raped some Mormon women, although several Mormons denied such reports, according to the *Missouri Republican* newspaper.[12]

Conditions improved immensely after Clark's arrival on the scene. A guard was placed around the town both to protect the Mormons from citizens and to keep all fugitives contained. When he learned of the food shortages, Clark shared militia rations to ensure that none of the Mormons starved. He made all the troops treat the prisoners with respect, and no atrocities were committed against the captive population. Clark even went as far as to modify the terms of the peace accord after he saw the dreadful state of the prisoners. First, the Mormons could remain in Missouri until a convenient time in the spring, but that under no circumstances could they put down a crop. Second, due to the extended time the Mormons were allowed to stay in their homes, the militia would no longer be able to provide an armed escort for their exodus but the state would guarantee their safety. Finally, the Mormons would receive back their arms when they left Missouri, but not a moment before.[13] Despite the concessions he gave them this advice, "You have brought these difficulties upon yourselves by being disaffected and not being subject to rule—. . . become as the other citizens, lest by recurrence of these events you bring upon yourselves irretrievable ruin."[14] Clark's efforts appeared to succeed. When the legislature later took up its investigation, several Mormons reported the fair treatment they received while in the custody of Clark and his men.[15]

John B. Clark was the over-all commander of the Missouri militia during the Mormon War. He became a U.S. congressman in 1857, but was expelled in 1861 for siding with the Confederacy during the Civil War. (*Library of Congress*)

Having dealt with the immediate military situation General Clark turned his attention to the legal side of things. He ensured that the treaty was completed and signed, including a deed of trust provision that would obligate all property of the Mormons in Caldwell County to satisfy their debt, due to their violent and aggressive acts, to the displaced citizens of Daviess County. He also began interviewing all remaining Mormons in Far West to scour for additional wrongdoers against whom charges could be made. All interviewees were told they would not be compelled to incriminate themselves, and at first his investigation went nowhere. People were simply too scared to talk. It was not until after Danite leader Sampson Avard, who had been skulking around the settlement to continue to exact his influence, was captured and brought into custody by Colonel Hall of the Platte County company that witnesses felt at ease talking and the information poured out. After two days and nights of interrogation, Clark was able to locate an additional fifty perpetrators. Of those Clark believed there to be sufficient evidence against forty-six to hold them in custody and transport them to Richmond to be arraigned in front of Judge King. Clark simultaneously hand-picked Brigadier General Wilson, also an attorney, to head to Adam-ondi-Ahman and conduct a similar investigation.[16]

General Wilson reported when he arrived in Adam-ondi-Ahman on November 8 that no militia troops were left in the city. The Mormons were free to come and go, and Wilson feared that most of the wanted men had already escaped. He immediately placed a guard around the town to ensure that no further fugitives were permitted to leave. A census of the Mormon men was then conducted; two hundred men entered their names. Justice Adam Black had taken up residence in the city, and the general took all men suspected of a crime directly to the judge for arraignment. Most of the guilty had escaped during the period when the city was left unguarded, and Wilson did not hold out hope of his presence making much of a difference. The scene around the county was one of devastation. With the exception of Adam-ondi-Ahman all non-Mormon communities had been sacked and burnt to ashes. People were without houses, beds, furniture, or even clothing, all in the face of unusually cold temperatures.[17]

Wilson said that he was shocked at the sheer brutality of the scene. "These Mormons . . . have acted more like demons from the infernal regions than human beings." Under the circumstances Wilson lacked adequate troops

to protect the Mormons from the retribution he was sure
would come. He concocted a plan to safely evacuate the
Mormons. "I told them I should remain in Daviess County
for ten days and would endeavour to protect them during
that time—at the end of ten days I would leave and was
not authorized to provide further protection in Daviess
County." General Clark had promised further protection
for Mormons in Caldwell County, and thus if they wished
to move to Caldwell or out of state, "I would give them a
permit to that effect and would guarantee their safety on
the rout." All Mormons in the county applied for permits
to leave and at the end of ten days all but a handful of
Mormons fled to Caldwell County.[18]

Wilson also discovered huge amounts of stolen property piled up around the town. It had been brought in by the
Mormons from all over the county, and despite the many
obvious piles on several occasions the Mormons concealed
stolen property underground. "I've been doing everything
to collect and preserve it for the true owners . . . but I find
it hard to do as these dirty thieves are more skilful in the
pilfering line than any I have yet seen," reported the general. Despite the insults and injuries heaped on the
Daviess County residents, General Wilson reported that
the citizens had shown a degree of compassion and char-
ity to the Mormons unparalleled under the circumstances.
They cheerfully obeyed all the general's orders. The citizens and their peace were restored to the county.[19]

Once Joseph Smith, Jr., Sidney Rigdon, Lyman Wight,
Amos Lyman, George Robinson, Parley Pratt, and Hyrum
Smith were marched to Richmond along with the forty-six
prisoners from Caldwell, the legal process began. They
were to be tried before Judge Austin A. King on charges of
treason, murder, arson, burglary, robbery, larceny, and per-
jury. They immediately took steps to retain Alexander
Doniphan and Amos Rees as their defense counsels. The
pair accepted the representation and immediately went to
work on behalf of the Mormons.[20] Circuit Attorney
Thomas Burch and Colonel W. T. Wood made up the prosecution team. General Clark described the major hurdles

the prosecution faced in getting successfully to trial against
the defendants. First, the defendants had to be tried in the
county in which they could be found or where the offense
was committed, and initially the prosecution felt Caldwell
County was their only option, meaning that Smith and the
others would have to be tried in that county. Clark stated
the obvious: until there was a change in population no one
would indict a Mormon in Caldwell County. The logical
solution to this problem was to try them in Daviess
County, but the question then became what offenses were
committed in Daviess that could be attributed to the prisoners. There was the visit to Adam Black's house for which
they had an affidavit, but that was hardly the type of case
the prosecution wanted for their trouble, and they did not
have the evidence for the defendant's participation in the
raid on Gallatin and other communities at this point. It
needed to be something worthy of the struggle of the militia.

The feather the prosecution sought for their hat was a
treason conviction. The question facing the prosecution
was whether they had sufficient evidence. Particularly difficult was going to be proving the defendants' plan to
overthrow the government. Clark pointed out, "the
enquiry takes a very extensive range and involves many
important legal principles, not often addressed in our
practice."[21] The main issue was whether or not the Danite
organization and steps taken by them showed a plan to
overthrow the government and establish a new one.
Governor Boggs sent his advice that the issues were
unprecedented, except for the case of Aaron Burr, and
would certainly be new ground for the Missouri courts to
tackle.[22] Judge King arraigned each of the defendants,
determining whether to grant them bail.

Doniphan and Rees did an admirable job. Of the forty-
six brought down from Caldwell, twenty-three were set
free with their charges dropped. The other men (also
numbering twenty-three) were arraigned on charges, and
thirteen of them were allowed bail. The remaining ten
prisoners included Smith, Rigdon, and the other leaders.

Four were kept in Richmond jail and six were transferred to the Liberty jail. Smith arrived in Liberty on November 30. Over the following months, Doniphan and Rees ran into a brick wall. Every sympathetic witness they subpoenaed would be arrested on some new charge. The prosecution was not creating false charges to malign the defense; however, it got to a point where no Mormon would voluntarily appear to defend Smith. Doniphan vented his frustration saying, "If a cohort of angels were to come down and declare you innocent it would make no difference, Judge King is determined to see you in prison."[23]

The Liberty jail was a small jail with a basement in which to contain prisoners. The walls were made of one-foot-thick wooden logs reinforced by a one-foot-layer of stone and another one-foot-thick board to make the outer wall. It was impenetrable by tool. The ceiling of the basement had a trap door that was opened to give the prisoners their food and to provide a clean waste bucket. This hole is where Smith and his fellow prisoners would live for the next four months awaiting trial.

With plenty of free time for writing, light through the jail bars, and ample writing supplies from guests or the jailer, Smith began composing a defense and apology to his people. Although he encouraged, approved, and directed the Danites in secret, Smith publicly repudiated the group.[24] He blamed his failure on Sampson Avard for the secret activities among the Danites. These things done by the Danites were "false and pernicious" and Smith claimed he was "ignorant and innocent."[25] Many looked at him as a fallen prophet due to this setback, and he had his work cut out to dispel that belief. Among the naysayers was his younger brother William Smith, who told fellow Mormons he hoped his brother rotted in jail, "if I had the disposing of my brother I would have hung him years ago!"[26] In fact one Mormon named Isaac Russell had already set up a reform church, and the High Council wanted answers from the prophet as to how his downfall could have happened if he was still favored by God.[27] Among the guests early on at the jail was Brigham Young, who was Smith's defender to the church and in a couple of months was able to quell the minor uprising. Despite Young's success, a schism was beginning to form within the church leadership.

Brigham Young also gathered information and shared it with Smith in jail visits. Young was responsible for leading the Mormon group to Illinois and used his visits to plan those activities. Also visiting was Smith's wife Emma and their son Joseph Smith, III, who would later become the leader of an offshoot of his father's church. And although Smith denied the practice of polygamy at this point and would not make the practice doctrine until his arrival in Illinois several months later, he was visited by his plural wife, Prescindia Huntington Buell, during his stay in Liberty.[28]

The liberal *Missouri Republican Daily* published in St. Louis picked up the story of the Haun's Mill attack and characterized it as cold-blooded murder just as the legislators were arriving in Jefferson City for a joint session of the General Assembly. They demanded an explanation from the governor.[29] The paper also reported that in Daviess County the citizens were organizing a public auction of all Mormon lands and intended to keep the proceeds. Undoubtedly unfamiliar with the treatment of the citizens at the hands of Mormons, the editors of the newspaper vehemently vilified the Daviess County residents, saying they "got up this crusade in order to obtain possession of the houses and lands of their victims."[30] Such stories raised a public outcry and outpouring of support for the Mormons. Many demanded an appropriation by the legislature for the Mormons' rehabilitation.[31]

John Corrill, present in the legislature, introduced a measure on behalf of the Mormons seeking aid from the state. His address began by explaining the problems Mormons had had in Jackson County in 1833. He claimed that Mormons had never received any compensation for

the property taken nor any satis-
faction of having the wrongdoers
brought to justice. His story followed them in to Clay and finally
Caldwell County, where he again
detailed the problems Mormons
had with their non-Mormon
neighbors. Now they were
wronged again and without any
compensation. Corrill said,
"Mormons are a poor and afflict-
ed people. If we are compelled to
leave the State next spring it will
have to be at the State's expense."
He explained how the property
they did still own was pledged by
deed of trust to satisfy any debts
they were found to owe at the

Brigham Young became the
leader of the largest faction
of Mormons after the death
of Joseph Smith, Jr. He led
his church to Utah where
they established Salt Lake
City. (*Library of Congress*)

conclusion of the legal action then pending. Corrill concluded, "We believe all problems brought about were
because of our religious faith."[32] The legislators listened
respectfully and then moved that the matter be brought
up after the Turner Committee, the joint committee from
the Missouri State House and Senate officially appointed
to investigate the Mormon disturbance, made its recom-
mendation.[33]

The Turner Committee reviewed the letters, affidavits,
dispatches, and orders that the governor had assembled
during the "Mormon War." After careful consideration
they determined it unwise to make the record public. They
also determined that due to the ongoing court case pending in front of Judge King in the Fifth Circuit it would be
untimely for them to release a full report and recommen-
dation on the topic as it might interfere with due
process.[34] They did, however, recommend that an appropriation be made to the Mormons to help defray their travel expenses. The legislature approved $2,000 for the
Mormons and then within a week approved the $200,000
requested by the governor to cover the Missouri militia

costs of the war. The governor's extermination order was
not rescinded despite requests.[35] The editor of the
Republican erupted, "The very members who first cried
loudest for investigation . . . have solemnly declared, they
will have no investigation."[36] These harsh words were
hardly accurate, as the Turner Committee did conduct its
investigation and seemingly reached the conclusion that
the governor's ultimate reaction was appropriate under
the circumstances. They felt no need to justify their conclusion in the arena of public opinion and expected that
the constituents who sent them to the legislature would
trust their judgment when it came to maintaining the
honor of the state.

While in jail, Smith was approached by speculators
regarding land for sale at a low price in Illinois and Iowa
along the Mississippi River. One salesman said the offer
was so good due to their recent misfortunes in Missouri,
but it later proved the price was low due to the seller's
problems with clear title to the land. Smith, flattered by
the solicitation, immediately instructed Young to investigate a move to Illinois. Flush with the grant of $2,000 from
the legislature, Young made arrangements for the
Mormons to trek across Missouri to Quincy, Illinois,
approximately 160 miles due east from Caldwell County
on the Mississippi River. By February Young too was a
wanted man facing the same charges as Smith and other
church leaders. He left Missouri to prepare a place in
Illinois. The people of Quincy were genuinely concerned
for the Mormons and warmly received them. However it
was not long before it was obvious the Mormons were too
numerous to all find space in Quincy, a town of approximately 1,600 inhabitants.[37] Finally locating appropriate
space just to the north, the group settled in a town called
Commerce which Smith renamed Nauvoo, an anglicized
version of the Hebrew word for beautiful.[38]

Smith's wife, children, parents, and brothers moved to Quincy in February 1839. Their crossing was plagued by cold and rainy weather. The lodging along the way was often miserable, without even the comfort of a fire. After nearly ten arduous days the group arrived on the western bank of the Mississippi. By this time the temperature had dropped and the rain had turned to snow, and the group made their beds on the accumulated six inches on the ground. The following day Smith's family was ferried across to their new home in Quincy. In the following two months the majority of Smith's followers left for Illinois by the same route.[39]

After the exodus, Smith became very melancholy. The trial seemed to be dragging on with no end in sight and he was losing faith in his attorneys. Doniphan had succeeded in getting Rigdon released on a writ of habeas corpus, but as soon as the bail was posted Rigdon fled the state and gave the judge all the more reason to refuse bail for the remaining prisoners. Fearful that Rigdon might be up to his old tricks of subjugating the church to his will, Smith wrote Brigham Young and warned him that all decisions should be made by a council and not one man so as to limit Rigdon's influence.[40]

Finally the prisoners determined to attempt a jail break. One night as the jailer was bringing them their food, Joseph Smith's older brother, Hyrum, rushed the guard, attempting to bowl him over and secure the door. Unfortunately at the same time the guard was delivering dinner, several guests came to visit the Mormon prisoners and for that reason the jailer had increased the guard. With the additional security the jail break failed. A couple of weeks later the prisoners had an auger smuggled into them by a visitor, and they attempted to bore through the jail walls. The equipment broke before they even made it through the first layer.[41]

Finally in April 1839 the prisoners found the freedom they sought. They were moved to Daviess County for a hearing on a motion to transfer venue to Boone County. This hearing was held at the schoolhouse, and many former enemies were present—not to condemn but to commiserate with the prisoners. They brought whiskey and began reliving old times. By the time of the hearing most of the witnesses were completely drunk. The motion to transfer venue was granted. As the sheriff prepared to take the prisoners to Boone County, the Smith brothers made their move. About twenty-five miles outside Adam-ondi-Ahman Hyrum offered the sheriff and his men some honey-sweetened whiskey he had bought. Joseph Smith offered the sheriff $800 to take a nap and allow the Mormons to take their horses. It was enough. The sheriff took his money and whiskey and told his men it looked like they had found a nice place for a nap. Joseph Smith and the other prisoners galloped away. First Smith proceeded to Far West, where he met up with the last Mormons to leave the state, and then made all speed for Illinois.[42]

FIFTEEN

Nauvoo

U PON ARRIVING IN ILLINOIS, Smith was reunited with his beloved "Saints," as fellow Mormons called one another. At Nauvoo, Hancock County, Illinois, Smith quickly established a formidable militia force, called the Nauvoo Legion, with himself at the head as general. It was estimated that by 1844 as a military force in America it was second only in size to the army of the United States.[1] The population of Nauvoo swelled from a sleepy town to one with nearly 12,000 Mormons by 1844, which rivaled the size of Chicago.[2] With the boom in population Smith encouraged his followers to fill all Nauvoo elected positions with Mormon candidates, from municipal judge to constable. Clearly Smith viewed a large military force and political dominance as necessary to maintain Mormon autonomy.

Turning their attention to the mistreatment they received while in Missouri, Hyrum Smith suggested that they buy goods on credit from Missourians and refuse to pay them back. "The Missourians have robbed, plundered and murdered our people . . . our merchants would go to St. Louis and take their large quantities of goods on credit and then, when the notes became due, simply not pay them."[3] Not satisfied to stop there, Mormons began stealing livestock and other goods they needed from their Missouri, Illinois, and Iowa neighbors as well.[4] The Mormons were safe from legal process in Hancock County since the sheriff, Jacob B. Backenstos, was a Mormon sympathizer and never served a writ from an outsider.[5] Outside process servers and bill collectors soon discovered that it was a dangerous and unproductive proposition to attempt collection from a Mormon in Nauvoo.[6]

A band of intimidators called a whittling and whistling brigade was created to keep out non-Mormons.[7] Hosea Stout, a large man as his name might imply, and a group of twelve others would take large bowie knives and a pine board and whittle away with large intimidating strokes next to the faces of the intruders. Then a group of boys would run up with whistles, bells, and other noise-makers to drown out anything the outsider might have to say. They never touched the object of their derision, and soon enough that person would get the idea and get out of town before they were injured. With no fear of legal retribution, the system effectively shielded Mormons from non-Mormon lawsuits.[8]

It was rumored that Smith or his followers longed for revenge against Governor Lilburn Boggs, which took the form of an assassination attempt. In 1842 as he was running for one of the United States Senate seats for the state of Missouri, Boggs was shot one evening in his home in Independence. It was reported that one of Smith's bodyguards, Porter Rockwell, had gone to Independence some weeks before the attack and reappeared in Nauvoo two days after the shooting. The Mormon newspaper, *The Wasp*, inaccurately stated, "Boggs is undoubtedly killed according to report; but who did the noble deed remains to be found out."[9] Smith denied any culpability but a wealthy Canadian convert, William Law, his second counselor at the time, swore an affidavit on July 17, 1885, stating that "Joseph told me that he sent a man to kill Governor Boggs of Missouri. The fellow shot the governor in his own house."[10]

Joseph Smith at the head of the Nauvoo Legion from the April 1853 issue of *Harper's New Monthly Magazine*. The Mormon temple in the background was not completed in Smith's lifetime. Smith was said to have worn a military uniform as the leader of the legion, but this romantic image does not capture the true appearance of the Mormon armed force.

In March 1844, six weeks after having been nominated by the Twelve Apostles as a candidate for president of the United States, Smith organized a secret society called the Council of Fifty. This group was made up mostly of Danites (there were three non-Mormon members) and had similar oaths, including the death penalty for unfaithful members.[11] The council's purpose was to represent the political kingdom of God on earth and was to be the tool by which Smith hoped to run for the presidency. In April, Smith, "prophecied the entire overthrow of this nation in a few years."[12]

Despite his embrace of political and military power it was a social issue that would ultimately lead to Smith's demise. Officially polygamy was not the doctrine of the Mormon church from 1835 to 1844.[13] However, it has been suggested that Smith first engaged in polygamy in Ohio in 1833 with Fanny Alger and again in Missouri in 1838; the majority of his plural marriages were said to have occurred in Nauvoo between 1841 and 1844.[14] The practice was kept secret it is supposed because it was illegal in Illinois, but after the Mormons moved to Utah, in 1847, it was practiced openly until the church officially banned the practice in 1890.[15] Sidney Rigdon, Smith's longtime associate, was vehemently opposed to the practice of polygamy and ultimately lost favor with Smith because of it. By 1844 Rigdon had abandoned Nauvoo to return to Pennsylvania.[16]

One evening in late 1843 on a night when Smith knew William Law, Smith's second counselor, would be away, he is said to have propositioned Law's wife Jane to become his polyandrous spouse. She refused, and when she told her husband what had transpired he believed that Smith had become a fallen prophet.[17] By January 1844, Smith had Law and his wife excommunicated for slander. Smith told the church the Laws were apostates because they lied about Smith's sexual advances on Jane Law.[18] After a drawn out ecclesiastical political wrangling, their excommunications were confirmed. Law wasted no time forming the True Church of Jesus Christ of Latter Day Saints, which held the same beliefs as Smith's church minus an adherence to polygamy or interest in secular politics, with himself as the president. Law also created his own newspaper called the *Nauvoo Expositor* in which he published an article decrying Smith's involvement with polygamy and mixture of church and state in the paper's one and only edition of June 7, 1844.[19]

The story so incensed Smith that he convened a session of the municipal court to condemn Law's newspaper as a nuisance and then upon such finding ordered its printing presses destroyed.[20] The order was carried out on June 10, 1844, under the force of the Nauvoo Legion, after which Smith declared martial law in Nauvoo and held several individuals prisoner without charges.[21] Reacting quickly, Augustine Spencer, a witness to the events in Nauvoo, traveled the Carthage, the county seat of Hancock, and swore out an affidavit before the justice of the peace, R. F. Smith. The justice of the peace issued a warrant for the arrest of those involved on charges of treason.[22]

Illinois Governor Thomas Ford took a much more hands-on approach to the Mormons than Missouri Governor Boggs had and quickly issued an ultimatum to Smith on June 22, 1844. The fact that Smith had an army many more times the size of anything the state of Illinois could readily muster had to have been a major concern.

I now express to you my opinion that your conduct in the destruction of the press was a very gross outrage upon the laws and the liberties of the people. It may have been full of libels, but this did not authorize you to destroy it.

There are many newspapers in this state which have been wrongfully abusing me for more than a year, and yet such is my regard for the liberty of the press and the rights of a free people in a republican government that I would shed the last drop of my blood to protect those presses from any illegal violence. You have violated the Constitution. . . .

You have violated that part of it which declares that the printing presses shall be free, being responsible for the abuse thereof, and that the truth may be given in evidence. This article of the Constitution contemplates that the proprietors of a libelous press may be sued for private damages, or may be indicted criminally, and that upon trial they should have the right to give the truth in evidence. In this case the proprietors had no notice of the proceeding.

The Constitution also provides that the people shall be protected against unreasonable searches and seizures of their property and "That no man shall be deprived of life, liberty or property, except by the judgment of his peers (which means a jury trial) and the law of the land," which means due process of law and notice to the accused.

You have also violated the Constitution and your own charter in this: Your Council, which has no judicial powers, and can only pass ordinances of a general nature, have undertaken to pass judgment as a court and convict without a jury a press of being libelous and a nuisance to the city.

The Council at most could only define a nuisance by general ordinance, and leave it to the courts to determine whether individuals or particulars accused came within such definition.

The Constitution abhors and will not tolerate the union of legislative and judicial power in the same body of magistracy, because, as in this case, they will first make a tyrannical law, and then execute it in a tyrannical manner.

You have also assumed to yourselves more power than you are entitled to in relation to writs of *habeas* under your charter. I know that you have been told by lawyers; for the purpose of gaining your favor that you have this power to any extent. In this they have deceived you for their own base purposes. Your charter supposes that you may pass ordinances, a breach of which will result in the imprisonment of the offender.

For the purpose of insuring more speedy relief to such persons, authority was given to the Municipal Court to issue writs of *habeas corpus* in all cases arising under the ordinances of the city.

It was never supposed by the Legislature, nor can the language of your charter be tortured to mean that a jurisdiction was intended to be conferred which would apply to all cases of imprisonment under the general laws of the state or of the United States, as well as the city ordinances.

It has also been reserved to you to make the discovery that a newspaper charged to be scurrilous and libelous may be legally abated or removed as a nuisance. In no other state, county, city, town or territory in the United States has ever such a thing been thought of before. Such an act at this day would not be tolerated even in England. Just such another act in 1830 hurled the king of France from his throne, and caused the imprisonment of four of his principal ministers for life. No civilized country can tolerate such conduct; much less can it be tolerated in this free country of the United States.

The result of my deliberations on this subject is, that I will have to require you and all persons in Nauvoo accused or sued to submit in all cases implicitly to the process of the court, and to interpose no obstacles to an arrest, either by writ of *habeas corpus* or otherwise; and that all of the people of the city of Nauvoo shall make and continue the most complete submission to the laws of the state, and the process of the courts and justices of the peace.

In the particular case now under consideration, I require any and all of you who are or shall be accused to submit yourselves to be arrested by the same constable, by virtue of the same warrant and be tried before the same magistrate whose authority has heretofore been resisted. Nothing short of this can vindicate the dignity of violated law and allay the just excitement of the people.[23]

Governor Ford concluded his letter to Smith stating that if Smith did not surrender, the militia would be called up to enforce the arrest warrant and the governor could make no guarantee of safety for Smith or the citizens of Nauvoo. If, however, Smith voluntarily surrendered, Governor Ford assured Smith of his safety and fair trial on the charges.[24]

Upon receiving the governor's letter Smith crafted a long and somewhat disingenuous reply and sent it to Ford the same day. Here we can clearly see the difficulty Smith's church faced, since at the same time they believed and made abundantly clear they were the chosen race and above man-made laws—a stance which insulted and antagonized some—they were forced to remain on the defensive, in isolation, and constantly under real or perceived threats from the outside.

Our "insisting to be accountable only before our own Municipal Court." is totally incorrect. We plead a *habeas corpus* as a last resort to save us from being thrown into the power of the mobocrats, who were then threatening us with death, and it was with neat reluctance we went before the Municipal Court, on

account of the prejudice which might arise in the
minds of the unbiased; and we did not petition for a
habeas corpus until we had told the constable that on
our lives we dare not go to Carthage for trial, and
plead with him to go before any county magistrate he
pleased in our vicinity, (which occurrence is common
in legal proceedings) and not a member of our society, so that our lives might be saved from the threats
thus already issued against us.

The press was declared a nuisance under the
authority of the charter as written in 7th section of
Addenda, the same as in the Springfield charter, so
that if the act declaring the press a nuisance was
unconstitutional, we cannot see how it is that the
charter itself is not unconstitutional: and if we have
erred in judgment, it is an official act, and belongs to
the Supreme Court to correct it, and assess damages
versus the city to restore property abated as a nuisance. If we have erred in this thing, we have done it
in good company; for Blackstone on "Wrongs,"
asserts the doctrine that scurrilous prints may be
abated as nuisances.

As to martial law, we truly say that we were obliged
to call out the forces to protect our lives; and the
Constitution guarantees to every man that privilege;
and our measures were active and efficient, as the
necessity or the case required; but the city is and has
been continually under the special direction of the
marshal all the time. No person, to our knowledge,
has been arrested only for violation of the peace, and
those some of our own citizens, all of whom we
believe are now discharged.

And if any property has been taken for public benefit without a compensation, or against the will of the
owner, it has been done without our knowledge or
consent and when shown shall be corrected, if the
people will permit us to resume our usual labors.

If we "have committed a gross outrage upon the
laws and liberties of the people," as your Excellency
represents, we are ready to correct that outrage when
the testimony is forthcoming. All men are bound to

act in their sphere on their own judgment, and it would be quite impossible for us to know what your Excellency's judgment would have been in the case referred to; consequently acted on our own and according to our best judgment, after having taken able counsel in the case. If we have erred, we again say we will make all right if we can have the privilege.

"The Constitution also provides that the people shall be protected against all unreasonable search and seizure." True. The doctrine we believe most fully, and have acted upon it; but we do not believe it unreasonable to search so far as it is necessary to protect life and property from destruction.

We do not believe in the "union of legislative and judicial power," and we have not so understood the action of the case in question.

Whatever power we have exercised in the *habeas corpus* has been done in accordance with the letter of the charter and Constitution as we confidently understood them, and that, too, with the ablest counsel; but if it be so that we have erred in this thing, let the Supreme Court correct the evil. We have never gone contrary to constitutional law, so far as we have been able to learn it. If lawyers have belied their profession to abuse us, the evil be on their heads.

You have intimated that no press has been abated as a nuisance in the United States. We refer your Excellency to Humphrey versus Press in Ohio, who abated the press by his own arm for libel, and the courts decided on prosecution no cause of action. And we do know that it is common for police in Boston, New York, &c., to destroy scurrilous prints: and we think the loss of character by libel and the loss of life by mobocratic prints to be a greater loss than a little property, all of which, life alone excepted, we have sustained, brought upon us by the most unprincipled outlaws, gamblers, counterfeiters, and such characters as have been standing by me, and probably are now standing around your Excellency—namely, those men who have brought these evils upon us.

We have no knowledge of men's being sworn to pass our city. And upon receipt of your last message the Legion was disbanded and the city left to your Excellency's disposal.

How it could be possible for us now to be tried constitutionally by the same magistrate who first issued the writ at Carthage we cannot see, for the Constitution expressly says no man shall twice be put in jeopardy of life and limb for the same offense; and all you refer to, have been, since the issuance of the *habeas corpus*, complied with for the same offense, and trial before Daniel H. Wells, justice of the peace for Hancock county, and, after a full investigation, were discharged. But, notwithstanding this, we would not hesitate to stand another trial according to your Excellency's wish, were it not that we are confident our lives would be in danger. We dare not come. Writs, we are assured, are issued against us in various parts of the country. For what? To drag us from place to place, from court to court, across the creeks and prairies, till some bloodthirsty villain could find his opportunity to shoot us. We dare not come, though your Excellency promises protection. Yet, at the same time, you have expressed fears that you could not control the mob, in which case we are left to the mercy of the merciless. Sir, we dare not come, for our lives would be in danger, and we are guilty of no crime.

You say, "It will be against orders to be accompanied by others, if we come to trial." This we have been obliged to act upon in Missouri; and when our witnesses were sent for by the court, (as your honor promises to do) they were thrust into prison, and we left without witnesses. Sir, you must not blame us, for "a burnt child dreads the fire." And although your Excellency might be well-disposed in the matter, the appearance of the mob forbids our coming. We dare not do it.

We have been advised by legal and high-minded gentlemen from abroad, who came on the boat this

evening to lay our grievances before the Federal
Government, as the appearance of things is not only
treasonable against us, but against the state on the
part of Missouri, unless the same has been requested
of Governor Ford by the Federal Government. And
we suppose your Excellency is well aware by this time
that the mass-meetings of the county declared utter
extermination of the Mormons, and that the Legion
was not called out until complaints were made to the
Mayor, and the citizens were afraid of their lives, and
losing their confidence in the authorities of the city,
and that nothing on the part of the city authorities
had been wanting, legally and judiciously, to allay
excitement and restore peace. We shall leave the city
forthwith to lay the facts before the General
Government, and, as before stated, the city is left
open and unprotected; and by everything that is
sacred, we implore your Excellency to cause our helpless women and children to be protected from mob
violence, and let not the blood of innocence cry to
heaven against you. We again say, if anything wrong
has been done on our part, and we know of nothing,
we will make all things right if the Government will
give us the opportunity. Disperse the mob, and secure
to us our constitutional privileges, that our lives may
not be endangered when on trial.[25]

Fearing a lynching or worse, Joseph and Hyrum Smith
made plans to escape Illinois and travel to the Great
Basin region west of the Rocky Mountains. On the
evening of June 22 the pair and several accomplices
crossed into Iowa to avoid officers sent by the governor to
arrest them. The Smith brothers charged W. W. Phelps
with the duty of making arrangements for their families
to catch up to them. As messages passed back and forth
across the Mississippi River, Smith's wife Emma sent a
note imploring Joseph to return and surrender himself to
the authorities.

Reynolds Cahoon, the messenger carrying Emma's letter, informed Smith that the Illinois militia intended to

harass the town of Nauvoo until Smith gave himself up. Cahoon urged Smith to surrender based upon the governor's promise "to protect him while he underwent a legal and fair trial." Cahoon, Lorenzo D. Wasson, and Hiram Kimball accused Joseph of cowardice for wishing to leave the people, adding that their property would be destroyed, and they left without house or home, as in the fable where the shepherd ran from the flock when the wolves came, and left the sheep to be devoured. To which Joseph replied, 'If my life is of no value to my friends it is of none to myself.'"[26]

According to witness Willard Richards, Joseph Smith asked Porter Rockwell, "What shall I do!" Rockwell replied, "You are the oldest and ought to know best; and as you make your bed, I will lie with you." Joseph then turned to his brother Hyrum, and asked, "Brother Hyrum, you are the oldest, what shall we do!" Hyrum said, "Let us go back and give ourselves up, and see the thing out." After studying a few moments, Joseph said, "If you go back I will go with you, but we shall be butchered." Hyrum said, "No, no; let us go back and put our trust in God, and we shall not be harmed. The Lord is in it. If we live or have to die, we will be reconciled to our fate."[27]

Smith was convinced it was madness to do so, but nonetheless he went along with his brother Hyrum and other church leaders. Smith surrendered himself to the governor in Carthage on June 25, 1844.[28] He was detained in the two-story Carthage jail.

Smith, no longer one to wait around in jail, called on the commander of the Mormon militia to rescue him and his fellow prisoners Hyrum Smith and John Taylor. (Taylor was an English-born Canadian convert who in 1844 was a member of the Mormon church leadership. He would eventually become the third president of the church after the death of Brigham Young.) Smith's commander refused to execute the order for fear of a bloodbath with the citizens.[29]

After enduring more than five years of what they felt was an intimidating, blasphemous, and dishonest presence in their state, Smith's arrest gave the angry citizens of Illinois their opportunity to destroy the Mormon leader, and that is what they did on June 27, 1844.[30] Governor Ford left the town of Carthage, after obtaining a vote from his officers and soldiers to strictly follow the law and do their best to protect the Mormon prisoners under their watch, to travel to Nauvoo where he endeavored to disarm the Nauvoo Legion before all-out war descended upon the state.[31] To effect the surrender he took most of the jail guard and militia, leaving the prisoners nearly unguarded. A division of Illinois militiamen from Warsaw (a town in Hancock County that was very antagonistic toward Mormons and Smith) disobeyed Governor Ford's orders and returned to Carthage intent on killing Smith.[32] Joseph and Hyrum Smith were in possession of two pistols, smuggled to them by friends. When the militia mobbed up to the second floor, where the prisoners were held, the brothers produced their weapons and shot three men, killing two. The militia deserters opened fire into the room housing the prisoners; one shot striking Hyrum Smith in the head, killing him instantly. Taylor was shot four times, but not fatally. Joseph, seeing his slain brother, made an attempt to escape through the window.[33] As he prepared to make the two-story leap he was shot in the back. Smith slumped forward and tumbled to the ground below. Once there a militia soldier dragged Smith's limp body against the well-curb, and orders were issued to fire on the helpless man. Four men leveled their rifles and executed the Mormon leader.[34]

Governor Ford would later remark that neither he nor the prisoners had anticipated any problems from an attack, nor had the governor feared any attempt to escape by the prisoners. In fact Governor Ford had concocted a plan to rid himself of the Mormons, which was thwarted by Joseph Smith's untimely death. He planned to allow Smith to escape, just as in Missouri. Smith would thus be in great fear of ever returning to the state, and Ford believed his church would follow him in his flight. Although Ford claims he never spoke of the plan, appar-

ently many Illinois citizens were intent on preventing
Smith's escape to the point they would rather see him
murdered than free.[35]

It was assumed that the state would erupt into war, and
the instigators intended the news of the Smith murders
to reach Nauvoo while the governor was present so that
he in turn would be assassinated, thereby creating great
sympathy for the Illinois cause.[36] In fact, the governor
intercepted the messengers to Nauvoo on his way back to
Carthage and delayed the news of Joseph's and Hyrum's
deaths until after preparations could be begun for a possible all-out war. The Illinois troops numbered only seven-
teen hundred compared to the three to four thousand
Mormon troops.[37] The situation was dire and it was unclear
at this moment who was responsible for the acts or
whether the governor's life could be defended from
Mormon vengeance. No war erupted, but tensions did not
ease between Mormon and non-Mormon residents in
Illinois.[38] By the time the fear of war had subsided it was
discovered that a force of two hundred men from Warsaw
(whom the governor had ordered to disband) proceeded to
Carthage on June 27, intent on killing Joseph Smith. The
Warsaw mob conspired with the jail guard, a company of
militia troops known as the Carthage Greys, to pretend an
assault on the jail. After each side fired blanks at the other,
the Greys feigned being overwhelmed and allowed the
Warsaw men access to the prisoners.[39] In October the same
year, Governor Ford attempted to capture the responsible
parties from their hideout in Missouri so they would face
trial for the murders, but without authority to extradite the
prisoners and faced with an armed conflict over the
arrests, his posse returned home empty-handed.[40]

Smith's death did not end the conflict. The newspapers
decried the murders and vilified the Illinois citizens.[41]
Mormons, however, were accused of continuing to consider themselves above any law outside of Nauvoo and took

advantage of their neighbors by seizing property without compensation and refusing to honor obligations to repay debts to non-Mormons.[42] Mormons, under the leadership of Sheriff Backenstos, and non-Mormons regularly intimidated one another, culminating in raids where homes were burned to ashes and plundered.[43] On September 22, 1845, delegates from nine counties met in Quincy, Illinois, and adopted a resolution requesting that the Mormons leave Illinois.[44] The Illinois residents recorded their sentiments as follows:

> No people, however quietly disposed, can live in the immediate neighborhood of the Mormons without being drawn into collision with them, and without resort to arms for self-protection. We utterly repudiate the imprudent assertion so often and constantly put forth by the Mormons, that they are persecuted for righteousness sake. We do not believe them to be a persecuted people. We know they are not; but that whatever grievances they may suffer are the necessary, and legitimate consequences of their illegal, wicked and dishonest acts.[45]

After the death of Smith, the church that Smith had worked so hard to keep together split under different leaderships.[46] In February 1846, 12,000 Mormons followed Brigham Young to Utah to establish a new country.[47] In Utah the Mormons again came into conflict with non-Mormons, this time in the Utah Territory.[48] In September 1857 a group of approximately 140 pioneers traveling from the Ozark Mountains of northwest Arkansas and southwest Missouri were killed in southern Utah in what became known as the Mountain Meadows Massacre. Mormons led by John D. Lee, a man present in Missouri during the war in 1838, concocted a plan to dress as Piute Indians and steal the settlers' cattle and other wealth. A standoff ensued and, fearful that the pioneers had seen through their disguises, the Mormons tricked the travelers into surrendering their arms under promise of protection—only to summarily execute each member of the train

over the age of seven.[49] John D. Lee was later convicted
before an all-Mormon jury for the murder of his victims
and shot by firing squad.[50]

A larger conflict broke out between Mormon settlers
and the U.S. government from May 1857 until July 1858.
Mormons fought to prevent federal troops under orders of
President James Buchanan from entering Utah. As long as
the Mormons had been allowed to choose their own leadership and run the Utah Territory according to their cus-
toms, they did not have much problem with the U.S. claim
of sovereignty. However, the Mormons rebelled against the
federally appointed territorial leadership, which they saw
as a non-Mormon threat to their self-determination.[51] In
contrast many Americans and, by extension, the federal
government distrusted the "theodemocracy" practiced in
Utah politics as a violation of the principle of separation
of church and state.[52] The conflict ended peacefully with
the U.S. excercising its control over the emigration routes
to California as well as federal law over all persons within
its boundaries. (The precedent Buchanan created by forcing the Mormons to submit to the authority of the federal
government despite the Mormons' claim of independence
was used again by President Abraham Lincoln against the
southern states when they seceded from the Union.) At
the conclusion of the Utah Mormon War, all Mormons
were pardoned for sedition and treason. Utah would ultimately become a state on January 4, 1896.

The thousand Mormons who objected to the leadership
of Brigham Young and what they considered the false doctrine of polygamy, chose not to follow Young to Utah. They
were driven out of Illinois in the fall of 1846 in what
became known as the Battle of Nauvoo.[53] The resort to
arms was chiefly caused when a group of Mormons went
out to harvest their fields and were waylaid by a group of
non-Mormons. The harvesters were whipped and sent
back to Nauvoo without their crop. In retaliation, the

Mormons formed a posse and captured each of the non-Mormon perpetrators individually and held them in Nauvoo without charge or bail. The non-Mormons then captured a group of Mormons to hold without bail or charge until their comrades were released. Both sides released their prisoners, but the non-Mormons schemed to kidnap the Mormon leader, William Pickett, who was actually not a member of the Mormon faith.[54] Those willing to take Pickett swelled to six hundred men, and instead they tried to capture Nauvoo by force on September 12, 1846. Cannons were fired by both sides and the firefight lasted an hour and fifteen minutes, with three Mormons and one non-Mormon killed. Nothing decisive was accomplished.[55] The following day the non-Mormons assaulted the town again but had to retreat after their ammunition was exhausted. A committee from Quincy rushed to Nauvoo and helped negotiate a truce, and thereafter most of the remaining Mormons left Nauvoo for good.[56]

In 1860, those antipolygamous Mormons now in Lamoni, Iowa, would form a new church under the leadership of Joseph Smith III, Smith's eldest son. The new church was called the Reorganized Church of Jesus Christ of Latter Day Saints, or RLDS, and today is known as the Community of Christ.[57] That church would later splinter in 1984 when a group would break off calling themselves the Remnant Church of Jesus Christ of Latter Day Saints.[58] Both groups differ from mainstream Mormonism in various areas focused mainly on post–Joseph Smith teachings, and both are headquartered in their Zion: Independence, Jackson County, Missouri.

NOTES

PREFACE

1. Lapham, "Interview with the Father of Joseph Smith."
2. Smith, Jr. and Smith III, *The History of the Reorganized Church of Jesus Christ of Latter Day Saints*, 1:9. (Hereafter, this source will be abbreviated as *RLDS Church History*.)
3. Brodie, *No Man Knows My History*, vii.
4. *Book of Commandments* 67; *Doctrine and Covenants* 28:2. See also Bushman, *Joseph Smith*, 514–522.

CHAPTER ONE: FOUNDATION

1. Butler, "Magic, Astrology and the Early American Religious Heritage 1600–1700," 318; "Second Great Awakening," Ohio History Central, http://www.ohiohistorycentral.org/entry.php?rec=1532; Quinn, *Early Mormonism*, 24.
2. Quinn, *Early Mormonism*, 2, 14, 27; Gaustad, *The Rise of Adventism*, xiii; Finke and Stark, "Turning Pews into People."
3. Cross, *The Burned-over District*, 3; Finney, *Autobiography*, 76–78; Porter, "Notes on the Folklore of the Mountain Whites of the Alleghanies."
4. Cross, *The Burned-over District*, 44, 252–53.
5. Quinn, *Early Mormonism*, 14, 25; Estes, *The History of Holden, Massachusetts*; Rev. Joseph Avery, Letter to Chester Dewey, 1821, on blank page of Dewey's original letter to Avery, April 26, 1821, described in Grunder, *The Mormons*.
6. Thatcher, *An Essay on Demonology*, 4; Quinn, *Early Mormonism*, 11.
7. Quinn, *Early Mormonism*, 12; Swedenborg, *Arcana Coelestia*; Backman, *Joseph Smith's First Vision*.
8. Cross, *The Burned-over District*, 142; Bushman, *Joseph Smith*, 51.
9. Quinn, *Early Mormonism*, 27; Willey, "Observation on Magical Practices."
10. L. Smith, *Biographical Sketches*, 54–57; Quinn, *Mormon Hierarchy*, 2.

11. Bushman, *Joseph Smith*, 25, 26, 36; L. Smith, *Biographical Sketches*, 74.

12. Quinn, *Early Mormonism*, 28; Anderson, "Circumstantial Confirmation of the First Vision."

13. Bushman, *Joseph Smith*, 36; Prince, "Psychological Tests for the Auhorship of the Book of Mormon," 374.

14. Quinn, *Early Mormonism*, 29; "The Divining Rod," *American Journal of Science and Arts*; "The Divining Rod," *Worcester Magazine and Historical Record*.

15. Bushman, *Joseph Smith*, 26, 567n63; Cross, *The Burned-over District*, 38–39.

16. Quinn, *Early Mormonism*, 31; "The Rodsmen," *Middlebury Vermont American*, May 7, 1828; Frisbie, *History of Middletown, Vermont*, 52, Hemenway, *Vermont Historical Gazetteer* (1877), 3:814; emphasis original.

17. Quinn, *Early Mormonism*, 31; "The Rodsmen"; Frisbie, *History of Middletown, Vermont*, 54–55.

18. Bushman, *Joseph Smith*, 28–29.

19. Benton, *Warning Out in New England*, 55, 106–13, 115, 117.

20. Ibid.

21. Bushman, *Joseph Smith*, 48–52; Cross, *The Burned-over District*, 142; Quinn, *Early Mormonism*, 36; Willard Chase, Affidavit, 11 Dec. 1833 (in Howe, *Mormonism Unvailed*, 240); *Hamilton Child Gazetteer for 1867–1868*, 53; Tucker, *Origin, Rise, and Progress of Mormonism*, 20–21; McIntosh, *History of Wayne County, New York*, 150; Howe, *Mormonism Unvailed*, 12; Barber and Howe, *Historical Collections of the State of New York*, 581; Ford, *History of Illinois*, 252; Mather, "The Early Days of Mormonism," 198–99; Christopher M. Stafford, Affidavit, March 23, 1885, *Naked Truths About Mormonism* April 1, 1888: 1; Mrs. S. F. Anderick, Affidavit, June 24, 1887, *Truths About Mormonism* April 1, 1888: 2; Kennedy, *Early Days of Mormonism*; Daniel Hendrix, Statement, Feb. 2, 1897, *St. Louis Globe-Democrat*, Feb. 21, 1897.

22. Purple, "Reminiscence," 2:365; *RLDS Church History*, 3:29; Quinn, *Early Mormonism*, 36; Joseph Smith, Jr. 1838.

23. *RLDS Church History*, 3:29.

24. Quinn, *Early Mormonism*, 13; Jessee, *Personal Writings of Joseph Smith*, 4–5; Smith, ed. Faulring, *An American Prophet's Record*, 4.

25. Quinn, *Mormon Hierarchy*, 3.

26. Quinn, *Early Mormonism*, 12–13; Backman, *Joseph Smith's First Vision*, 67; Morgan, *Dale Morgan on Early Mormonism*, 256.

27. Quinn, *Early Mormonism*, 39, 37; Defoe, *System of Magic*, 3.

28. Quinn, *Early Mormonism*, 36; Purple, "Reminiscence," 2:365.

29. Quinn, *Early Mormonism*, 39; Vanderhoof, *Historical Sketches of Western New York*, 13–39.

30. Quinn, *Early Mormonism,* 39; Vanderhoof, *Historical Sketches of Western New York,* 13–39.

31. Quinn, *Early Mormonism,* 43; Cowdery, Letter, *Messenger and Advocate* 2, 1835: 203–4.

32. Quinn, *Early Mormonism,* 38, 40; Blackman, *History of Susquehanna County, Pennsylvania,* 577.

33. Bushman, *Joseph Smith,* 52; Quinn, *Early Mormonism,* 44; Lewis and Lewis, "Mormon History"; Wyl, *Mormon Portraits,* 79–81.

34. Quinn, *Early Mormonism,* 45; Walters, "Joseph Smith's Bainbridge, NY Court Trials," 129; Tanner and Tanner, *Joseph Smith's 1826 Trial.*

35. See the legal definition of "Disorderly Persons," *The Justice's Manual,* Albany, New York, 1829, 144.

36. Benton, "Mormonites"; Quinn, *Early Mormonism,* 44.

37. Bushman, *Joseph Smith,* 52; Quinn, *Early Mormonism,* 45; Marshall, "The Original Prophet," 229–30; L. Smith, *Biographical Sketches,* 103.

38. Bushman, *Joseph Smith,* 52; Quinn, *Early Mormonism,* 45; L. Smith, *Biographical Sketches,* 103.

39. Brodie, *No Man Knows My History,* 34; *Palmyra Register,* Jan. 21, 1818; *Palmyra Herald,* Feb. 19, 1823.

40. Brodie, *No Man Knows My History,* 35; Clinton, "Discourse," 93. See also Squier, *Antiquities of the State of New York,* 213.

41. Brodie, *No Man Knows My History,* 37; L. Smith, *Biographical Sketches,* 89, Cowdery, Letters, 47. See also *Messenger and Advocate* 2 [Oct. 1835]: 195–202.

42. *The Book of Mormon* (Palmyra, 1830), 72, 144–145.

43. *Western Farmer* (Palmyra, New York), Sept. 19, 1821.

44. Peter Ingersoll, Affidavit, Dec. 9, 1833, first published in Howe's *Mormonism Unvailed* in 1834 and subsequently Bennett's *Mormonism Exposed* in 1842; Brodie, *No Man Knows My History,* 35.

45. L. Smith, *Biographical Sketches,* 85; Brodie, *No Man Knows My History,* 35.

46. L. Smith, *Biographical Sketches,* 85.

47. Affidavit of Peter Ingersoll, Dec. 9, 1833; Brodie, *No Man Knows My History,* 37.

48. L. Smith, *Biographical Sketches,* 113, 120–22; Brodie, *No Man Knows My History,* 40.

49. Adams, *Dictionary of All Religions and Religious Denominations,* 202; Paul, "Joseph Smith and the Manchester (New York) Library," 347.

50. Swedenborg, in *Western Repository,* Dec. 6, 1808; Adams, *Dictionary of All Religions and Religious Denominations,* 202; Paul, "Joseph Smith and the Manchester (New York) Library," 347.

51. L. Smith, *Biographical Sketches,* 117; Brodie, *No Man Knows My History,* 37.

52. See Clark, *Gleanings by the Way*, 224–25; *Rochester Gem* article, Sept. 5, 1829. See also Kirkham, *A New Witness for Christ in America*, 151–52; Brodie, *No Man Knows My History*, 41.

53. L. Smith, *Biographical Sketches*, 135; affidavit of Issac Hale, March 20, 1834, published in Swartzell, *Mormonism Exposed*; Brodie, *No Man Knows My History*, 41.

54. *Saints Herald*, 26 (Oct. 1, 1879), 289; Brodie, *No Man Knows My History*, 42–43.

55. Quinn, *Early Mormonism*, 32; *Doctrine and Covenants* 6:10–12.

56. Quinn, *Mormon Hierarchy*, 5; *Doctrine and Covenants* 10:67–68.

57. Brodie, *No Man Knows My History*, 39; *RLDS Church History*, vol. 1.

58. Quinn, *Mormon Hierarchy*, 8; Whitmer, *An Address to All Believers in Christ*, 32, 33; *Doctrine and Covenants* 21:1.

59. *Rhode-Island American*, April 16, 1830.

Chapter Two: Missouri

1. Stevens, *Missouri the Center State*, 46.

2. Ibid., 2, viii, 1.

3. Shoemaker, *Missouri's Struggle for Statehood*, 69; *Missouri Intelligencer*, April 16, 1821; *Switzler's Illustrated History of Missouri*, 495.

4. Stevens, *Missouri the Center State*, 1.

5. Ibid., viii; *Switzler's Illustrated History of Missouri*, 495.

6. Stevens, *Missouri the Center State*, 2; *Switzler's Illustrated History of Missouri*, 197.

7. Stevens, *Missouri the Center State*, 2; *Switzler's Illustrated History of Missouri*, 202–4.

8. Stevens, *Missouri the Center State*, 3.

9. Ibid.

10. Jefferson, *The Writings of Thomas Jefferson*, letter to John Adams Dec. 10, 1819, 7:145.

11. Jefferson, *Writings of Thomas Jefferson*, letter to John Adams, Dec. 10, 1819, 7:145. Foley, *The Jeffersonian Cyclopedia*, Letter to Hugh Nelson, p. 564.

12. Stevens, *Missouri the Center State*, 4.

13. Schurz, *Henry Clay*, 180; Stevens, *Missouri the Center State*, 4.

14. Stevens, *Missouri the Center State*, 5.

15. Ibid., 6, 10.

16. *Switzler's Illustrated History of Missouri*, 210; Stevens, *Missouri the Center State*, 3.

17. Stevens, *Missouri the Center State*, 29, 26.

18. Sandweiss, *St. Louis in the Century of Henry Shaw*, 53; Stevens, *Missouri the Center State*, 26.

19. Stevens, *Missouri the Center State,* 25.

20. *Switzler's Illustrated History of Missouri,* 202; Stevens, *Missouri the Center State,* 15.

21. Stevens, *Missouri the Center State,* 9.

22. *Campbell's Gazetteer of Missouri,* 528; Stevens, *Missouri the Center State,* 7.

23. Stevens, *Missouri the Center State,* 25, 26.

24. Ibid., 12.

25. Lovejoy and Lovejoy, *Memoir of the Reverend Elijah P. Lovejoy,* Letter to His Parents, April 2, 1832; Stevens, *Missouri the Center State,* 26.

26. *Alton Observer,* Alton, Illinois, Nov. 7, 1837; Stevens, *Missouri the Center State,* 26.

27. Stevens, *Missouri the Center State,* 46.

28. Ibid., 8.

29. Barton, *Life of Andrew Jackson,* 3:551; Stevens, *Missouri the Center State,* 367.

30. Violette, *History of Missouri,* 144; Stevens, *Missouri the Center State,* 370.

31. Violette, *History of Missouri,* 145; Stevens, *Missouri the Center State,* 15.

32. Violette, *History of Missouri,* 146; Stevens, *Missouri the Center State,* 370.

33. Stevens, *Missouri the Center State,* 367.

34. Violette, *History of Missouri,* 146.

35. Stevens, *Missouri the Center State,* 125.

36. Violette, *History of Missouri,* 144; Stevens, *Missouri the Center State,* 371.

37. Stevens, *Missouri the Center State,* 370.

38. Ibid., 367.

39. *Campbell's Gazetteer of Missouri,* 165.

40. Stevens, *Missouri the Center State,* 366, 367, 85.

41. Ibid., 147; *Campbell's Gazetteer of Missouri,* 700.

42. Houck, *Spanish Regime in Missouri,* 1:292; Stevens, *Missouri the Center State,* 68.

43. *Switzler's Illustrated History of Missouri,* 165.

44. Stevens, *Missouri the Center State,* 69.

45. Ibid., 147.

46. *Switzler's Illustrated History of Missouri,* 174; Stevens, *Missouri the Center State,* 147.

47. Stevens, *Missouri the Center State,* 162.

48. *Campbell's Gazetteer of Missouri,* 55; Stevens, *Missouri the Center State,* 69.

CHAPTER THREE: KIRTLAND, OHIO

1. L. Smith, *Biographical Sketches*, 207.
2. *RLDS Church History,* 3:31, 166–68, 170–72, 215, 232, 284, 287; Document Containing the Correspondence, Orders, etc. in Relation to the Disturbances with the Mormons; and the Evidence Given before the Hon. Austin A. King; Quinn, *Mormon Hierarchy,* 23.
3. *RLDS Church History,* 1:86–99, with footnote of Smith's lawyer's account in 1:95n and 6:394–95; *Times and Seasons* 5 (June 1, 1844); Walters, "Joseph Smith's Bainbridge, N.Y. Court Trials," 123–55; Quinn, *Mormon Hierarchy,* 23.
4. *RLDS Church History,* 1:95n, and 6:394–95.
5. Ibid.
6. Ibid.
7. *RLDS Church History,* 1:97.
8. Ibid.
9. Campbellite refers to followers of Thomas and Alexander Campbell, who began a restoration movement in the United States during the early nineteenth century which was designed to reject the various Christian denominations and support only teachings drawn directly from the Bible. See Allen and Hughes, *Discovering Our Roots.*
10. Brodie, *No Man Knows My History*, 141–42.
11. "Fanaticism," *Connecticut Mirror*, February 19, 1831, including a column reprinted from the *Painesville* (Ohio) *Gazette*.
12. *Doctrine and Covenants* 28:2; Quinn, *Mormon Hierarchy,* 9.
13. *Doctrine and Covenants* 43:3–4; Quinn, *Mormon Hierarchy,* 9.
14. *Book of Commandments* 10.
15. *Doctrine and Covenants* 5:4 (emphasis added); *Book of Commandments* 4:2. Smith's son, Joseph Smith, III would explain the discrepancy after his father's death, stating that the *Book of Commandments* was never authorized by the Church and so only the *Doctrine and Covenants* controlled.
16. Smith, III, *Book of Commandments vs. Doctrine and Covenants,* pamphlet.
17. *Journal of Discourses* 16:156 (Orson Pratt 1873), 19:114 (Orson Pratt 1877), 22:32 (Orson Pratt, 1880) in Brodie, *No Man Knows My History*, as Appendix A; Quinn, *Mormon Hierarchy,* 5.
18. Oliver Cowdery Statement, Sept. 28, 1835, in Joseph Smith, Sr., *Patriarchal Blessing Book*, 1:9, also in J. F. Smith, ed., *Teaching of the Prophet Joseph Smith*, 39; Quinn, *Mormon Hierarchy,* 9–10.
19. *Messenger and Advocate*, August 1836, 353–54; Brodie, *No Man Knows My History*, 143.
20. Howe, *Mormonism Unvailed*, 83, 128, 176 (affidavits contained in book were collected by Hurlbut).

21. Howe, *Mormonism Unvailed*, 232–68. Brodie, *No Man Knows My History*, 143–44.

22. Quitman, *A Treatise on Magic*, iii, 26; Quinn; *Early Mormonism,* 193.

23. *RLDS Church History,* 1:475; *Times and Seasons* 6:771; Brodie, *No Man Knows My History*, 144.

24. *Times and Seasons*, 6:992; Brodie, *No Man Knows My History*, 144.

25. Brodie, *No Man Knows My History*, 144, 145.

26. Mormons teach that Satan is the brother of Jesus and coequal in stature. Jesus and Satan, or Lucifer, competed for the opportunity to become the savior of planet Earth. Jesus's plan won approval and Lucifer rebelled and became the tempter and deceiver of planet Earth. (Book of Abraham 3: 27, 28.)

27. *Messenger and Advocate,* December 1835, 227; *Boston Journal,* May 27, 1839; Mayhew, *History of the Mormons,* 45–48; Brodie, *No Man Knows My History*, 145.

28. *Journal of Discourses,* 4:78 (Brigham Young statement from Nov. 9, 1856); Brodie, *No Man Knows My History*, 145–46.

29. Whitmer, "History of the Church," manuscript, chapter viii, and "Newel Knight's Journal," 70; Brodie, *No Man Knows My History*, 112.

30. "Newel Knight's Journal," 70; Brodie, *No Man Knows My History*, 112.

31. *Doctrine and Covenants* 52; Brodie, *No Man Knows My History*, 113.

32. *RLDS Church History,* 7:250–52, 254–55, 261; Quinn, *Mormon Hierarchy,* 13.

33. *Doctrine and Covenants* 52; Brodie, *No Man Knows My History*, 113.

34. *Doctrine and Covenants* 56. See also Ezra Booth letter no. 5 reprinted in Howe, *Mormonism Unvailed*, 194; Brodie, *No Man Knows My History*, 113.

35. Brodie, *No Man Knows My History*, 113. *Doctrine and Covenants* 56, "Wo unto you rich men, that will not give your substance to the poor, for your riches will canker your souls . . . Wo unto you poor men, whose hearts are not broken, whose spirits are not contrite, and whose bellies are not satisfied, and whose hands are not stayed from laying hold upon other men's goods, whose eyes are full of greediness, and who will not labor with your own hands! But blessed are the poor who are pure in heart, whose hearts are broken, and whose spirits are contrite, for they shall see the kingdome of God coming in power and great glory unto their deliverance; for the fatness of the earth shall be theirs."

36. Ezra Booth letter of Nov. 21, 1831 published in *Ohio Star* 2 (Nov. 24, 1831); Quinn, *Mormon Hierarchy,* 44.

37. Jackson, *Mormonism Explained*, 34. See also *Doctrine and Covenants* 28:9.

38. Woodford, "Jesse Gause: Counselor to the Prophet," *BYU Studies,* Spring 1975, 15 (3): 362–64 (citing Kirtland Revelation Book, March 8, 1832).

39. Matthew Houston to Seth Y. Wells, Aug. 10, 1832; Zebedee Coltrin diary on Aug. 20, 1832, LDS archives; Cook and Cannon, ed., *Far West Record,* 47; Joseph Smith diary, Dec. 3, 1832, in Faulring, ed., *An American Prophet's Record,* 10; Quinn, *Mormon Hierarchy,* 42.

40. Reynolds Cahoon diary, July 5–6, 1832; Van Wagoner, *Sidney Rigdon: A Portrait of Religious Excess*; Quinn, *Mormon Hierarchy,* 42.

41. Hyrum Smith diary, July 28, 1832, Special Collections and Manuscripts Department, Harold B. Lee Library; Joseph Smith to W. W. Phelps, July 31, 1832, in Jessee, *Personal Writings of Joseph Smith,* 247; Quinn, *Mormon Hierarchy,* 42.

42. Cook, *Revelations of Joseph Smith,* 362; Quinn, *Mormon Hierarchy,* 42.

43. Flake, *Prophets and Apostles of the Last Dispensation,* 239–41; Williams, "Frederick Granger Williams of the First Presidency of the Church," 259.

44. Kirtland Council Book, 16, *RLDS Church History,* 1:334; Quinn, *Mormon Hierarchy,* 43.

45. *RLDS Church History,* 1:465; Jessee, *Personal Writings of Joseph Smith,* 23; Jessee, *Papers of Joseph Smith,* 2:15–16; Quinn, *Mormon Hierarchy,* 44.

46. *Doctrine and Covenants* 100:9; Jessee, Papers of Joseph Smith, 1:21, 24; Quinn, *Mormon Hierarchy,* 44.

47. Oliver Cowdery statement, Sept. 28, 1835, in Smith, Sr., *Patriarchal Blessing Book,* 1:1, with transcription in 1834 typescripts, 1, Prince Papers, Marriott Library, University of Utah; Quinn, *Mormon Hierarchy,* 47.

48. Brewster, *To the Mormon Money Diggers,* 2, 5; cf. Anderson, "The Mature Joseph Smith and Treasure Searching," 497–98; Quinn, *Early Mormonism,* 209.

49. Oliver Cowdery to Warren Cowdery, Jan. 21, 1838, Cowdery Letter Book, 81, Henry E. Huntington Library, San Marino, Calif.; Thomas B. Marsh to Joseph Smith, Feb. 15, 1838, in *Elders' Journal* 1 (July 1838): 45; Cook and Cannon, ed., *Far West Record,* 167; Quinn, *Mormon Hierarchy,* 45.

50. *Doctrine and Covenants* 98:4–11, 134:9; Quinn, *Mormon Hierarchy,* 80.

51. *Book of Commandments* 67; *Doctrine and Covenants* 28:2; Quinn, *Mormon Hierarchy,* 80.

52. Stegner, *The Gathering of Zion,* vii.

53. *Doctrine and Covenants* 101:50, 102:3, 104:21, 107:27; Quinn, *Mormon Hierarchy,* 86.

54. Kirtland Township Trustees' Minutes, 129 (Oct. 14, 1834); *RLDS Church History*, 2:167–68; Quinn, *Mormon Hierarchy*, 87.

55. Sketch of the Life of Newel Knight, 6, fd 2, draft #1, archives, Historical Department of the Church of Jesus Christ of Latter-day Saints, Salt Lake City, Utah; Gates, *Lydia Knight's History*, 31; Quinn, *Mormon Hierarchy*, 88.

CHAPTER FOUR: EXPULSION

1. Quinn, *Mormon Hierarchy*, 70–71; *Doctrine and Covenants* 107:65–68.

2. *Campbell's Gazetteer of Missouri*, 119; Brodie, *No Man Knows My History*, 130.

3. Brodie, *No Man Knows My History*, 130.

4. Ibid., 131.

5. *The Evening and the Morning Star*, 2 (July 1833), 218–21. The name of this newspaper was shortened to the *Evening and Morning Star* when the editions were collected, edited, and reprinted beginning in 1835.

6. This assertion that Mormon immigrants were poor is also confirmed by *Portsmouth Journal* and *Rockingham Gazette*, May 11, 1833. *RLDS Church History*, 1:375; Pratt, *History of the Late Persecution*.

7. *Campbell's Gazetteer of Missouri*, 528; Stevens, *Missouri the Center State*, 7.

8. *RLDS Church History*, 1:372–73; *Western Monitor* (Fayette, Missouri), Aug. 2, 1833.

9. *Western Monitor*, Aug. 2, 1833 (Summary of grievances of the "old settlers").

10. Ibid. Brodie, *No Man Knows My History*, 131.

11. *RLDS Church History*, 1:180–81; Brodie, *No Man Knows My History*, 130.

12. Brodie, *No Man Knows My History*, 132.

13. *RLDS Church History*, 1:378.

14. *RLDS Church History*, 1:378–79. All branches of the Mormon church have been vocal that this was simply Phelps's opinion and not the official position of the church.

15. *Western Monitor*, August 2, 1833.

16. *RLDS Church History*, 1:390; Brodie, *No Man Knows My History*, 133.

17. *RLDS Church History*, , 1:394–95; Brodie, *No Man Knows My History*, 133–134.

18. Joseph Smith letter to Vienna Jacques, Sept. 4, 1833, *Personal Writings of Joseph Smith*, 318–19; Brodie, *No Man Knows My History*, 133–34.

19. *RLDS Church History*, 1:425; Journal of Newel K. Knight, 80; Brodie, *No Man Knows My History*, 135–36.

20. Brodie, *No Man Knows My History*, 136.

21. Quinn, *Mormon Hierarchy*, 82.

22. Brodie, *No Man Knows My History*, 136.

23. *RLDS Church History*, 1:428; *Evening and Morning Star*, Jan. 1834; Brodie, *No Man Knows My History*, 136. See also Diary of John Corrill, 19.

24. *RLDS Church History*, 1:430–31; Brodie, *No Man Knows My History*, 136.

25. *RLDS Church History*, 1:435–36; Brodie, *No Man Knows My History*, 136.

26. *Missouri Intelligencer and Boon's Lick Advertiser* (Dec. 21, 1833).

27. Jenson, *Church Chronology*, 7; Brodie, *No Man Knows My History*, 135, 141.

28. *RLDS Church History*, 1:432–35; Brodie, *No Man Knows My History*, 136–37.

29. J. F. Smith, "Essentials in Church History," 165; Brodie, *No Man Knows My History*, 137.

30. J. F. Smith, "Essentials in Church History," 165; Brodie, *No Man Knows My History*, 137.

31. Cannon and Knapp, *Brigham Young and His Mormon Empire*, chap. 5.

32. J. F. Smith, "Essentials in Church History," 166; Brodie, *No Man Knows My History*, 137.

33. Brodie, *No Man Knows My History*, 138; McCullough, *Truman*, 22. Tens or even hundreds of thousands of meteors crossed the night sky and are an annual occurrence. See also David Olson, "1833 meteor shower's effects are seen to this day in religion," *The Press-Enterprise*, November 16, 2009.

34. Firmage and Mangrum, *Zion in the Courts*, 66, citing *Missouri Republican*, Nov. 1833.

35. *Missouri Intelligencer*, Nov. 16, 1833; *Niles Register*, Sept. 14, 1833; *Salt River Journal* and *Liberty Enquirer* over the same period.

36. Brodie, *No Man Knows My History*, 137, 138.

37. *RLDS Church History*, 1:449–50; Brodie, *No Man Knows My History*, 138.

38. *RLDS Church History*, 1:449–50.

39. *Doctrine and Covenants* 101: 41 "Behold, here is wisdom concerning the children of Zion, even many, but not all; they were found transgressors; therefore they must needs be chastened. . . .

40. *Doctrine and Covenants* 101; Brodie, *No Man Knows My History*, 139.

CHAPTER FIVE: ZION'S MARCH

1. Brodie, *No Man Knows My History*, 146.

2. *Doctrine and Covenants* section 103.

3. *Doctrine and Covenants* 103:1, 26, 28, 34; Quinn, *Mormon Hierarchy*, 84.

4. Howe, *Mormonism Unvailed*, 155–56.

5. Brooks, *On the Mormon Frontier*, 1:12; Brodie, *No Man Knows My History*, 147.

6. *Doctrine and Covenants* 104:84–85.

7. Stevens, *Centennial History of Missouri: The Center State*, 2:105; Brodie, *No Man Knows My History*, 147.

8. Brodie, *No Man Knows My History*, 147; Bancroft, *History of Utah* (1889), 107–8.

9. Brodie, *No Man Knows My History*, 148.

10. L. Smith, *Biographical Sketches*, 60–63.

11. Brodie, *No Man Knows My History*, 148; Bushman, *Joseph Smith: Rough Stone Rolling*, 238.

12. *Connecticut Courant*, July 21 and Aug. 4, 1834; *Independent Inquirer*, July 26, 1834.

13. *RLDS Church History*, 2:92n.

14. *Independent Inquirer*, July 26, 1834.

15. *RLDS Church History*, 2:79-80. The Lamanites are a people described in the Book of Mormon as ancestors of the American Indians.

16. Brodie, *No Man Knows My History*, 149.

17. *RLDS Church History*, 2:150–60; Brodie, *No Man Knows My History*, 149–50.

18. *RLDS Church History*, 2:150–60; Brodie, *No Man Knows My History*, 150.

19. *RLDS Church History*, 2:56 (Letter from Gov. Dunklin to W. W. Phelps, June 9, 1834); Brodie, *No Man Knows My History*, 146.

20. *RLDS Church History*, 2:492; Brodie, *No Man Knows My History*, 150.

21. *Latter-day Saints Millennial Star* (1853) 15:68; Brodie, *No Man Knows My History*, 150, 152.

22. *RLDS Church History*, 2:100, 101, 154, 159; Brodie, *No Man Knows My History*, 152.

23. *RLDS Church History*, 2:100, 101, 154, 159.

24. *Connecticut Courant*, Aug. 4, 1834; Brodie, *No Man Knows My History*, 153–54.

25. Genesis 25: 25-34; Esau, a son of Isaac and Rebekah and the grandson of Abraham and Sarah, was the twin brother of Jacob also known as Israel. Esau traded his birthright as firstborn to his brother Jacob for a meal when he returned starving from an unsuccessful hunting trip.

26. *RLDS Church History*, 1:492; Brodie, *No Man Knows My History*, 152–53.

27. *RLDS Church History*, 2:107; Brodie, *No Man Knows My History*, 154.

28. *RLDS Church History,* 2:120, 146; Brodie, *No Man Knows My History,* 152, 157.

29. Edgar and Gill, ed., *St. Louis Medical and Surgical Journal,* 384; Brodie, *No Man Knows My History,* 157.

30. *Connecticut Courant,* Aug. 4, 1834; Brodie, *No Man Knows My History,* 155.

31. Brodie, *No Man Knows My History,* 154. See also *RLDS Church History,* 1:498 and Smith, "Current Opinions ad Reports of Early Days," *Journal of History* 9 (1916): 63.

32. Smith, *Journal of History* 9 (1916): 66 (Letter of Daniel Dunklin to Col. J. Thornton).

33. *Connecticut Courant,* Aug. 4, 1834.

34. *Independent Inquirer,* July 26, 1834 (quoting *Liberty Enquirer*); Brodie, *No Man Knows My History,* 155–56, 158.

35. *Doctrine and Covenants* section 105.

36. Brodie, *No Man Knows My History,* 157. See also Reed Peck Manuscript, entry dated Sept. 18, 1839.

37. Reed Peck Manuscript, entry dated Sept. 18, 1839.

38. Letter from Smith to High Council drafted Aug. 16, 1834. *RLDS Church History,* 2:145.

39. *Liberty Enquirer* 1, nos. 1–4 (1834): 51; *Missouri Intelligencer,* July 19, 1834; Brodie, *No Man Knows My History,* 157, 158.

40. Parkin, "A History of Latter Day Saints in Clay County Missouri 1833-1837."

41. *Messenger Advocate,* Jan. 1, 1835. See also *Baltimore Patriot,* July 24, 1834.

42. "Early Days in the West: Along the Missouri One Hundred Years Ago" (reprinted from *Liberty Tribune,* Liberty Missouri), 1924, 79. See also *Baltimore Patriot,* July 24, 1834.

43. *Far West* (Liberty, Missouri), Aug. 25, 1836; Le Sueur, *The 1838 Mormon War in Missouri,* 18–19.

44. *Far West* (Liberty, Missouri), Aug. 25, 1836.

45. Ibid.

46. Corrill, *Brief History of the Church,* 26; *Missouri Argus* (St. Louis), Sept. 27, 1838; and Reed Peck Manuscript, 4.

47. *RLDS Church History,* 2:445 (June 2, 1836).

CHAPTER SIX: THE SAFETY SOCIETY BANK

1. *RDLS Church History,* 2:142–44.

2. Brodie, *No Man Knows My History,* 159–60.

3. *Pittsfield Sun,* Sept. 4, 1835; Larson, *By His Own Hand on Papyrus.*

4. Book of Abraham 3–5. In summary the new teachings were as fol-

lows: Each man's soul was created in heaven and not in his mother's womb as described by David in Psalms. There were many gods, each one a man who had successfully completed his life and as a reward received his own planet to control. Likewise each of them had the ability to later become a god of his own planet.

5. *RDLS Church History* 2:236; Smith, "Truth Will Prevail"; see *Messenger and Advocate*, Dec. 1835, 236.

6. Peterson, *Story of the Book of Abraham*, 6, 16. (Peterson described the history of the scrolls as follows: After Joseph Smith's death, the Egyptian artifacts were in the possession of his mother, Lucy Mack Smith, until her death on May 14, 1856. Joseph Smith's widow, Emma Hale Smith Bidamon, her second husband Lewis C. Bidamon, and her son Joseph Smith III, sold "four Egyptian mummies with the records with them" to Mr. Abel Combs on May 26, 1856. The St. Louis Museum was closed in July 1863 and its collection moved to the Chicago Museum, which was sold to Joseph H. Wood in 1864. The renamed Wood's Museum was destroyed in the Great Chicago Fire of 1871. Combs kept at least some of the mounted papyri fragments, which passed into the possession of his housekeeper, Charlotte Weaver Huntsman, and then to her daughter, Alice Combs Weaver Heusser. In 1918, Alice Heusser approached the Metropolitan Museum of Art, New York, about acquiring some papyri in her possession, which the museum declined. In 1947, Ludlow Bull, associate curator of Department of Egyptian Art at the Metropolitan, acquired them from Edward Heusser, Alice's widower.)

7. "The Facsimile Found," 64.

8. Turner and Turner, *Salt Lake City Messenger*, Sept. 1992, 1–4.

9. *RDLS Church History* 2:569 (later included in the book entitled *Pearl of Great Price*).

10. *Saints Herald*, 1860, 270.

11. *Doctrine and Covenants* 110; Brodie, *No Man Knows My History*, 159–60.

12. Brodie, *No Man Knows My History*, 160.

13. *RDLS Church History* 2:439.

14. *Doctrine and Covenants* 107; Corrill, *Brief History of the Church*, 25; Brodie, *No Man Knows My History*, 161.

15. *Doctrine and Covenants* 107; Corrill, *Brief History of the Church*, 25.

16. See *Doctrine and Covenants* 105.

17. *RLDS Church History*, 2:47, 100.

18. "I have much treasure in this city for you, for the benefit of Zion, and many people in this city, whom I will gather out in due time for the benefit of Zion, through your instrumentality . . . and it shall

come to pass in due time that I will give this city into your hands, that you shall have power over it, insomuch that they shall not discover your secret parts; and its wealth, pertaining to gold and silver shall be yours. Concern not yourselves about your debts, for I will give you power to pay them. . . . And the place where it is my will that you would tarry, for the main, shall be signalized unto you by the peace and power of my Spirit, that shall flow unto you. This place you may obtain by hire. And inquire diligently concerning the more ancient inhabitants and founders of this city. For there are more treasures than one for you in this city" (*Doctrine and Covenants* 111). This prophecy was given on Aug. 6, 1836, in Salem Massachusetts. *RLDS Church History*, 2:463.

19. *RLDS Church History*, 2:100. See also Brodie, *No Man Knows My History*, 193.

20. Linn, *Story of the Mormons*, 148.

21. Brodie, *No Man Knows My History*, 193. See also Hansen, *The RLDS Church: Is It Christian?*, 8.

22. Corrill, *Brief History of the Church*, 26–27; Brodie, *No Man Knows My History*, 194.

23. Lee, *The Mormons, or Knavery Exposed*, 14.

24. Ibid.; Brodie, *No Man Knows My History*, 194.

25. *RLDS Church History*, 2:471–73 (*Messenger and Advocate*, Jan. 1837). The cashier was responsible for the issuance of bank notes and considered second only to the bank president in the leadership hierarchy (Golembe, *State Banks and the Economic Development of the West*).

26. Letter of William Parrish dated March 6, 1838, and published in *Zion's Watchman*, March 24, 1838. Smith is referencing the book of Exodus in the Bible wherein Aaron, brother of Moses and acting on his instructions, uses God's power to turn his staff into a serpent which consumes the snakes of the Pharaoh's sorcerers thereby displaying God's superiority over the Egyptian gods. Smith seems to imply that his bank will act as a manifestation of the correctness of his faith's gospel and that it will outlast the other banks, though it is not specified what religion those banks are supposed to represent.

27. Brodie, *No Man Knows My History*, 194.

28. Rerick, *History of Ohio*, 273.

29. Ibid., 272; Huntington, "A History of Banking and Currency in Ohio before the Civil War," 358, 377; Coover, "Ohio Banking Institutions 1803-1866," 296.

30. *Painesville Telegraph*, Jan. 27, 1837. See also Olney, *The Absurdities of Mormonism Portrayed*, 4.

31. Roseboom, *History of Ohio*, 160.

32. Linn, *Story of the Mormons*, 148; Brodie, *No Man Knows My History*, 196.

33. Wyl, *Mormon Portraits*, 36. See also Olney, *Absurdities of Mormonism Portrayed*, 4, and the letter of Cyrus Smalling (a resident of Kirtland, Ohio, familiar with but not a member of the Mormon church) in Lee, *The Mormons, or Knavery Exposed*, 14.

34. Letter of William Parrish dated March 6, 1838 and published in *Zion's Watchman*, March 24, 1838.

35. *Painesville Telegraph*, Jan. 19, 1837.

36. *Ohio City Argus*, Jan. 19, 1837.

37. Ibid.; *Brodie, No Man Knows My History*, 197.

38. *Painesville Telegraph*, Jan. 27, 1837.

39. According to Cyrus Smalling; Lee, *The Mormons, or Knavery Exposed*, 14. See also Harris, *Mormonism Portrayed*, 30.

40. Brodie, *No Man Knows My History*, 198.

41. Chardon, Ohio, Courthouse, vol. I, 362.

42. *Elders' Journal*, Aug. 1838, 56.

43. Ibid.

44. Wyl, *Mormon Portraits*, 35.

45. *Messenger and Advocate*, June 1837. See also Brodie, *No Man Knows My History*, 198 (citing diary of Willard Richie).

46. *Zion's Watchman*, March 24, 1838.

47. Brodie, *No Man Knows My History*, 198–201 (referencing records in archives of RLDS Church in Independence, Missouri).

48. Brodie, *No Man Knows My History*, 202. See also *Latter-day Saints Messenger and Advocate*, April 1837, 488.

49. *Latter-day Saints Messenger and Advocate*, April 1837, 488.

50. *Zion's Watchman*, March 24, 1838; *Elders' Journal*, August 1838.

51. *RLDS Church History*, 2:486.

52. *Painesville Telegraph*, May 19, 26, June 9, 16, 30, 1837. See also *Painesville Republican*, July 6, 1837.

53. Heber Kimball, Sermon delivered Sept. 28, 1856; *Journal of Discourses*, 4:105.

54. Johns Hopkins University, Second Catalogue of the Library of the Peabody Institute, vol. 4 (1899), 2577; Brodie, *No Man Knows My History*, 203–4.

55. Brodie, *No Man Knows My History*, 204. See also *Messenger and Advocate*, July 1837.

56. *Messenger and Advocate*, July 1837.

57. L. Smith, *Biographical Sketches*, 261.

58. L. Smith: *Biographical Sketches*, 211–13.

59. Crary, *Pioneer and Personal Reminiscences*, 44.

60. L. Smith, *Biographical Sketches*, 266–67; Brodie, *No Man Knows My History*, 205.

61. E. Snow, *Biography and Family Record of Lorenzo Snow*.

62. Harper, Harper, and Harper, "Van Wagoner's *Sidney Rigdon*," 261–74.

63. *Elders' Journal*, August 1838.

64. Kennedy, *Early Days of Mormonism*, 166–67.

65. *Latter-Day Saints Messenger and Advocate*, Jan. 1838, 438.

66. Brodie, *No Man Knows My History*, 207; *Zion's Watchman*, March 24, 1838.

67. *Zion's Watchman*, March 24, 1838.

CHAPTER SEVEN: FAR WEST

1. *RLDS Church History*, 3:1; Matthew 10:23.

2. Ibid.

3. Ibid., 3:3.

4. Ibid., 3:13.

5. *RLDS Church History*, 3:3.

6. Hill, *Quest for Refuge*, 70; Quinn, *Mormon Hierarchy*, 93.

7. John Smith diary, Aug. 4, Sept. 1, 1838, George A. Smith family papers, Marriott Library; Thompson, "Chronology of Danite Meetings in Adam-ondi-Ahman"; *Deseret News 1993-1994 Church Almanac*, 52; *RLDS Church History*, 3:38, Quinn, *Mormon Hierarchy*. 92.

8. *Painesville (Ohio) Telegraph*, June 9, 1837; Court of Common Pleas book T, 52-53 (June 5, 1837), Geauga County Courthouse, Cardon, Ohio; Firmage and Mangrum, *Zion in the Courts*, 55–56, 382n17; and a brief discussion of the case in Roberts, *Comprehensive History*, 1:405; Quinn, *Mormon Hierarchy*, 91.

9. Swartzell, *Mormonism Exposed*, 17 (quoting Lyman Wight).

10. *RLDS Church History*, 3:11.

11. It has been suggested that Joseph Smith had an affair with George Harris's wife, Lucinda. Brodie, *No Man Knows My History*, 209. Wyl, *Mormon Portraits*, 60. In 1844, after Mrs. Sarah Pratt confided to W. Wyl in an interview that Joseph Smith had attempted to seduce her in 1842, and Mrs. Pratt had turned to Lucinda Harris for support. According to Mrs. Pratt, Mrs. Harris replied, "How foolish you are! Why, I am his [Smith's] mistress since four years." Dr. William Wyl was a well-known and highly respected German physician who visited Salt Lake City and who claimed no intent to disparage the Mormons. He wrote, "I do not wish to insult anybody in this book, or to hurt anybody's feelings. I desire to do my simple duty as a writer. That is all; to do it as a critic and observer, having the courage of my opin-

ions, and being happily free from 'all entangling alliances.'" Benjamin Johnson, a future patriarch of the church in Utah, claimed that Smith became a polygamist after revealing the practice in the Book of Abraham while still in Kirtland. According to Johnson, Smith's first plural wife was a seventeen-year-old neighbor, Fanny Alger. Fanny eventually left Kirtland and did not travel to Missouri. Letter from Benjamin Johnson to George S. Gibbs, 1903, quoted in Brodie, *No Man Knows My History*, Appendix C, 458.

12. *Times and Seasons*, 7:785–87, 800; Brodie, *No Man Knows My History*, 210, 209.

13. Violette, *History of Missouri*, 219; Brodie, *No Man Knows My History*, 209.

14. *RLDS Church History*, 3:20, Brodie, *No Man Knows My History*, 212.

15. *Missouri Argus* (Feb. 15, 1839, Speech of Cornelius Gilliam); *Kansas City Journal* June 12, 1881 (Interview of Gen. Doniphan).

16. Brodie, *No Man Knows My History* 210.

17. Ibid., 217; Testimony of John Whitmer, in *Correspondence, Orders, etc.*, 138–39.

18. See letter of Brother Winchester, composed between Sept. 6 and Nov. 19, 1838 and copied into the *Journal History* in Salt Lake City under the date Nov. 19, 1838. See also Swartzell, *Mormonism Exposed*, 24, and Reed Peck Manuscript, 42; Brodie, *No Man Knows My History*, 221–22.

19. *RLDS Church History*, 3:18n.

20. Reed Peck Manuscript 25–26; Brodie, *No Man Knows My History*, 217.

21. *RLDS Church History*, 3:8, 17, 19–20; Quinn, *Mormon Hierarchy* 93.

22. *RLDS Church History*, 3:13, 15.

23. Ibid., 3:16, 18–19.

24. *RLDS Church History*, 3:8, 17, 19–20; Brodie, *No Man Knows My History*, 213. Quinn, *Mormon Hierarchy*, 93.

25. Daniel 2:44–45; Quinn, *Mormon Hierarchy*, 93.

26. Joseph Smith Diary, July 27, 1838, in Faulring, ed., *An American Prophet's Record*, 198, and in Jessee, *Papers of Joseph Smith*, 2:262; Quinn, *Mormon Hierarchy*, 93.

27. D. Whitmer, *Address to All Believers in Christ*, 27; Cowdery, *Defense in a Rehearsal*; Robinson, Account in the *Return* 1:36; Brodie, *No Man Knows My History*, 214, 216.

28. *RLDS Church History*, 3: 180–81; Brodie, *No Man Knows My History*, 215.

29. Jessee, Ashurst-McGee, and Jensen, "Biographical Directory," 398; Bushman, *Joseph Smith*, 351.

30. Reed Peck Manuscript, 49–50. See also Peck, *Correspondence, Orders*, 116–20.

31. Robinson, "Items of Personal History of the Editor," 1:217; Quinn, *Mormon Hierarchy*, 93.

32. Corrill, *Brief History of the Church*, 31.

33. D. Whitmer, *Address to All Believers in Christ,* 27; Cowdery, *Defense in a Rehearsal.*

34. D. Whitmer and Cowdery, *Address to All Believers in Christ*, 27. See also Brodie, *No Man Knows My History*, 214.

35. *RLDS Church History,* 3:180–81.

36. Brodie, *No Man Knows My History*, 215, 216. See also *RLDS Church History,* 3: 180–81.

37. Reed Peck Manuscript, 25–26. See also Brodie, *No Man Knows My History*, 217–18.

38. *Doctrine and Covenants* 103:8–10.

39. *Doctrine and Covenants* 103, February 1834.

40. Reed Peck Manuscript, 25–26; Brodie, *No Man Knows My History*, 218.

41. Reed Peck Manuscript, 25–26. See also Brodie, *No Man Knows My History*, 218. Matthew 27:3–5 in the New International Version states that Judas, feeling remorse for betraying Jesus, hung himself. No reference to revenge, retribution, or Peter is made.

42. Corrill, Testimony in *Correspondence, Orders, etc.*, 138–39.

43. J. Whitmer in *Correspondences, Orders, etc.*, 138–39. See also Brodie, *No Man Knows My History*, 218.

44. Robinson, "Items of Personal History of the Editor"; Quinn, *Mormon Hierarchy*, 94.

45. *Correspondence, Orders, etc.*, 103–6; Brodie, *No Man Knows My History*, 219.

46. Quinn, *Mormon Hierarchy*, 94.

47. Whitmer, *History of the Church,* manuscript, ch. XXII; Brodie, *No Man Knows My History*, 219.

48. Ibid.

49. David Whitmer to "Dear Brethren," ca. Dec. 9, 1886, in *Saints' Herald* 34 (Feb. 5,1887): 91; Quinn, *Mormon Hierarchy,* 94–95.

CHAPTER EIGHT: THE ELECTION BRAWL

1. *RLDS Church History,* 3:44.

2. *Doctrine and Covenants* 119, 120; *RLDS Church History,* 3: 44n.; Lee, *Mormonism Unveiled*, 46; Reed Peck Manuscript, 34.

3. Lee, *Mormonism Unveiled*, 46; Reed Peck Manuscript, 34.

4. Brodie, *No Man Knows My History*, 220–21. See also Lee, *Mormonism Unveiled*, 60–61.

5. Lee, *Mormonism Unveiled*, 60–61.

6. Lee, *Mormonism Unveiled*, 60–61.

7. In Acts 5, Ananias and Sapphira secretly held back a portion of their real estate proceeds that they were to donate to the church. God revealed the deception and punished them with death.

8. Reed Peck Manuscript, 52.

9. Swartzell, *Mormonism Exposed*, 24; Reed Peck Manuscript, 52.

10. Ibid. Letter of Brother Winchester composed between Sept. 6 and Nov. 19, 1838, published in *Journal History* in Salt Lake City. See also Brodie, *No Man Knows My History*, 221.

11. Brodie, *No Man Knows My History*, 221.

12. Ibid.

13. Ibid., 210.

14. Ibid., 211. *RLDS Church History,* 3:35; *Doctrine and Covenants* 117; Corrill, *Brief History of the Church*, 28.

15. Swartzell, *Mormonism Exposed*, 12.

16. Quinn, *Mormon Hierarchy,* 95 (quoting John Corrill); *Correspondence, Orders, etc.*, 111; Jessee and Whittaker, *Last Months of Mormonism in Missouri*, 13, 23.

17. Corrill, *Brief History of the Church*, 26.

18. Ibid., 29.

19. Swartzell, *Mormonism Exposed*, 12; Brodie, *No Man Knows My History*, 222.

20. *RLDS Church History,* 3:56; Quinn, *Mormon Hierarchy*, 95–96.

21. *Church History* (Lamoni, Iowa), 2:157–65.

22. *RLDS Church History,* 3:41.

23. Brodie, *No Man Knows My History*, 223. See also Young, *Wife No. 19*, 44.

24. *RLDS Church History,* 3:41.

25. Ibid.

26. *Church History* (Lamoni, IA), 2:157–165; Rigdon speech quoted in Brodie, *No Man Knows My History*, 223.

27. Brodie, *No Man Knows My History*, 223. See also Young, *Wife No. 19*, 44.

28. *RLDS Church History,* 3: 43–44; Brodie, *No Man Knows My History*, 223 (citing *Church History,* Lamoni, IA, 2:157–165).

29. Oration Delivered by Mr. S. Rigdon on the 4th of July 1838, *Elders' Journal* 1 (Aug. 1838): 54; Quinn, *Mormon Hierarchy*, 96.

30. *RLDS Church History,* 3:47–48.

31. Ibid.

32. Ibid., 3:56.

33. Ibid., 3:56, 57.

34. Ibid., 3:57.
35. John L. Butler statement, Aug. 6, 1838, in *Journal History of the Church of Jesus Christ of Latter-day Saints*; Quinn, *Mormon Hierarchy*, 96.
36. Butler statement, Aug. 6, 1838; Lee, *Mormonism Unveiled*, 58–60; Brodie, *No Man Knows My History*, 225.
37. Butler statement, Aug. 6, 1838; Lee, *Mormonism Unveiled*, 58–60.
38. *RLDS Church History*, 3:57.
39. Lee, *Mormonism Unveiled*, 58–60.
40. *RLDS Church History*, 3:58.
41. Ibid.

CHAPTER NINE: CONFLICT

1. *RLDS Church History*, 3:58.
2. Swartzell, *Mormonism Exposed*, 29.
3. *RLDS Church History*, 3:59.
4. Ibid.
5. Ibid.
6. Swartzell, *Mormonism Exposed*, 29; Brodie, *No Man Knows My History*, 226.
7. *RLDS Church History*, 3:59; *Richmond, MO, Inquirer*, Sept. 28, 1838.
8. Affidavit of Adam Black, Aug. 28, 1838, Missouri State Archives—Mormon War; *Richmond, MO, Inquirer*, Sept. 28, 1838.
9. Rigdon, *An Appeal to the American People*, 24: "I Adam Black, a justice of the peace of Daviess County, do hereby sertify to the people coled Mormin, that he is bound to support the constitution of this State and of the United State, and he is not attached to any mob nor will not attach himself to any such people. And so long as they will not molest me, I will not molest them. This the 8th day of August, 1838. (Signed) ADAM BLACK, J. P."
10. *RLDS Church History*, 3:59–60.
11. Ibid., 3:60.
12. Ibid., 3:61; Affidavit of William Penniston, Aug. 10, 1838, Missouri State Archives—Mormon War.
13. Brodie, *No Man Knows My History*, 227; Affidavit of William Penniston, Aug. 10, 1838, Missouri State Archives—Mormon War.
14. *RLDS Church History*, 3:62, 63.
15. The concept of probable cause comes from the Fourth Amendment, which was a backlash against British random searches. However, the first time the test for probable cause was enunciated was in *Draper v. United States*, 358 U.S. 307 (1959). The test used to determine whether probable cause existed for purposes of arrest is based on whether facts and circumstances within a law enforcement

officer's knowledge are sufficient to warrant a prudent person to believe a suspect has committed, is committing, or is about to commit a crime. *United States v. Puerta*, 982 F.2d 1297, 1300 (9th Cir. 1992).

16. Brodie, *No Man Knows My History*, 227; *Richmond, MO, Inquirer,* Sept. 28, 1838.

17. *RLDS Church History*, 3:63.

18. Brodie, *No Man Knows My History*, 227; *Richmond, MO, Inquirer*, Sept. 28, 1838.

19. *RLDS Church History*, 3:63.

20. Bergera, "Buckeye's Laments."

21. *RLDS Church History*, 3:63.

22. Order of Adjutant Gen. B. M. Lisle dated Aug. 30, 1838, Missouri State Archives—Mormon War.

23. Letter of Judge King to Gen. Atchison dated Sept. 10, 1838, Missouri State Archives—Mormon War.

24. Affidavit of Daniel Ashby, Sept. 1, 1838, Missouri State Archives—Mormon War.

25. Affidavit of Daniel Ashby, Sept. 1, 1838, Missouri State Archives—Mormon War.

26. *RLDS Church History*, 3:28–30; Brodie, *No Man Knows My History*, 130.

27. Affidavit of John Sapp, Sept. 6, 1838, Missouri State Archives—Mormon War.

28. Petition of William Dryden, Sept. 15, 1838, and Affidavit of Adam Black, Aug. 28, 1838, Missouri State Archives—Mormon War.

29. Letter from Citizens of Daviess and Livingston Counties, Sept. 12, 1838, Missouri State Archives—Mormon War.

30. Ibid.

31. Letter from Judge King to Gen. Atchison, Sept. 10, 1838, Missouri State Archives—Mormon War.

32. Ibid.

33. Letter of Gen. Atchison to Gov. Boggs, Sept. 12, 1838, Missouri State Archives—Mormon War.

34. Ibid.

35. Order of Gov. Boggs to Ad. Gen. Lisle, Sept. 15, 1838, Missouri State Archives—Mormon War.

CHAPTER TEN: MILITIA ON THE MOVE

1. Letter from B. M. Lisle to Boonville Guards, Sept. 15, 1838, Missouri State Archives—Mormon War.

2. Order of Lisle to Lucas et al., Sept. 18, 1838, Missouri State Archives—Mormon War.

3. Daviess and Livingston County Residents to Gov. Boggs, Sept. 12, 1838, Missouri State Archives — Mormon War.

4. *Richmond Inquirer,* Sept. 28, 1838.

5. Report of Gen. Doniphan to Gen. Atchison, Sept. 15, 1838, Missouri State Archives — Mormon War.

6. Rigdon, *An Appeal to the American People,* 32–33; Gen. Doniphan to Gen. Atchison, Sept. 15, 1838, Missouri State Archives — Mormon War.

7. Gen. Doniphan to Gen. Atchison, Sept. 15, 1838, Missouri State Archives — Mormon War.

8. Ibid.

9. The opposite was reported in the *Richmond Inquirer*, Sept. 28, 1838, that Smith had surrendered but that Lyman Wight refused to surrender.

10. Letter from Gen. Doniphan to Gen. Atchison, Sept. 15, 1838, Missouri State Archives — Mormon War.

11. Gen. Atchison to Gov. Boggs, Sept. 17, 1838, Missouri State Archives — Mormon War.

12. Philo Dibble, "Philo Dibble's Narrative," 82.

13. G.A. Smith, *History*; Brodie, *No Man Knows My History*, 227.

14. Gen. Atchison to Gov. Boggs, Sept. 20, 1838, Missouri State Archives — Mormon War.

15. Gen. Atchison to Gov. Boggs, Sept. 20, 1838, Missouri State Archives — Mormon War.

16. Ibid.

17. Gen. Atchison to Gov. Boggs, Sept. 20, 1838, Missouri State Archives — Mormon War.

18. Gen. Parks to Gov. Boggs, Sept. 25, 1838, Missouri State Archives — Mormon War.

19. Ibid.

20. Ibid.

21. Ibid.

22. Gen. Atchison to Gov. Boggs, Sept. 27, 1838, Missouri State Archives — Mormon War.

23. Secy. Glover to Gov. Boggs, Sept. 22, 1838, Missouri State Archives — Mormon War.

24. Ad. Gen. Lisle to Gen. Clark Sept. 24, 1838, Missouri State Archives — Mormon War.

CHAPTER ELEVEN: THE DEWITT STAND-OFF

1. Gen. Atchison to Gov. Boggs, September 20, 1838, Missouri State Archives — Mormon War.

2. Brodie, *No Man Knows My History*, 227.

3. Richard Bennett, Master's Thesis. http://historytogo.utah.gov/people/ethnic_cultures/the_peoples_of_utah/theoft-crossedborder.html. See also *The Daily Picayune*, Sept. 14, 1838 (referencing 1000-1500 additional fighting men available to Smith).

4. Smith and Smith, *Journal of History* (Jan. 1911), Vol. 4, 94; Brodie, *No Man Knows My History*, 227.

5. Smith and Smith, *Journal of History* (Jan. 1911), Vol. 4, 94.

6. Gen. Atchison to Gov. Boggs, Sept. 20, 1838, Missouri State Archives—Mormon War.

7. Brodie, *No Man Knows My History*, 228 (quoting Brother Winchester letter of Nov. 19, 1838).

8. Gen. Doniphan to Gen. Atchison, Sept. 15, 1838, Missouri State Archives—Mormon War; Brodie, *No Man Knows My History*, 228.

9. *LDS History of the Church*, Vol. III, 65.

10. *LDS History of the Church*, Vol. III, 66.

11. Ibid., 66.

12. Corrill, *Brief History of the Church*.

13. Johnson, *Mormon Redress Petitions*, 666; Baugh, *A Call to Arms*, 65.

14. *Missouri Republican*, August 18, 1838.

15. Johnson, *Mormon Redress Petitions*, 470.

16. Gen. Atchison to Gov. Boggs, Oct. 5, 1838, Missouri State Archives—Mormon War. See also letter of Howard County citizens, Oct. 7, 1838, Missouri State Archives—Mormon War; Brodie, *No Man Knows My History*, 228.

17. Petition of DeWitt Mormons to Governor Boggs, Sept. 22, 1838, Missouri State Archives—Mormon War.

18. Gen. Parks to Gen. Atchison, Oct. 3, 1838, Missouri State Archives—Mormon War.

19. Lucas to Gov. Boggs, Oct. 4, 1838, Missouri State Archives—Mormon War.

20. Gen. Lucas to Gov. Boggs, Oct. 4, 1838, Missouri State Archives—Mormon War.

21. Gen. Atchison to Gov. Boggs, Oct. 5, 1838, Missouri State Archives—Mormon War

22. Affidavit of Adam C. Woods, Oct. 6, 1838, Missouri State Archives—Mormon War.

23. Letter of Chariton County Committee, Oct. 5, 1838, Missouri State Archives—Mormon War.

24. Letter of Howard County Committee, Oct. 7, 1838, Missouri State Archives—Mormon War.

25. Letter of Howard County citizens, Oct. 7, 1838, Missouri State Archives—Mormon War.

26. *Missouri Republican*, Oct. 11, 1838; Autobiography of Zadok Knapp Judd, 8-9; *LDS History of the Church*, Vol. III, 452, Sidney Rigdon Affidavit, July 1, 1843.

27. Gen. Parks to Gen. Atchison, Oct. 7, 1838, Missouri State Archives—Mormon War.

28. Ibid.

29. Gen. Parks to Gov. Boggs, Oct. 7, 1838, Missouri State Archives—Mormon War.

30. Gen. Atchison to Gov. Boggs, Oct. 9, 1838, Missouri State Archives—Mormon War.

31. Brodie, *No Man Knows My History*, 228; *LDS History of the Church*, Vol. III, 452

32. Brodie, *No Man Knows My History*, 228; Rigdon, *An Appeal to the American People*, 30; *Missouri Republican*, Oct. 18, 1838, Nov. 1, 1838.

33. Letter from Capt. Bogart to Gov. Boggs, Oct. 9, 1838, Missouri State Archives—Mormon War.

34. Ibid.

35. Ibid., 229.

36. *LDS History of the Church*, Vol. III, 167.

37. Brodie, *No Man Knows My History*, 229; *LDS History of the Church*, Vol. III, 167; *Correspondence, Orders, etc.*, 57–9, 97–129 (specifically referring to the affidavits of Thomas March and Orson Hyde); Reed Peck Manuscript, 80.

38. *LDS History of the Church*, Vol. III, 167. The word blackleg was an insult, referring to a bacterial infection common among cattle and sheep much like gangrene.

39. Affidavits of T.B. Marsh, Orson Hyde, George M. Hinkle, John Corrill, W.W. Phelps, Sampson Avard, and Reed Peck in *Correspondence, Orders, etc.*, 57–9, 91–129. See also *LDS History of the Church*, Vol. III, 162, 167 and Reed Peck Manuscript, 80; Brodie, *No Man Knows My History*, 230. Smith was closely paraphrasing John 15:13 in the King James Version of the Bible: "Greater love hath no man than this, that a man lay down his life for his friends."

40. Affidavits of T.B. Marsh, Orson Hyde, George M. Hinkle, John Corrill, W.W. Phelps, Sampson Avard, and Reed Peck in *Correspondence, Orders, etc.*, 57–9, 91–129. See also *LDS History of the Church*, Vol. III, 162, 167 and Reed Peck Manuscript, 80; Brodie, *No Man Knows My History*, 230.

41. Ibid.

CHAPTER TWELVE: THE RAID ON GALLATIN

1. Letter from Gen. Atchison to Gov. Boggs, Oct. 7, 1838, Missouri State Archives—Mormon War.

2. Ibid.

3. Ibid.

4. Letter from Gen. Clark to Gov. Boggs, Oct. 9, 1838, Missouri State Archives—Mormon War.

5. Ibid.

6. Gen. Atchison to Gov. Boggs, Oct. 9, 1838, Missouri State Archives—Mormon War.

7. Testimony of George Hinkle and James B. Turner, *Correspondence, Orders, Etc.*, 125–29, 134–40; Lee, *Mormonism Unveiled*, 73–74; Brodie, *No Man Knows My History*, 231.

8. Testimony of Hinkle and Turner, *Correspondence, Orders, etc.*, 125–29, 134–40; Lee, *Mormonism Unveiled*, 73–74.

9. Testimony of Hinkle and Turner, *Correspondence, Orders, etc.*, 125–29, 134–40.

10. Lee, *Mormonism Unveiled*, 73–74.

11. Trial Testimony of Reed Peck, Nov. 12, 1838, Missouri State Archives—Mormon War.

12. *Farmers Cabinet,* Oct. 5, 1838; *Public Ledger,* Oct. 11, 1838.

13. Affidavit of Adam Black, Oct. 24, 1838, Missouri State Archives—Mormon War. Henry Lee sought out Adam Black to report this information as Black was a justice of the peace and a member of Daviess County's leadership.

14. Testimony of Hinkle and Turner, *Correspondence, Orders, etc.*, 125–29, 134–40. See also Brodie, *No Man Knows My History,* 232.

15. Oliver B. Huntington, unpublished diary of Oliver B. Huntington, Utah State Historical Society Library, vol. I, 31–34.

16. Ibid.

17. Affidavit of James Stone, Oct. 22, 1838, Missouri State Archives—Mormon War. *Correspondence, Orders, etc.*, 53–54.

18. Letter from Sheriff Morgan to Gov. Boggs, Oct. 21, 1838; letter from Justice Covington to Gov. Boggs, Oct. 22, 1838, Missouri State Archives—Mormon War.

19. Letter from Justice Covington to Gov. Boggs, Oct. 22, 1838, Missouri State Archives—Mormon War.

20. Affidavit of Adam Black, Oct. 24, 1838, Missouri State Archives—Mormon War.

21. Ibid.

22. Affidavit of Jonathan L. Dryden, Oct. 22, 1838, Missouri State Archives—Mormon War.

23. Affidavit of Samuel Venable, Oct. 22, 1838, Missouri State Archives—Mormon War.

24. *Correspondence, Orders, etc.,* Affidavit of Sam Venable, 44.

25. *Correspondence, Orders, etc.*, Report of Messrs. Morehead, Thornton and Gudgel, 57–58.

26. Testimony of W. W. Phelps, Nov. 12, 1838, Missouri State Archives—Mormon War; Brodie, *No Man Knows My History,* 232.

27. Ibid. This statement means that they cut a man's throat and left his dead body in the brush. Rigdon concludes his remark by threatening to kill anyone who mentions it to the authorities. Trial Testimony of Reed Peck, Nov. 12, 1838, Missouri State Archives—Mormon War.

28. Affidavit of Henry Marks, Oct. 24, 1838, Missouri State Archives—Mormon War.

29. Affidavit of Thomas B. Marsh, Oct. 24, 1838, Missouri State Archives—Mormon War.

30. Testimony of W.W. Phelps, Nov. 12, 1838, Missouri State Archives—Mormon War. According to Mormon teachings saints are spiritually descended from the twelve tribes of Israel and are therefore by spiritual husbandry members of God's chosen people as described in the Old Testament; accordingly all non-Mormons are Gentiles.

31. See Testimony of Sampson Avard, Nov. 12, 1838, Missouri State Archives—Mormon War.

32. Affidavit of Thomas B. Marsh, Oct. 24, 1838, Missouri State Archives—Mormon War. Marsh was excommunicated from the Church in absentia on March 17, 1839, in Quincy, Illinois. In 1857, Thomas Marsh was rebaptized into The Church of Jesus Christ of Latter-day Saints. After Marsh moved to Utah and rejoined the Latter-day Saints, he looked back at his decision to leave the church with regret, recanting the 1838 affidavit. (Young and Marsh, "Return of Thomas B. Marsh to the Church", in Watt, *Journal of Discourses,* 5.) Thomas B. Marsh died in Ogden, Utah Territory in January 1866, apparently a pauper. He is buried at the Ogden Cemetery.

33. Affidavit of Thomas B. Marsh, Oct. 24, 1838, Missouri State Archives—Mormon War.

34. Ibid.

35. Affidavit of Thomas I. Martin, Oct. 22, 1838, Missouri State Archives—Mormon War.

36. Affidavit of James Stone, Oct. 22, 1838, Missouri State Archives—Mormon War.

37. Affidavit of Adam Black, Oct. 24, 1838, Missouri State Archives—Mormon War.

38. Letter from Col. Penniston to Gov. Boggs, Oct. 21, 1838, Missouri State Archives—Mormon War. The early Canadian converts came from cities along the St. Lawrence River, a rather well populated and

civilized region. They would not have been the rough and tumble fur trappers one imagines coming from the Northwest Territories. Bennett, "Canada: From Struggling Seed," 30.

39. Letter from Gen. Atchison to Gov. Boggs, Oct. 22, 1838, Missouri State Archives — Mormon War.

40. Letter from Gen. Parks to Gen. Atchison, Oct. 21, 1838, Missouri State Archives — Mormon War.

41. Letter from Gen. Parks to Gen. Atchison, Oct. 21, 1838, Missouri State Archives — Mormon War.

42. Ibid. See also Testimony of Reed Peck, Sampson Avard and John Corrill, Nov. 12, 1838, Missouri State Archives — Mormon War.

43. Testimony of Reed Peck, Sampson Avard, and John Corrill, Nov. 12, 1838, Missouri State Archives — Mormon War.

44. Letter from Capt. Bogart to Gen. Atchison, Oct. 23, 1838, Missouri State Archives — Mormon War.

45. Letter from Citizens of Ray to Gov. Boggs, Oct. 23, 1838, Missouri State Archives — Mormon War.

46. Ibid.

47. Letter from Pros. Thomas C. Burch to Gov. Boggs, Oct. 23, 1838, Missouri State Archives — Mormon War.

48. The Veiled Prophet of Khorassan is a reference to Moore, *La lia Rookh*, 1817. Al Mokanna [Hakem Ibn Hashem], styled the Veiled Prophet, was an Islamic imposter of Persia in the eighth century. He attributed to himself divine powers, and gained many followers, so that at last the caliph was compelled to send an armed force against him. He retired to a fortress in Transoxiana, where he first poisoned and burned his family, and then burned himself. His followers continued to pay him divine honors after his death.

49. Letter from Pros. Thomas C. Burch to Gov. Boggs, Oct. 23, 1838, Missouri State Archives — Mormon War.

CHAPTER THIRTEEN: MASSACRE AND CAPITULATION

1. Report of Morehead, Thornton and Gudgel, *Correspondence, Orders, etc.*, 57–58.

2. Report of Morehead, Thornton and Gudgel, Oct. 24, 1838, Missouri State Archives — Mormon War.

3. Ibid.

4. Public Meeting, Ray Co., Oct. 24, 1838, Missouri State Archives — Mormon War.

5. Letter from Judge King to Gov. Boggs, Oct. 24, 1838, Missouri State Archives — Mormon War.

6. Ibid.

7. Lee, *Mormonism Unveiled*, 73; Brodie, *No Man Knows My History*, 233.

8. Zimmerman, ed., *I Knew the Prophets*, 27; Nathan Turner reminiscence, 386; Quinn, *Mormon Hierarchy*, 99.

9. Brodie, *No Man Knows My History*, 233; Rich and Kimball, "History of David W. Patten."

10. Lee, *Mormonism Unveiled*, 73; Reed Peck Manuscript, 99–100; Brodie, *No Man Knows My History*, 234.

11. Quinn, *Mormon Hierarchy*, 99; Lee, *Mormonism Unveiled*, 93–94; Hunt, *Mormonism*, 190–91.

12. Lee, *Mormonism Unveiled*, 75; Brodie, *No Man Knows My History*, 234.

13. Report of Sashel Woods and Joseph Dickson, Oct. 24, 1838, Missouri State Archives—Mormon War.

14. Wiley Williams and Amos Rees to Gen. Clark, Oct. 25, 1838, Missouri State Archives—Mormon War.

15. E. M. Ryland to Rees and Williams, Oct. 25, 1838, Missouri State Archives—Mormon War.

16. Order No. 44; Oct. 27, 1838, Gov. Boggs to Gen. Clark, Missouri State Archives—Mormon War.

17. Ibid.

18. *Laws of a Public and General Nature of the District of Louisiana*, 150, 161.

19. Adjutant Gen. Lisle to 1st, 4th, 5th, 6th and 12th Divisions, Oct. 26, 1838, Missouri State Archives—Mormon War.

20. Brooks, *John Doyle Lee*, 34; Brodie, *No Man Knows My History*, 235.

21. Brodie, *No Man Knows My History*, 237 (Diary of Winchester from Journal History all published under date Nov. 19, 1838).

22. Lee, *Mormonism Unveiled*, 78; Brodie, *No Man Knows My History*, 236 (quoting Diary of John D. Lee).

23. Lee, *Mormonism Unveiled*, 79–80; Brodie, *No Man Knows My History*, 237.

24. Lee, *Mormonism Unveiled*, 79–80.

25. Sen. Ashby to Gen. Clark, Nov. 28, 1838, Missouri State Archives—Mormon War.

26. Sen. Ashby to Gen. Clark, Nov. 28, 1838, Missouri State Archives—Mormon War; Lee, *Mormonism Unveiled*, 80; Brodie, *No Man Knows My History*, 237.

27. Lee, *Mormonism Unveiled*, 80; *RLDS Church History*, 3:184-87, 326n, 175; Ludlow, *Encyclopedia of Mormonism* 2:577; Brodie, *No Man Knows My History*, 237; Quinn, *Mormon Hierarchy*, 100.

28. Sen. Ashby to Gen. Clark, Nov. 28, 1838, Missouri State Archives—Mormon War.

29. Lee, *Mormonism Unveiled*, 80; Brodie, *No Man Knows My History*, 237 and Quinn, *Mormon Hierarchy*, 100 (quoting survivor Joseph Young). Letter of S. M. Smith to Gov. Boggs, March 21, 1839, Missouri State Archives—Mormon War.

30. Sen. Ashby to Gen. Clark, Nov. 28, 1838, Missouri State Archives—Mormon War.

31. Lee, *Mormonism Unveiled*, 80; Brodie, *No Man Knows My History*, 237; Quinn, *Mormon Hierarchy*, 100 (quoting survivor Joseph Young). Letter of S. M. Smith to Gov. Boggs, March 21, 1839, Missouri State Archives—Mormon War.

32. Bushman, *Joseph Smith*, 43; Brodie, *No Man Knows My History*, 238.

33. Reed Peck Manuscript, 103; Brodie, *No Man Knows My History*, 238.

34. Reed Peck Manuscript 103, quoted by Brodie, *No Man Knows My History*, 238.

35. Reed Peck Manuscript, 108–109, quoted in Brodie, *No Man Knows My History*, 238.

36. Gen. Lucas to Gov. Boggs, Nov. 2, 1838, and Gen. Lucas to Gov. Boggs, Nov. 5, 1838, Missouri State Archives—Mormon War.

37. Gen. Clark to Gov. Boggs, Nov. 29, 1838, Missouri State Archives—Mormon War.

38. Gen. Lucas to Gov. Boggs, Nov. 2, 1838, Missouri State Archives—Mormon War.

39. Ibid.

40. Reed Peck Manuscript 108-109; Letter of Col. Hinkle to W. W. Phelps, Aug. 14, 1844, published in *Messenger and Advocate*, Pittsburgh Aug. 1, 1845. See also Brodie, *No Man Knows My History*, 239.

41. Lee, *Mormonism Unveiled*, 81. (Hinkle had been riding with scouts as militia approached Goose Creek and was seen turning his coat inside out, indicating his intention to switch sides.)

42. Gen. Lucas to Gov. Boggs, Nov. 2, 1838, Missouri State Archives—Mormon War.

43. Ibid.

44. Miller B. Huntington Diary manuscript Vol. I 34. See also Brodie, *No Man Knows My History*, 239.

45. Lee, *Mormonism Unveiled*, 82. See also Brodie, *No Man Knows My History*, 239.

46. Pratt, *Autobiography*, 204. See also Brodie, *No Man Knows My History*, 240.

47. Roberts, "History of the Mormon Church," *Americana* 5 (Jan. 1910): 1047. See also Brodie, *No Man Knows My History*, 240.

48. *Latter-Day Saints Millennial Star* 21, no. 1 (Jan. 1859): 539.

49. Gov. Boggs to Gen. Clark, Nov. 6, 1838, Missouri State Archives—Mormon War.

50. Gen. Lucas to Gov. Boggs, Nov. 2, 1838, Missouri State Archives — Mormon War.

51. Ibid.

CHAPTER FOURTEEN: EXODUS

1. Lee, *Mormonism Unveiled*, 83; Pratt, *Autobiography*, 205; Brodie, *No Man Knows My History*, 241.

2. Lucas to Clark, Nov. 5, 1838, Missouri State Archives — Mormon War.

3. Brodie, *No Man Knows My History,* 242–43 and Library Archives of RLDS Church in Independence, Missouri.

4. Gov. Boggs to Gen. Clark, Nov. 6, 1838, Missouri State Archives — Mormon War.

5. Gen. Lucas to Gov. Boggs, Nov. 7, 1838, Missouri State Archives — Mormon War.

6. Gen. Clark to Gov. Boggs, Nov. 29, 1838, Missouri State Archives — Mormon War.

7. Ibid.

8. Gov. Boggs to Gen. Clark, Nov. 6, 1838, Missouri State Archives — Mormon War.

9. Gen. Clark to Gov. Boggs, Nov. 14, 1838, Missouri State Archives — Mormon War.

10. *Far West Record,* 211, entry on Dec. 10, 1838.

11. Gen. Clark to Gov. Boggs, Nov. 10, 1838, Missouri State Archives — Mormon War.

12. Brodie, *No Man Knows My History*, 242; Moorehead, *Missouri Republican*, Dec. 29, 1838.

13. Gen. Clark to Gov. Boggs, Nov. 29, 1838, Missouri State Archives — Mormon War.

14. *History of Caldwell and Livingston Counties*, 140.

15. Mormon Report to Legislature, Nov. 23, 1838, Missouri State Archives — Mormon War.

16. Gen. Clark to Gov. Boggs, Nov. 29, 1838, Missouri State Archives — Mormon War.

17. Gen. Wilson to Gen. Clark, Nov. 14, 1838, Missouri State Archives — Mormon War.

18. Ibid.

19. Ibid.

20. Gen. Clark to Gov. Boggs, Nov. 14, 1838, Missouri State Archives — Mormon War.

21. Ibid.

22. Gov. Boggs to Gen. Clark, Nov. 19, 1838, Missouri State Archives — Mormon War.

23. West, *Kingdom of the Saints,* 97; Brodie, *No Man Knows My History,* 245.
24. *RLDS Church History,* 3:58–322; Quinn, *Mormon Hierarchy,* 101.
25. *RLDS Church History,* 3:226-33; Brodie, *No Man Knows My History,* 246.
26. Brigham Young, *Millennial Star* 27 (Oct. 21, 1865): 658.
27. *RLDS Church History,* 3:224–26.
28. Brodie, *No Man Knows My History,* 246, 250, 252; *RLDS Church History,* 3:226–33.
29. *Missouri Republican Daily,* Dec. 12, 1838.
30. Ibid.
31. *Missouri Republican Daily,* Feb. 4, 1839; Brodie, *No Man Knows My History*, 247.
32. *Far West Record,* Dec. 10, 1838, 217–18. See also Mormon Petition to Legislature, Nov. 1838, Missouri State Archives — Mormon War.
33. *RLDS Church History,* 3:238.
34. Turner Committee Report, Dec. 9, 1838, Missouri State Archives — Mormon War.
35. Letter from Sylvester M. Smith from Kirtland, OH to Gov. Boggs, March 21, 1839, Missouri State Archives — Mormon War; Brodie, *No Man Knows My History*, 248. The governor's Extermination Order was not rescinded until 1976.
36. *Missouri Republican Daily*, Feb. 4, 1839.
37. Black, "Quincy — A City of Refuge," 76, and Bennett, "'Quincy, the Home of Our Adoption'," 86 (1,600 residents for Quincy in 1839 is used by two authors).
38. Brodie, *No Man Knows My History,* 248; *Historical Encyclopedia of Illinois and History of Hancock County,* vol. 2; Isaiah 52:7, "How beautiful upon the mountains . . . ."
39. L. M. Smith, *Biographical Sketches,* 322–25.
40. Brodie, *No Man Knows My History*, 250–52; G. A. Smith, *Journal Discourses* 18: 109; *RLDS Church History,* Church 3: 295, 301, 303.
41. Brodie, *No Man Knows My History*, 250–51; McRae, *Deseret News,* Oct. 9 and Nov. 1, 1854.
42. Brodie, *No Man Knows My History*, 253–55; Burnett, *Recollections and Opinions of an Old Pioneer,* 65; Memoirs of Joseph Smith, III (*Saints Herald*) 81 (Nov. 13, 1934): 1454.

CHAPTER FIFTEEN: NAUVOO

1. *Public Ledger* (Philadelphia) Nov. 18, 1843 (describing size of Nauvoo Legion as some 4,000 to 5,000 men). The U.S. Army had a total of 8,730 active duty officers and enlisted men in 1844. *Historical Statistics of the United States, Colonial Times to 1970*, Part 2, 1142.

2. Hoyt, *One Hundred Years of Land Values in Chicago*, 49–50.

3. *Salt Lake Tribune*, July 31, 1887, Interview of William Law; Hallwas and Launius, *Cultures of Conflict*, 76.

4. *Emancipator*, Aug. 13, 1840; *New Bedford Mercury*, Aug. 7, 1840.

5. Ford, *History of Illinois*, 287; Wilson and Davis, eds., "Mormons in Hancock County" by Eudocia Baldwin Marsh, *Journal of the Illinois State Historical Society* 64 (1971): 27 (quoting an anecdote of one Mrs. Murphy, a resident of Hancock County at the time).

6. *New York Sun*, Sept. 13, 1843.

7. Whitney, *History of Utah*, 4:49; Ford, *History of Illinois*, 287; Wilson and Davis, eds., "Mormons in Hancock County," *Journal of the Illinois State Historical Society* 64 (1971): 27.

8. *New-Hampshire Patriot*, Oct. 12, 1843; Ford, *History of Illinois*, 287; Wilson and Davis, eds., "Mormons in Hancock County," *Journal of the Illinois State Historical Society* 64 (1971): 27.

9. Brodie, *No Man Knows My History*, 323; *The Wasp* May 28, 1842.

10. Law's affidavit was published in Shook, *True Origin of Mormon Polygamy*, 125–29; Brodie, *No Man Knows My History*, 331.

11. William Clayton Diary, March 1, 1845, in Smith, *An Intimate Chronicle*, 158; Quinn, *Mormon Hierarchy*, 124, 128–29; Bushman, *Joseph Smith*, 514, 519-20.

12. John Taylor revelation, June 27, 1882, in Annie Taylor Hyde note-book, 64; Collier, unpublished revelations, 133, v. 18; *Public Ledger* (Phila.), Mar. 15, 1844 (Smith declaring as a candidate); Bushman, *Joseph Smith*, 521.

13. *Doctrine and Covenants* 101: 251, 1835 edition. "Inasmuch as this church of Christ has been reproached with the crime of fornication, and polygamy: we declare that we believe, that one man should have one wife; and one woman, but one husband, except in the case of death, when either is at liberty to marry again."

14. Van Wagoner, *Mormon Polygamy*, 83.

15. U.S. Congress, Executive Documents of the House of Representatives, United States Congressional serial set, Issue 2726 (1890), 427.

16. Rigdon, "Apostates and Rebellious Spirits at Nauvoo," *Latter Day Saints Messenger and Advocate*, Jan. 1, 1845, 1.

17. Schindler, "Polygamy, Persecution and Power," *Salt Lake Tribune*, June 16, 1996, paragraph 16, 17; Young, *Wife no. 19*, 61.

18. Letter of William Law to Dr. Wyl, Jan. 20, 1887.

19. *Nauvoo Expositor*, June 7, 1844.

20. Letter from Gov. Ford to Joseph Smith, June 22, 1844, *LDS History of the Church*, Vol. VI, 533-537. *Sangamo Journal*, 13, no. 45 June 20, 1844.

21. Letter from Gov. Ford to Joseph Smith (June 22, 1844), *LDS History of the Church*, Vol. VI, 533-537. "The following-named persons are reported to me as being detained against their will by martial law: John A. Hicks, H. O. Norton, A. J. Higbee, John Eagle, P. J. Rolf, Peter Lemon, and T. J. Rolf. It will tend greatly to allay excitement if they shall be immediately discharged and suffered to go without molestation."

22. Warrant for Arrest of Joseph Smith on the Charge of Treason, June 25, 1844, *LDS History of the Church*, Vol. VI.

23. Letter from Gov. Ford to Joseph Smith, June 22, 1844, *LDS History of the Church*, Vol. VI, 533-537.

24. Ibid.

25. Letter from Joseph Smith to Gov. Ford, June 22, 1844, *LDS History of the Church*, Vol. VI, 538-541.

26. Willard Richards, Account of the Arrest and Imprisonment of Joseph Smith (June 22–25, 1844); *LDS History of the Church*, Vol. VI, 547-573. The author, a Mormon, does claim to have been present during the events, although his account may contain some bias.

27. Ibid.

28. Ibid.

29. Tanner and Tanner, *Salt Lake City Messenger*, May 1995, 13.

30. Bergera, "Joseph Smith and the Hazards of Charismatic Leadership," *John Whitmer Historical Association Journal* 6 (1986): 35.

31. Ford, *History of Illinois*, 332.

32. *Warsaw Sentinel*, May 29, 1844; Ford, *History of Illinois*, 329 (reference to the rumor that Hyrum Smith had offered a reward to anyone who destroyed the *Warsaw Sentinel* newspaper).

33. "Zina Huntington Jacobs," *Latter Day Saints Biographical Encyclopaedia*, 1: 698. (Jacobs was a plural wife of Joseph Smith.) See also John Taylor, *Correct Account of the Murder of Generals Joseph and Hyrum Smith, Nauvoo 1845* (Taylor was also a prisoner in jail at the time of the murders). Recorded in Brodie, *No Man Knows My History*, 393-94.

34. Brodie, *No Man Knows My History*, 394. Smith claimed it had been revealed to him by God that he could not die for a period of five years from 1843 and it was an unconditional promise (Hallwas and Launius, *Cultures of Conflict*, 256-57). "Zina Huntington Jacobs," *Latter Day Saints Biographical Encyclopaedia*, 1: 698. See also Taylor, *Correct Account of the Murder of Generals Joseph and Hyrum Smith*; recorded in Brodie, *No Man Knows My History*, 393-94.

35. Ford, *History of Illinois*, 338-39.

36. Ibid., 349.

37. Ibid., 341.

38. Ibid., 349. *Pittsfield Sun,* July 18, 1844.

39. Ford, *History of Illinois,* 354.

40. Ibid., 366.

41. *Southern Patriot,* July 18, 1844; *New-Hampshire Patriot,* July 18, 1844.

42. Conyers, *A Brief History of the Leading Causes of the Hancock Mob in the Year 1846,* 17–21; Hallwas and Launius, *Cultures in Conflict,* 305.

43. Hallwas and Launius, *Cultures in Conflict,* 302; Brigham Young, Letter to Quincy Committee of 9 Counties dated Sept. 24, 1845.

44. Conyers, *A Brief History of the Leading Causes of the Hancock Mob in the Year 1846,* 15–17.

45. Ibid.; Hallwas and Launius, *Cultures in Conflict,* 306.

46. Smith, Jr., *LDS History of the Church,* 6: 408–09 "I have more to boast of than ever any man had. I am the only man that has ever been able to keep a whole church together since the days of Adam. . . . Neither Paul, Peter, nor Jesus ever did it. I boast that no man ever did such a work as I. The followers of Jesus ran away from Him; but the Latter-day-Saints never ran away from me yet."

47. *RLDS Church History,* 3: 201.

48. Carleton, *Special Report on the Mountain Meadows Massacre (The first published federal report on the events of September 1857 in Utah),* May 25, 1859.

49. The age of seven has significance in the Mormon faith as the age of accountability, and all children younger than seven would have been considered innocent and unaccountable for their sins. "And their children shall be baptized for the remission of their sins when eight years old, and receive the laying on of the hands." *Doctrine and Covenants* 68:27.

50. Carleton, *Special Report on the Mountain Meadows Massacre.*

51. Gordon, *The Mormon Question,* 6.

52. Furniss, *The Mormon Conflict: 1850-1859,* 70–71. Theodemocracy is a combination of theocracy and democracy that was created by Joseph Smith, *Times and Seasons,* 5:510.

53. Conyers, *A Brief History of the Leading Causes of the Hancock Mob in the Year 1846,* 15–17. Hallwas and Launius, *Cultures in Conflict,* 302.

54. X.Y.Z., "Nauvoo—Then and Now," *Carthage Gazette,* Jan. 19, 1876, 1; Hallwas and Launius, *Cultures in Conflict,* 329. William Pickett, a lawyer and owner of a printing press in St. Louis, had moved to Illinois in order to cover the murder of Joseph Smith, Jr.; while there he met and married Agnes Moulton, the widow of Don Carlos Smith, one of Joseph Smith's brothers. He never converted to Mormonism

but given his education and command of words would have been a
natural selection as a leader.
55. X.Y.Z., "Nauvoo—Then and Now," *Carthage Gazette,* Jan. 19, 1876,
1.
56. Conyers, *A Brief History of the Leading Causes of the Hancock Mob in
the Year 1846,* 62.
57. Community of Christ Web site. http://www.cofchrist.org.
58. Remnant Church of Jesus Christ of Latter Day Saints Web site.
http://www.theremnantchurch.com.

BIBLIOGRAPHY

ARCHIVES

Historical Department of the Church of Jesus Christ of Latter-day Saints, Salt Lake City, UT.

Mormon War Papers, 1837–1841; Office of the Secretary of State, Record Group 5, Missouri State Archives, Jefferson City, MO.

Reorganized Church of Jesus Christ of Latter Day Saints Archives, Independence, MO.

PUBLISHED SOURCES

Adams, Hannah. *Dictionary of All Religions and Religious Denominations.* 4th ed. New York: James Eastburn & Co., 1817.

Allen, Leonard, and Richard T. Hughes. *Discovering Our Roots: The Ancestry of the Churches of Christ.* Abilene: Abilene Christian University Press, 1988.

Anderson, R. L. "Circumstantial Confirmation of the First Vision Through Reminiscences." *BYU Studies* 9 (Spring 1969): 373–404.

_____. "The Mature Joseph Smith and Treasure Searching." *BYU Studies* 24 (Fall 1984): 497–98.

Backman, Milton V. *Joseph Smith's First Vision: The First Vision in Historical Context.* Salt Lake City: Bookcraft, 1971.

Bancroft, Hubert Howe. *The Works of Hubert Howe Bancroft: History of Utah.* San Francisco: The History Company, 1889.

Barber, John W., and Henry Howe. *Historical Collections of the State of New York.* New York: S. Tuttle, 1841.

Barton, James. *The Life of Andrew Jackson,* Vol. III. New York: Mason Brothers, 1860.

Baugh, Alexander L. *A Call to Arms: The 1838 Mormon Defense of Northern Missouri.* Salt Lake City: BYU Studies, 2000.

Bennett. John C. *The History of the Saints; or, An Exposé of Joe Smith and Mormonism.* 3rd ed. Boston: Leland and Whiting, 1842.

Bennett, Richard E. "Canada: From Struggling Seed, the Church Has Risen to Branching Maple." *Ensign* (Sept. 1988): 30.

_____. "'Quincy, the Home of Our Adoption': A Study of the Mormons in Quincy, Illinois 1838–1840." In Black and Bennett, *A City of Refuge*, 86.

_____. "A Study of The Church of Jesus Christ of Latter-day Saints in Upper Canada, 1830–1850." Master's thesis, Brigham Young University, 1975.

Benton, Abram W. "Mormonites." *Evangelical Magazine and Gospel Advocate.* Vol. 2. Utica, N.Y., April 9, 1831, 120.

Benton, Josiah Henry. *Warning Out in New England.* Boston: W. B. Clarke, 1911.

Bergera, Gary James. "Buckeye's Laments: Two Early Insider Exposés of Mormon Polygamy and Their Authorship." *Journal of the Illinois State Historical Society*, Winter 2003.

_____. "Joseph Smith and the Hazards of Charismatic Leadership." *John Whitmer Historical Association Journal* 6 (1986): 35.

Black, Susan Easton, and Richard E. Bennett. *A City of Refuge: Quincy, Illinois.* Millennial Press, 2000.

Blackman, Emily C. *History of Susquehanna County, Pennsylvania.* Philadelphia: Claxton, Remsen & Haffelfinger, 1873.

Book of Commandments 10, contained in *Manuscript Revelation Books, facsimile edition, the Revelations and Translations series of The Joseph Smith Papers.* Joseph Smith, Dean C. Jessee, Ronald K. Esplin and Richard Bushman. Church Historian's Press, 2009.

Brewster, J. C. *Very Important! To the Mormon Money Diggers.* Springfield, Ill., 1843.

Brodie, Fawn, *No Man Knows My History.* New York: Vintage Books, 1995.

Brooks, Juanita, ed. *On the Mormon Frontier: Diary of Hosea Stout 1844–1861,* Vol. I. Salt Lake City: University of Utah Press, 1964.

Brooks, Juanita. *John Doyle Lee: Zealot, Pioneer-Builder, Scapegoat.* Glendale, Calif.: A. H. Clark Co., 1962.

Buck, H. A., M.D. "Asiatic Cholera: Its History, Causes, and Prevention." *St. Louis Medical and Surgical Journal* 10 (1873): 384.

Burnett, Peter. *Recollections and Opinions of an Old Pioneer.* New York, 1880.

Bushman, Richard. *Joseph Smith: Rough Stone Rolling.* New York: Alfred A. Knopf, 2005.

Butler, Jon. "Magic, Astrology and the Early American Religious Heritage 1600–1700." *American Historical Review* 84 (April 1979): 317–46.

Campbell, R. A. *Campbell's Gazetteer of Missouri.* St. Louis, 1875.

Cannon, Donald Q., and Lyndon W. Cook, ed. *Far West Record: Minutes of the Church of Jesus Christ of Latter-day Saints, 1830–1844.* Salt Lake City: Deseret Book Co., 1983.

Cannon, Frank J., and George L. Knapp. *Brigham Young and His Mormon Empire.* New York: Fleming H. Revell, 1913.

Carleton, Brevet Major J. H., U.S.A. *Special Report on the Mountain Meadows Massacre (The first published federal report on the events of September 1857 in Utah).* May 25, 1859.

Church Almanac: The Church of Jesus Christ of Latter Day Saints. Salt Lake City: Deseret News, 1992.

Clark, John A. *Gleanings by the Way.* Philadelphia, 1842.

Clinton, DeWitt. "Discourse." *New-York Historical Society Publications* 2 (1811): 93.

Coltrin, Zebedee. Diary. Salt Lake City: LDS Archives.

Conyers, Josiah B. *A Brief History of the Leading Causes of the Hancock Mob in the Year 1846.* St. Louis, 1846.

Cook, Lyndon W. *The Revelations of the Prophet Joseph Smith.* Salt Lake City: Deseret Book Co., 1985.

Coover, A. B. "Ohio Banking Institutions 1803–1866." *Archeological and Historical Publications* 21 (1912): 296.

Correspondence, Orders, etc. in Relation to the Disturbances with the Mormons; and the Evidence Given before the Hon. Austin A. King. Fayette, MO: Office of the Boon's Lick Democrat, 1841.

Corrill, John. *A Brief History of the Church of Christ of Latter Day Saints.* St. Louis: For the Author, 1839. Salt Lake City: Mormon Microfilm Co., 1964.

Cowdery, Oliver. *Defense in a Rehersal of my Grounds for Separating Myself from the Latter Day Saints.* Norton: Pressley's Job Office, 1839.

_____. *Letters of Oliver Cowdery.* Independence, MO: Price Publishing Co., 2002.

_____. "The Record of the Nephites." *Messenger and Advocate* 2, 1835: 203–4.

Crary, C. G. *Pioneer and Personal Reminiscences.* Marshalltown, Iowa, 1893.

Cross, Whitney R. *The Burned-over District: The Social and Intellectual History of Enthusiastic Religion in Western New York, 1800–1850.* Ithaca: Cornell University Press, 1950.

Defoe, Daniel. *System of Magic; or a History of the Black Art,* 1727.

Dening, A. B., ed. *The Naked Truth About Mormonism.* Oakland, CA, 1888.

"The Divining Rod." *American Journal of Science and Arts* 11 (Oct. 1826): 201–12,

"The Divining Rod." *Worcester Magazine and Historical Record* 1 (Oct. 1825): 27–29.

Doctrine and Covenants of the Church of Jesus Christ of Latter Day Saints. Salt Lake City: Church of Jesus Christ of Latter-day Saints, revised 1981.

"Early Days in the West: Along the Missouri One Hundred Years Ago." Liberty, MO: Liberty Tribune, 1924.

Estes, David Foster. *The History of Holden, Massachusetts, 1684–1894.* Worchester, MA: C. F. Lawrence and Co., 1894.

"The Facsimile Found: The Recovery of Joseph Smith's Papyrus Manuscripts." *Dialogue: A Journal of Mormon Thought* (Winter 1967): 64.

Finke Roger, and Rodney Stark. "Turning Pews into People: Estimating Church Membership in Nineteenth Century America." *Journal for the Scientific Study of Religion* 25 (June 1986).

Finney, Charles G. *An Autobiography.* 1876.

Firmage, Edwin Brown, and Richard Collin Mangrum. *Zion in the Courts: A Legal History of the Church of Jesus Christ of Latter-day Saints, 1830–1900.* Urbana, IL: University of Illinois Press, 1988, 2001.

Flake, Lawrence R. *Prophets and Apostles of the Last Dispensation.* Provo, UT: Religious Studies Center, Brigham Young University, 2001.

Ford, Thomas. *History of Illinois From its Commencement as a State in 1818 to 1847.* Chicago: S. G. Griggs and Co., 1854.

Frisbie, Barnes. *The History of Middletown, Vermont.* Rutland, VT: Tuttle & Co., 1867.

Furniss, Norman F. *The Mormon Conflict: 1850–1859.* New Haven: Yale University Press, 2005.

Gates, Susa Young. *Lydia Knight's History: The First Book of the Noble Women's Lives Series.* Salt Lake City: Juvenile Instructor Office, 1883.

Gaustad, Edwin Scott. *The Rise of Adventism: Religion and Society in Mid-Nineteenth Century America.* New York: Harper & Row, 1974.

Golembe, Carter Harry. *State Banks and the Economic Development of the West, 1830–1844.* New York: Arno Press, 1978.

Gordon, Sarah. *The Mormon Question: Polygamy and Constitutional Conflicts in Nineteenth Century America.* Chapel Hill: University of North Carolina Press, 2002.

Graffam, Merle H., ed. *Salt Lake School of the Prophets: Minute Book, 1883.* Palm Desert, CA: ULC Press, 1981.

Grunder, Rick. *The Mormons: Mormon List Twenty-one.* Ithaca, NY: Rick Grunder Books, 1986.

Hallwas, John F., and Roger D. Launius. *Cultures of Conflict: A Documentary History of the Mormon War in Illinois.* Logan, UT: Utah State University Press, 1995.

Hamilton Child Gazetteer and Business Directory of Wayne County, NY for 1867–1868. Syracuse, N.Y.: Journal Office, 1867.

Hansen, Carol. *Reorganized Latter Day Saint Church: Is It Christian?* Independence, MO: Refiner's Fire Ministry, 1999.

Harper, Howard K., Steven C. Harper, and David P. Harper. "Van Wagoner's *Sidney Rigdon:* A Portrait of Biographical Excess." *FARMS Review* 14, no. 1 (2004): 261–74.

Harris, William. *Mormonism Portrayed.* Warsaw, IL: Sharp and Gamble, 1841.

Hemenway, Abbey Maria. *The Vermont Historical Gazetteer.* 4 vols. Burlington, VT: Privately Published, 1877–1882.

Hill, Marvin S. *Quest for Refuge: The Mormon Flight from American Pluralism.* Salt Lake City: Signature Books, 1989.

History of Caldwell and Livingston Counties. St. Louis, 1886.

Houck, Louis. *Spanish Regime in Missouri.* Vol. I. Chicago: R. R. Donnelly and Sons, 1909.

Howe, Eber D. *Mormonism Unvailed.* Painesville, OH: By the Author, 1834.

Hoyt, Homer. *One Hundred Years of Land Values in Chicago.* Chicago: University of Chicago Press, 1933.

Hunt, James H. *Mormonism: Their Troubles in Missouri and Final Expulsion from the State.* St. Louis: Ustick & Davies, 1844.

Huntington, C. C. "A History of Banking and Currency in Ohio Before the Civil War." *Ohio Archeological and Historical Publications*, 24 (1915): 358. 377.

Huntington, Oliver B. Unpublished Diary of Oliver B. Huntington. Salt Lake City: Utah State Historical Society Library.

Jackson, Andrew. *Mormonism Explained.* Wheaton, IL: Crossway Books, 2008.

Jefferson, Thomas. *The Writings of Thomas Jefferson,* vol. VII, 1854.

Jenson, Andrew. *Church Chronology.* Salt Lake City, 1886.

_____. *Latter-Day Saint Biographical Encyclopedia.* Salt Lake City: A. Jenson History, Co., 1901

Jessee, Dean C. *The Personal Writings of Joseph Smith.* Salt Lake City: Deseret Book Co., 1984.

Jessee, Dean C., Mark Ashurst-McGee, Richard L. Jensen, eds., "Biographical Directory," *Journals, Volume 1: 1832–1839,* The Joseph Smith Papers. Salt Lake City: Church Historian's Press, 2008.

Jessee, Dean C., and David J. Whittaker, eds. "Last Months of Mormonism in Missouri: The Albert Perry Rockwood Journal." *BYU Studies* 28 (Winter 1988): 5–41.

Johnson, Clark V. *Mormon Redress Petitions: Documents of the 1833–1838 Missouri Conflict.* Religious Studies Center, Brigham Young University, 1992.

Journal History of the Church of Jesus Christ of Latter-day Saints (1830–1972), 246 reels, microfilm, J. Willard Marriott Library, The University of Utah.

Journal of Discourses, 26 vols. London: Latter-day Saints' Book Depot, 1855–86.

Judd, Zadok Knapp. Autobiography. Typescript. Salt Lake City: LDS Archives.

Kennedy, J. H. *Early Days of Mormonism: Palmyra, Kirtland, and Nauvoo.* New York: Charles Scribner's Sons, 1888.

Kirkham, Francis W. *A New Witness for Christ in America.* Salt Lake City: Utah Printing Co., 1959.

Knight, Newel K. "Newel Knight's Journal." *Scraps of Biography.* Salt Lake City, 1883.

Lapham, [La]Fayette. "Interview with the Father of Joseph Smith, the Mormon Prophet, Forty Years Ago. His Account of the Finding of the Sacred Plates," *Historical Magazine* [second series] 7 (May 1870): 305–9; republished in Dan

Vogel, *Early Mormon Documents*. Vol. 1. Salt Lake City: Signature Books, 1996.

Larson, Charles M. *By His Own Hand on Papyrus*. Grand Rapids, MI: Institute for Religious Research, rev. 1992.

Laws of a Public and General Nature of the District of Louisiana, of the Territory of Louisiana, of the Territory of Missouri and of the State of Missouri, up to the year 1824. Jefferson City, MO: W. Lusk and Son, 1842.

Lee, Ernest G. *The Mormons, or Knavery Exposed*. Frankford, PA: E. G. Lee, 1841.

Lee, John D. *Mormonism Unveiled*. St. Louis: Bryan, Brand, 1877.

LeSueur, Stephen C. *The 1838 Mormon War in Missouri*. Columbia, MO: University of Missouri Press, 1987.

Lewis, Joseph, and Hiel Lewis. "Mormon history, A New Chapter, About to be Published." *Amboy Journal*, April 30, 1879.

Linn, William Alexander. *The Story of the Mormons: From the Date of Their Origin to the Year 1901*. New York: Macmillan, Co., 1902.

Lovejoy, Joseph C., and Owen Lovejoy. Memoir of the Reverend Elijah P. Lovejoy. New York: John Taylor, 1838.

Ludlow, Daniel H., ed. *Encyclopedia of Mormonism*. New York: Macmillan, 1992.

Marshall, Charles. "The Original Prophet." *Frazer's Magazine* 87 (Feb. 1873).

Mather, Frederick G. "The Early Days of Mormonism." *Lippincott's* Aug. 26, 1880, 198–99.

Mayhew, Henry. *History of the Mormons*. Auburn: Derby and Miller, 1853.

McIntosh, W. H. *History of Wayne County, New York*. Philadelphia: Everts, Ensign and Everts, 1877.

McRae, Alexander. *Deseret News*, Oct. 9 and Nov. 1, 1854.

McCullough, David. *Truman*. New York: Simon & Schuster, 1992.

Moore, Thomas. *Lalia Rookh*. 1817. *The Poetical Works of Thomas Moore: with the life of the author, by Thomas Moore*, John Francis Waller. New York: P.F. Collier, 1884.

Morgan, Dale L. *Dale Morgan on Early Mormonism: Correspondence and A New History*. John Phillip Walker, ed. Salt Lake City: Signature Books, 1986.

Olney, Oliver. *The Absurdities of Mormonism Portrayed*. 1843.

Olsen, David. "1833 Meteor Shower's Effects Are Seen to This
    Day in Religion." *Press Enterprise*, Nov. 16, 2009.
Parkin, Max H. "A History of Latter Day Saints in Clay County
    Missouri 1833–1837." Ph.D. dissertation, Brigham Young
    University, 1976.
Paul, Robert. "Joseph Smith and the Manchester (New York)
    Library." *BYU Studies* 22 (Summer 1982): 333–56.
Peck, Reed. Reed Peck Manuscript. Salt Lake City: Utah
    Lightouse Ministry, reprint.
Peterson, H. Donl. *Story of the Book of Abraham: Mummies,
    Manuscripts, and Mormonism*, Salt Lake City: Deseret Book
    Co, 1995.
Philo Dibble, "Philo Dibble's Narrative," Early Scenes in
    Church History: Eighth Book of the Faith-Promoting Series
    (Salt Lake City: Juvenile Instructor Office, 1882), 82.
Porter, J. Hampden. "Notes on the Folklore of the Mountain
    Whites of the Alleghanies." *Journal of American Folklore*
    (April–June 1894): 105–17.
Pratt, Parley. *The Autobiography of Parley Parker Pratt.* New
    York: Russell Brothers, 1874.
_____. *History of the Late Persecution.* Detroit: By the author,
    1839.
Prince, Walter Franklin. "Psychological Tests for the
    Authorship of the Book of Mormon." *The American Journal
    of Psychology*, Vol. 28, No. 3 (Jul. 1917), 373–389.
Purple, W. D. Reminiscence, 1877. In Francis W. Kirkham, *A
    New Witness for Christ in America: The Book of Mormon.* 2 vols.
    Independence, MO: Zion's Printing and Publishing Co.,
    1951.
Quinn, D. Michael, *Early Mormonism and the Magic World View.*
    Salt Lake City: Signature Books, 1987.
_____ *The Mormon Hierarchy: Origins of Power.* Salt Lake City:
    Signature Books in association with Smith Research
    Associates, 1994.
Quitman, Frederick Henry. *A Treatise on Magic, or, On the
    Intercourse Between Spirits and Men: with Annotations.* Albany,
    NY: Balance Press, 1810.
Rerick, Rowland H. *History of Ohio.* Madison, Wisc.: Northwest
    Historical Association, 1902.
Rich, Charles C., and Heber C. Kimball. "History of David W.
    Patten." *Millennial Star* 26 (1864).

Rigdon, Sidney. "The Apostates and Rebellious Spirits at
    Nauvoo." *Latter Day Saints Messenger and Advocate,*
    Pittsburgh, January 1, 1845.
_____. *An Appeal to the American People.* Cincinnati: Printed by
    Shepard & Stearns, 1840.
Roberts, B. H. *A Comprehensive History of the Church of Jesus
    Christ of Latter-day Saints.* 6 vols. Provo, UT: Brigham Young
    University Press, 1957.
_____. "History of the Mormon Church," chapters XXX and
    XXXI. *Americana* 5 (Jan. 1910): 1047.
Robinson, E. "Items of Personal History of the Editor." *The
    Return* 1 (Oct. 1889): 145–47; (Feb. 1890): 218–19.
"The Rodsmen," *Middlebury Vermont American,* May 7, 1828.
Roseboom, E. H., and F. P. Weisenburger. *A History of Ohio.*
    New York: Prentice-Hall, 1934.
Sandweiss, Eric. *St. Louis in the Century of Henry Shaw.*
    Columbia, MO: University of Missouri Press, 2003.
Schindler, Hal. "Polygamy, Persecution and Power All Played
    Role in Nauvoo Exodus." *Salt Lake Tribune,* June 16, 1996.
Schurz, Carl. *Henry Clay.* Boston: Houghton Mifflin, 1887.
Scofield, Charles J., ed. *Historical Encyclopedia of Illinois and
    History of Hancock County,* Vol. II. Chicago: Munsell
    Publishing Company, 1921.
Shoemaker, Floyd Calvin. *Missouri's Struggle for Statehood,
    1804–1821.* Jefferson City, MO: Hugh Stephens, 1916.
Shook, Charles, *True Origin of Mormon Polygamy.* Cincinnati:
    Standard Publishing Company, 1914.
Sketch of the Life of Newel Knight, 6, fd 2, draft #1, archives,
    Historical Department of the Church of Jesus Christ of
    Latter-day Saints, Salt Lake City.
Smith, G[eorge]. A. *History.* n.p.
Smith, George A. *Journal of Discourses Vol. XIII,* published Oct.
    1868.
Smith Heman C., and Frederick M. Smith. *Journal of History* 4
    (Jan. 1911): 94.
Smith, Hyrum Diary, 28 July 1832, Special Collections and
    Manuscripts Department, Harold B. Lee Library, Brigham
    Young University.
Smith, Joseph, Sr. *Patriarchal Blessing Book.* Special
    Collections, J. Willard Marriott Library, University of Utah.
Smith, Joseph, Jr. *The Book of Mormon.* Palmyra, NY: Joseph
    Smith, 1830.

_____. *The Book of Mormon.* 1840.

_____. *History of the Church of Jesus Christ of Latter-day Saints.* 8
Vols. 2nd ed. Salt Lake City: Deseret Book Co., 1976.

_____. *An American Prophet's Record: The Diaries and Journals of
Joseph Smith.* Scott H. Faulring, ed. Salt Lake City:
Signature Books/Smith Research Associates, 1987.

Smith, Joseph, Jr., and Joseph Smith, III. *The History of the
Reorganized Church of Jesus Christ of Latter Day Saints,* 4 vols.
Independence, MO: Herald Publishing House, 1967.

Smith, III, Joseph. *Book of Commandments vs. Doctrine and
Covenants.* Independence, MO: Price Publishing Co. 2000.

_____. Memoirs of Joseph Smith, III (*Saints Herald*) 81 (Nov. 13,
1934): 1454.

Smith, Joseph Fielding. *Essentials in Church History.* Salt Lake
City: Deseret News Press, 1922.

Smith, Joseph Fielding, ed. *Teachings of the Prophet Joseph
Smith.* Salt Lake City: Deseret Book Co., 1938.

Smith, Lucy Mack. *Biographical Sketches: Joseph Smith the
Prophet and His Progenitors.* Independence, MO: Price
Publishing Co., 1998 (reprint of the 1912 edition).

Snow, Eliza R. *Biography & Family Record of Lorenzo Snow.* Salt
Lake City, 1884.

Squier, E. G. *Antiquities of the State of New York.* Buffalo, NY:
Geo. H. Derby & Co., 1851.

Stegner, Wallace. *The Gathering of Zion: The Story of the Mormon
Trail.* New York: McGraw-Hill, 1964.

Stevens, Walter Barlow. *Missouri the Center State.* 2 vols.
Chicago–St. Louis: S. J. Clarke, 1915.

Swartzell, William. *Mormonism Exposed.* Pekin, OH, 1840.

Swedenborg, Emanuel. *Arcana Coelestia; or, Heavenly Mysteries.*
12 vols. London: R. Hindmarsh, 1784–1804. Reprinted in
1789, 1800, 1807, 1819, etc.

_____. *Western Repository*, Dec. 6, 1808.

Switzler, William Franklin. *Switzler's Illustrated History of
Missouri, from 1541 to 1877.* St. Louis, 1879.

Tanner, Jerald, and Sandra Tanner. *Joseph Smith's 1826 Trial.*
Salt Lake City: Modern Microfilm, 1971.

_____. *Salt Lake City Messenger,* Sept. 1992, 1–4.

Taylor, John. *Correct Account of the Murder of Generals Joseph and
Hyrum Smith.* Nauvoo, IL, 1845.

Thatcher, James. *An Essay on Demonology, Ghost Apparitions, and
Popular Supersitions.* Boston: Carter and Hendee, 1831.

Thompson, John E. "A Chronology of Danite Meetings in Adam-ondi-Ahman, Missouri, July to September, 1838." *Restoration: News, Views, and History of the Latter Day Saint Movement* 4 (Jan. 1985): 11–14.

Tucker, Pomeroy. *Origin, Rise, and Progress of Mormonism: Biography of Its Founders and History of Its Church.* New York: D. Appleton & Co., 1867.

Turner, Nathan. Reminiscence. In George S. Tanner Family Association/Publishers Press, 1974.

U.S. Congress. Executive Documents of the House of Representatives, United States Congressional serial set, Issue 2726 (1890), 427.

Ursenbach, Maureen, and Richard L. Jensen. "The Oft-Crossed Border: Canadians in Utah." *The Peoples of Utah.* http://historytogo.utah.gov/people/ethnic_cultures/the_peoples_of_utah/theoft- crossedborder.html.

Vanderhoof, E.W. *Historical Sketches of Western New York.* Buffalo: Matthews-Northrup Works, 1907.

Van Wagoner, Richard S. *Mormon Polygamy: A History.* 2nd ed. Salt Lake City: Signature Books, 1992.

_____. *Sidney Rigdon: A Portrait of Religious Excess.* Salt Lake City: Signature Books, 1994.

Violette, Eugene Morrow. *History of Missouri.* Boston: D.C. Heath and Co., 1918.

Walters, Wesley P. "Joseph Smith's Bainbridge, N.Y. Court Trials." Westminster Technological Journal 36 (Winter 1974): 123–55.

Watt, G. D., et al. *Journal of Discourses Delivered by President Brigham Young, His Two Counsellors, and the Twelve Apostles, and Others.* Vol. 5. Liverpool: Asa Calkin, 1858.

West, Ray Benedict. *Kingdom of the Saints: The Story of Brigham Young and the Mormons.* New York: Viking Press, 1957.

Whitmer, David. *Address to All Believers in Christ.* Richmond, MO, 1887.

Whitmer, David to "Dear Brethren," ca. Dec. 9, 1886. *Saints' Herald* 34 (5 Feb. 1887): 91.

Whitmer, John. History of the Church. Manuscript. Salt Lake City: LDS Archives.

Whitney, Orson F. *History of Utah.* Vol. 4. Salt Lake City: George Q. Cannon, 1904.

Willey, Aaron C. "Observation on Magical Practices." *Medical Repository* 15 (1812): 377–82.

Williams, Frederick G. "Frederick Granger Williams of the First Presidency of the Church." *BYU Studies* 12, no. 3 (Spring 1972): 259.

Wilson, Douglas L., and Rodney O. Davis, eds. "Mormons in Hancock County" by Eudocia Baldwin Marsh. *Journal of the Illinois State Historical Society* 64 (1971).

Woodford, Robert. "Jesse Gause: Counselor to the Prophet." *BYU Studies* 15, no. 3 (Spring 1975): 362–64.

Wyl, W., pseud. [Wilhelm Ritter von Wymetal]. *Mormon Portraits: Joseph Smith the Prophet, his Family and Friends*, Salt Lake City: Tribune Printing and Publishing Co., 1886.

_____. *Mormon Portraits or the Truth about Mormon Leaders from 1830–1886*. Salt Lake City: Tribune Printing and Publishing Co., 1886.

X.Y.Z., "Nauvoo – Then and Now." *Carthage Gazette* (Jan. 19, 1876): 1.

Young, Ann Eliza. *Wife No. 19: or the Story of a Life in Bondage*. Hartford, Dustin, Gilman, 1875).

Young, Brigham and Orson Pratt. *Journal of Discourses by Brigham Young . . . His Two Counsellors, the Twelve Apostles and Others*. Liverpool: for Orson Pratt, 1856.

Zimmerman, Dean R. ed., *I Knew the Prophets: An Analysis of the Letter of Benjamin F. Johnson to George F.[S.] Gibbs, Reporting Doctrinal Views of Joseph Smith and Brigham Young.* Bountiful, Utah: Horizon Publishers, 1976.

Index

Abraham from Genesis, 59
Adams, John, 13
Adirondack Mountains, 1
Alger, Fanny, 31, 189
Algonquian tribes, 20
Allen, Charles, 38
Ashby, Daniel, 102, 162, 164
Atchison, David R.
    being skipped over for promotion and, 160, 175-176
    Bogart's report and, 130
    bringing Chief Big Neck to trial and, 21
    changing his tone regarding the Mormons and, 145-147
    combining forces with Lucas and, 166
    confirming the events in Carroll County and, 124, 129, 133-134
    describing the situation in Daviess and, 148
    description of the Mormons' arms and attitude, 118-119
    leadership of, 116
    militia called up to immediate "readiness" and, 101-102, 105-108
    military escort to the courthouse and, 48
    orders to unauthorized forces and, 111-112
    Parks disobeying the express orders of, 127-128
    petition for Mormons' rights in the courts and, 39
    photograph of, 105
    report to Governor Boggs and, 113-115, 117
    sympathy for Mormons and, 56
    using the state militia as an extension of mob justice and, 149
Atiya, Aziz S., 59
Austin, William, 111-112, 128
Avard, Sampson, 79-80, 86, 95, 143, 181

Backenstos, Jacob B., 188
Bank of Missouri, 18
banking, 17-18, 62–66, 69
Baptist Association, slavery and, 13
Barton, David, 16
Bates, Frederick, 18-19
Battle of Bunker Hill, 13
Battle of Nauvoo, 202
Benton, Thomas Hart, 16, 19
Big Neck, Chief, 20-21
Black, Adam
    Adamondi-Ahman and, 178
    affidavit to Judge King and, 102, 104
    attack on William Osbern's home and, 139
    Daviess County law enforcement and, 145
    destroying of his home and, 138, 180
    Mormon visit to Black's residence and, 97-100
    neutrality and, 96
    organizing anti-Mormon settlers and, 97

warrants within Daviess
County and, 96, 180
Blakely, Nathaniel H., 104
"Bleeding Kansas", crisis in, 105
Bogart, Samuel, 123, 127, 130,
135, 149, 155-157
Boggs, Lilburn
appointment of John B. Clark
and, 175-176, 180
assassination attempt and, 188
Atchison's reports and, 112-
114, 117, 130-131, 133-134
confirming the events in
Carroll County and, 124
court-martials and, 172
insurrection and, 106-107
letter from Col. Penniston to,
231n38
Mormon trouble in Jackson
County and, 108
Mormons in DeWitt and, 122
no orders to stop the Mormon
aggression and, 147-148
non-Mormon residents of
Daviess County and, 109
Order No. 44 (Extermination
Order) and, 158-160, 162, 166,
175, 184
Penniston's affidavit and, 99,
102-103
tension between Mormons and
their neighbors and, viii
Thomas Ford and, 190-191
wealthiest landowners in west-
ern Missouri and, 41-42
Bolton, Lewis, 101, 117
Book of Commandments, 23, 25,
38
Book of Mormon
Cowdery as scribe and, 31
Cowdery attempting to convert
Indians and, 103
distribution of, 10
Hurlbut's claims and, 26
Indians as progeny of the
Lamanites, 30

Martin Harris and, 70
naming of, 9
Nephite tribe and, 6
relying on old revelations and,
58
translation of, 5, 25, 27
Boonville Guard, 108
Braddock, Edward, 16
Brief History of the Church
(Corrill), 121
Brother, Richard, 2
Brown, A., 104
Brown, Samuel, 92
Brunson, Seymour, 137
Buchanan, James, 202
Buell, Prescindia Huntington, 182
Burch, Thomas C., 113, 150-151,
173, 179
Burnett, Sirenes, 29
Burr, Aaron, 31, 180
Butler, John L., 92-93, 104

Cahoon, Reynolds, 98, 197
Caldwell County, creation of, 56,
87
Cameron, Elisha, 56
Campbell, James, 54
Canada
missionary trips to, 40-41, 69
converts from, 76, 87, 91, 99,
105, 109-110, 119, 122, 127, 145,
188, 198
Carroll County Committee, 121
Carthage Greys, 200
Chamberlain, Joseph, 22
Chase, Sally, 5
Chief Big Neck, 20-21
Church of Jesus Christ of Latter-
day Saints, 59, 84, 190
Clark, John B.
Colonel Thompson and, 173
discharging of troops and, 117,
134-135
governor's extermination order
and, 162
head commander of militia

forces and, 160
interrogation of prisoners and, 178
militia called up to immediate "readiness" and, 101
Mormon atrocities in Daviess County and, 157
Order No. 44 and, 158
photograph of, 177
prosecution of defendants and, 180
protection for Mormons in Caldwell County and, 179
state's response to the insurrection and, 175-176
Clark, William, 18
Clay, Henry, 13-14, 16
Cleminson, John, 167
Comer, John, 106, 110-111
Community of Christ, 203
Copley, Leman, 28
Corrill, John
affidavits and, 229n39
church historian and, 78, 80, 120, 165
description of Mormons and, 183
false imprisonment charges and, 40
negotiating with militia and, 167
newly elected state representative for Caldwell County and, 120-121
organizational meetings of Danites and, 80
relations between Mormons and non-Mormons, 88
Rigdon's sermon and, 82
Council of Fifty, 189
Covington, Phillip, 139
Cowdery, Oliver
"acts of adultery" and, 31
breakaway faction and, 70
choice of the twelve apostles and, 29

convert Indians to Mormonism and, 103
Delaware Indians and, 36
excommunication of, 78
following Smiths to Palmyra and, 4
giving land to the church and, 77
"Golden Plates" and, 27
meeting Joseph Smith and, 8
Mormon church leader and, 3
Mormon expulsion from Zion and, 38
new church converts and, 23
persecution of dissenters and, 80-86
photograph of, 71
purchase of a new printing press and, 41
Smith's treasure seeking and, 61
traveled first to Missouri and, 30
Cowdery, William, 3-4, 8
Crawther, Henry W., 101
Crooked River, 56, 87, 147, 155-156

Danites
as true Mormons and, 143
Council of Fifty and, 189
description of forces and, 104
dissenters and, 150-151
Ebenezer Robinson and, 79
Elias Higbee and, 101
expanding the Danite organization and, 119
High Council and, 83
hostility toward settlers of Daviess County and, 88
John D. Lee and, 136
John L. Butler and, 92-93
Lyman Wight and, 87
Mormon festivities and, 89
organization of, 88

overthrowing the government
and, 180
prophecy in Daniel and, 78-79
raiding people's homes and, 84
retribution and, 85
"Salty Sermon" and, 81-82
Sampson Avard and, 79-80, 95,
178
Smith's public repudiation of,
181
violent rhetoric and, 80
Daughters of Zion, 79
Daviess County
Mormon population of, 118
reports of Mormon atrocities
in, 135
Delaware Indians, 20-21, 36
Doctrine and Covenants (1835),
25
Doniphan, Alexander
being suspicious of Austin's
motives and, 111-112
creation of Caldwell County as
Mormon homeland and, 110
extermination order and, 162
Hiram Parks and, 147, 161, 169-
170, 172-173
Mormon approach to Far West
and, 166
Mormon attorney and, 39, 179-
181, 185
Mormon sympathizer and, 56,
119, 131, 165
peace talks and, 167
photograph of, 111
refusal of orders to execute
Smith and, 174
reinforcements for General
Atchison and, 128-129
Smith's prisoners and, 110-111
terms of surrender and trial,
113, 120
working the Daviess County
settlers and, 121
Dryden, Jonathan L., 139
Dryden, William, 104, 106-107,

113, 116, 139-140
Dunklin, Daniel, 18, 39, 41, 43,
50-51, 99
Durphy, Perry, 92-93

Egyptian artifacts, 58-59
election brawl, 91-95, 97-98, 138
England
missionary trips to, 69, 91
converts from, 76, 119
Evening and the Morning Star,
Mormon newspaper, 34, 37
Extermination Order; see Order
No. 44

Far West
action at, 167-171
after surrender, 175-178
plans for, 76-77
surrender of, 169
Temple at, 88-90
financial panic of 1837, 19
Finney, Charles G., 1
Fishing River, 53
Ford, Thomas, 190, 193, 196, 198-
200, 237n21
Fort Duquesne, 16
Fraternity of Rodsmen, 3
French and Indian War, 16

Gallatin, 136-140, 143-145, 146,
148, 150, 155
Gause, Jesse, 30
general conference, first, 28
Gilliam, Cornelius, 54-55
Goose Creek, 166
Graham, Brigadier General, 167,
169, 170, 172-173
Grand River, 87, 105, 112, 121, 139
Grant, Thomas D., 101
Grindstone Fork, 136-137
Gudgel, Jacob, 152

habeas corpus, 185, 192-193, 195-
196

Hale, Emma. *see* Smith, Emma
    Hale
Harper's New Monthly Magazine,
    Nauvoo Legion and, 189
Harris, George W., 76
Harris, Martin, 8, 27, 70
Haun, Jacob, 162, 165-166
Haun's Mill, 162-163, 165, 182
hieroglyphs, 59
Higbee, Elias, 101
High Council, 60, 62, 68, 82-83,
    151, 181
Hinkle, George
    affidavits of, 229n39
    Carroll County Committee and,
    121
    General Doniphan and, 131
    Mormon military force and, 166
    Mormons in DeWitt and, 128-
    129
    peace talks and, 167, 171-172
Howe, Eber D., 27
Humphrey, Smith, 121
Huntington, Oliver, 138
Hurlbut, Philastus
    excommunication of, 26
    first-person accounts of the
    Smith family and, 7
    Smith's denouncing of, 27
Hyde, Orson, 26, 44, 68-69, 75,
    141

Illinois River, 50
Indians, American
    alleged conspiracy with, 102-
    103
    conversion of, 30, 36
    moundbuilders and, 6
    relations with, 19-20
Ingersoll, Peter, 7

Jackson, Andrew, 17-18, 34, 45
Jackson County
    attacks on Mormons and, 40
    expulsion of Mormons from, 39
    federal arsenal in, 51

Manifesto of Five Orders and,
    37-38, 42
    peace proposals of, 52-53
    petition of settlers in, 36-38
Jackson County Committee,
    Manifesto of Five Orders to
    Mormons and, 37-38, 42
Jefferson, Thomas, 13, 31
Johnson, Lyman E., 77-78, 80, 82-
    84, 86
Jones, William Claud, 121
Joseph of Egypt, 59

Kansas-Nebraska Act of 1854, 106
Keyte, James, 102
Kimball, Heber, 26, 68-69
Kimball, Hiram, 197
King, Austin
    communications from Grand
    River and, 105
    forty-six prisoners from
    Caldwell and, 178-180
    photograph of, 99
    prisoners being held by
    Mormons in Far West and, 106,
    111
    Ray County Circuit Judge and,
    98
    Ray County committee meet-
    ings and, 154
    siege preparations in Mormon-
    held areas and, 155
    Smith and Wight's surren-
    dered, 113
    Smith's request for a change of
    venue and, 101
    soliciting Atchison's forces and,
    106
    state of affairs in Caldwell and
    Daviess counties, 102
    Turner Committee and, 183
    warrant for Smith's arrest and,
    100
Kirtland, Ohio
    electing Mormons to political
    office and, 32

first general conference of
  Smith's Church (1831), 28
Hurlbut's lecturing in, 26
Smith's relocation to, 22
Kirtland Order, 23, 29
Kirtland Safety Society Bank, 19,
  62-65, 86
Kirtland Temple, 60-61
Knight, Newel, 22, 28, 32
Knight, Vinson, 96-98

Lake Erie, 22
Law, Jane, 190
Law, William, 188, 190
leadership hierarchy
  establishment of, 30-31
  expansion of, 60
Lee, Henry, 136
Lee, John D., 93, 136, 157, 162,
  201
Leonid meteor shower, 43
Lewis, Meriwether, 18
Liberty Enquirer
  effect of Smith's departure
  and, 55
  Jackson County residents and
  Mormons, 54
Lincoln, Abraham, 202
Lisle, B. M., 101-102, 107-108, 117,
  160-161
Lott, Cornelius, 104
Louisiana Purchase, 20
Louisiana Territory, 19
Lovejoy, Elijah, 16
Lucas, Samuel D.
  affidavits and warrants against
  Mormons, 101
  Carroll County affair and, 133
  disbanding of the militia and,
  117, 123, 172-173
  expulsion of Daviess County
  residents from their homes
  and, 160-161
  extermination order and, 166
  Far West and, 162, 166, 168,
  170-176

report to Governor Boggs and,
  123-124
terms to Smith's army and, 167
Lyman, Amos, 179

Manifesto of Five Orders to
  Mormons, 37-38, 42
March, Nathan, 103
Marks, Henry, 141-142
Marsh, Thomas B., 68, 141, 143-
  144
Martin, Thomas I., 144
McBride, Thomas, 163
McHaney, William, 106, 110
McKinney, Wilson, 153
McNair, Alexander, 18
Messenger and Advocate
  Kirtland Safety Society Bank
  and, 62
  Smith's apology and, 69
Metropolitan Museum of Art, 59
migration
  into Daviess County, 87, 91, 99
  free blacks and, 36-37
  seen as threat, 33-34
Miller, Adam, 106, 110
Miller, John, 18
Millport
  King on, 155
  raid on, 136-137, 140, 143, 146,
  150
  report on, 152-153
missionary trips, 68-69
Mississippi River, 31, 49, 54, 184-
  185, 197
Missouri
  early economy of, 16
  growing number of pro-slavery
  residents and, 15
  Henry Clay and, 13
  James Monroe and, 14
  Kirtland Order and, 41
  lead mining and, 17
  Mormon strong-hold of Far
  West and, 168
  purchase of, 11

removal of American Indians
from its borders and, 21
restrictions on General
Assembly and, 16
slavery and, 12, 14, 34
Western Missouri map and, 125
Missouri Compromise, 14
Missouri Gazette, Tallmadge's reso-
lution and, 12
Missouri Intelligencer, population
estimates and, 11
Missouri Republican Daily
Haun's Mill attack and, 182
Jackson County attacks on
Mormons and, 43
rape of Mormon women and,
176
Turner Committee and, 184
Missouri River, 20, 54, 105, 121
Monroe, James, 14-15
Morehead, Charles, 152
Morgan, William, 138
Moribund Library Association, 62
Morin, Josiah, 91, 98, 101, 113,
152-153
Mormon Army
march of, 48-49
problems encountered by, 50,
52
recruitment of, 46-47
secret, 78-79
see also Danites
Mormonism Unvailed (Howe), 27
Mormons
Battle of Nauvoo and, 202
Book of Commandments, 23,
25, 38
Church of Jesus Christ of
Latter-day Saints, 59, 84, 190
Council of Fifty, 189
Doctrine and Covenants (1835),
25
fleeing to Caldwell County and,
179
Fraternity of Rodsmen, 3
High Council, 60, 62, 68, 82-83,

151, 181
Manifesto of Five Orders and,
37-38, 42
polygamy and, 81, 182, 189-190,
202, 237n13
Quorum of Twelve Apostles, 49
Remnant Church of Jesus
Christ of Latter Day Saints, 203
Reorganized Church of Jesus
Christ of Latter Day Saints, 203
strong-hold of Far West and,
168
surrender of Far West and, 169
three-prong attack on Daviess
County and, 136-137
Utah Mormon War and, 201-
202
moundbuilders, 6-7, 26
Mountain Meadows Massacre, 201
Murdock, John, 121

Nauvoo Expositor, William Law's
newspaper and, 190
Nauvoo Legion, 187, 189-190, 199
Nelson, Abraham, 93, 104
Nelson, Hiram, 104
Newell, Grandison, 68, 71-72, 75
New York Rochester Republican,
condemnation of Smith and, 10

O'Fallon, John, 17-18
Order No. 44, 158-160, 162
Osage River, 18
Osbern, William, 139
Owens, Ephraim, 104
Ozark Mountains, 201
Page, Hiram, 24
Painesville (Ohio) Gazette, on
Smith's followers and, 23-24
Painesville Republican, currency
situation at Safety Society bank
and, 64
Painesville Telegraph
Grandison Newell and, 68
Kirtland colony and, 47
paying the temple bill and, 61

Safety Society Bank and, 65
Parks, Hiram
  Adam-ondi-Ahman and, 148
  arrival at DeWitt and, 128
  Atchison's initiative and, 116
  attack on Far West and, 168-173
  attitude of the Mormons and,
    115
  Carroll County and, 123-124,
    129
  Daviess County and, 147-149
  insurrection in DeWitt and,
    123
  joining Clark in Richmond
    and, 160-161
  mob spirit of troops and, 134
  Mormon reinforcements and,
    127
  peace talks and, 167
  Ray County committee and,
    154
  Ray Militia and, 114, 159
  report to General Atchison
    and, 148
Parrish, Warren, 64-66
Partridge, Edward, 29, 33, 37-38,
  100
Patten, David, 136, 139, 142-143,
  155-157
peace negotiations
  Clay County and, 52-54
  Daviess County and, 97-99
  at Far West, 100, 167-168
Pearl of Great Price, 59
Peck, Reed, 86, 165, 167
Penniston, William P.
  affidavit and, 98-100
  Canadian converts and, 231n38
  Daviess County settlers and,
    145
  Mormon visit to Judge Black's
    residence and, 98
  prohibiting Mormons from vot-
    ing in Daviess County and, 91-
    92
  property targeted by the

Mormons and, 153
  raid on Adam Black's house
    and, 98-99
  raising the resentment of Clay
    County settlers and, 55, 92, 94,
    96, 145
Phelps, William Wines
  affidavits and, 229n39
  Clay County Mormons and, 53
  Evening and Morning Star edi-
    tor, 34, 37, 57
  making arrangements for
    Smith brothers and, 197
  peace talks and, 167
  photograph of, 37
  renewed violence in Missouri
    and, 44
  showdown with Smith and, 77-
    78
  Sidney Rigdon and, 88
  tar and feathering of, 57
  testimony of, 230n30
  transgressors against the
    church and, 74-75
  U.S. Postmaster and, 84
Pickett, William, 203
Pitcher, Thomas, 42, 50-51
politics
  church-approved candidates
    and, 88
  in Missouri, 35-36
  in Nauvoo, 187
  Smith and, 31-32, 77, 189
  in Utah, 202
  voting and, 91-94
Polk, James K., 16
polygamy, 81, 182, 189-190, 202,
  237n13
Pratt, Orson, 25, 79
Pratt, Parley
  High Council and, 68
  hostages and, 171, 179
  marched to Richmond and, 179
  mission trip and, 68, 70
  peace talks and, 167

---

powers of persuasion and, 46, 68

real estate deal disagreement with Smith and, 68

restoration of arms in Jackson County and, 46

Sylvester Smith and, 50

wounding of Samuel Tarwater and, 156-157

Price, Sterling, 102

printing presses, destruction of, 16, 38, 71-72, 190-191, 195

property
  Kirtland Order and, 23, 29, 41
  overvaluation of, 63, 67
  raids and, 138-140, 142-143
  rescinded gifts of, 28-29
  theft of, 187-188
  United Order and, 77

Putnam, Benjamin, 2

Quakers, 30

Quorum of Twelve Apostles, 49

Randolph, John, 14

Ray County
  appeal from, 149-151, 154
  reconnaissance from, 152-153

Ray County Militia, 114

Redfield, H., 104

Rees, Amos, 39, 157-158, 173, 179, 181

Reid, John, 22

Remnant Church of Jesus Christ of Latter Day Saints, 203

Reorganized Church of Jesus Christ of Latter Day Saints, 203

Rhode-Island American, condemnation of Smith and, 10

Richards, Willard, 69, 198

Rigdon, Sidney, 224-225n9, 230n27
  address to Mormon army and, 48
  attack Hulburt's character and, 27
  attack on Rigdon and, 32
  Campbellite minister and, 23, 71, 79
  Canada trip and, 40-41, 91
  children of, 73
  church leadership and, 30
  Corrill's undermining of church leadership and, 120-121
  Danites and, 79-85, 104
  Daviess County Mormons and, 95
  dissenters taking over the temple and, 71
  elected postmaster and, 88
  election brawl and, 91-94
  escaping to Missouri and, 70-74
  extermination wording of, 158
  Far West speech and, 90, 132, 138, 141-142
  First Presidency and, 60, 90
  fleeing Kirtland and, 73
  hostages and, 179-181
  King's letter to Atchison and, 106
  Kirtland attack and, 32
  peace talks and, 167
  photograph of, 81
  polygamy and, 189-190
  released on a writ of habeas corpus and, 185
  renewing the communal economic approach and, 77
  rescinded gifts and, 28
  Safety Society Bank and, 62, 65-66
  Sampson Avard and, 78-79
  showdown between Smith and early followers, 77-78
  speech at Kirtland temple and, 71
  Smith's treasure hunt and, 61
  taking control of the church and, 30-31, 33
  war of extermination and, 124

Ripley, Andrew, 104

Robinson, Ebenezer, 79

Robinson, George, 100, 167, 179
Rockwell, Porter, 188, 198
Rocky Mountains, 132, 197
Root, Henry, 122-123
Rounds, Samuel D., 65
Russell, Isaac, 181
Ryland, E. M., 157-158

Safety Society Bank, 19, 62-65, 86
Salty Sermon, 81
Santa Fe Trail, 18
Sapp, John N., 103-104
seeing stones, 5-6
seer stones
    breakaway faction and, 70
    destruction of, 24
    Egyptian artifacts and, 59
    translation of plates and, 8
Shawnee tribes, 20-21
Shays's Rebellion, 159
Shoal Creek, 162
slavery
    Canadian Mormons and, 109-
        110
    Missouri Territory and, 14-15
    settlers and, 34
    statehood and, 12-14
Smalling, Cyrus, 63
Smith, Emma, 182, 197
Smith, George, 104
Smith, Hyrum
    brother's treasure hunting and,
        61
    Danites and, 83
    discovery of the plates and, 9
    escape attempt and, 185-186
    First Presidency and, 90
    High Council and, 83
    hostages and, 179
    killing of, 199-200
    managing church affairs in
        Kirtland and, 48
    mistreatment in Missouri and,
        187
    on Rigdon's actions and, 30

    plans to escape Illinois and,
        197-198
    reward for destroying the
        Warsaw Sentinel and, 238n32
    tales of theophanies and, 2
Smith, III, Joseph, 25, 53, 182, 203
Smith, John, 98
Smith, Joseph, Jr., 1, 3
    arrest of, 22
    arrival in Illinois and, 187
    becoming a seer and, 4
    children of, 73
    cholera outbreak and, 54
    Council of Fifty and, 189
    Doctrine and Covenants (1835)
        and, 25
    election brawl and, 91-94
    escaping Illinois and, 197-198
    first general conference of his
        Church (1831), 28
    "golden Bible" and, 7-10, 24, 26
    High Council and, 60, 62, 68,
        82-83, 151, 181
    "a history of the Indians" and,
        6
    influence of parents on, 2-3
    killing of, 199-200
    Kirtland attack and, 32
    moundbuilders and, 6-7
    move to upstate New York and,
        1
    Nauvoo Legion and, 189
    on finding the plates and, 9
    "peep stones" and, 5-6, 8, 24
    polygamy and, 81, 182, 189-190,
        202, 237n13
    portrait of, 53
    "Presidency and Two
        Counselors" and, 31, 60, 80-81,
        83, 85, 88, 90-91
    "Redemption of Zion" and, 46-
        48, 51, 55
    renewed dissension among his
        faithful and, 120-121
    second prong of his comeback
        and, 59-60

sexual advances on Jane Law
and, 190
sole prophet of the church and,
24-25
surrender at Far West and, 170-
171
surrendered himself to gover-
nor in Carthage and, 198
surrender of Far West and, 169
treasure digging and, 4
trial of, 22
United Order and, 77-78, 85-86
visions of God and, 4
"Zion's Camp" and, 52, 55, 58,
60, 86
Smith, Joseph, Sr., 2-4, 31, 71
Smith, Louisa, 28
Smith, Lucy Mack, 2, 6
Smith, R. F., 190
Smith, Sardius, 164
Smith, Sylvester, 50, 52, 58, 68,
164
Smith, Thaddeus, 28
Smith, William, 7, 181
Spaulding, Solomon, 26
Spencer, Augustine, 190
Stallings, Jacob, 138
Stewart, Riley, 93, 104
St. Louis Chamber of Commerce,
National Bank and, 17
Stone, James, 144
Stout, Hosea, 188
Stowell, Josiah, 6
Swartzell, William, 87
Swedenborg, Emanuel, 2, 7-8

Tallmadge, James, 12
Tallmadge Act, 15
Tanner, John, 60
Tarwater, Samuel, 156
Taylor, John, 198-199
Thayer, Ezra, 28
theocratic ethics, 32
theophanies, 2, 4
Thon, Andrew, 104
Thornton, G. W., 138

Thornton, William, 152
Thorp, Joseph, 56
Times and Seasons, Mormon news-
paper and, 59
Tubbs, Amos, 104
Turner Committee, 183-184
Turner, James B., 98
Two Counselors, 30-31

Umstead, Harvey, 104
United Order, 77-78, 85-86
United States Bank, 17
University of Utah, 59
Utah Mormon War, 201-202

Venable, Samuel, 140
violence, church-sanctioned, 75;
see also Danites
voting, see politics

War of 1812, 11, 20
Washington, George, 16
The Wasp, Mormon newspaper
and, 188
Wasson, Lorenzo D., 197
weapons
confiscation of, 104, 109
retrieval of, 110-111
Webb, C. G., 64
Welding, Richard, 92-93
Weldon, James, 105
Wells, Daniel H., 196
Western Missouri counties and
settlements, map of, 89
Western Monitor, anti-slavery can-
didates and, 35
Whiskey Rebellion, 159
Whiteacre, James, 104
Whitmer, David, 8, 25, 29, 40-41,
70, 77, 80-84, 86
Whitmer, John, 74, 77-78, 80-84,
86
Whitmer, Peter, 30
Wight, Lyman
Adam-ondi-Ahman and, 135-
136

Danites and, 87, 95, 104, 135-
136
description of, 114
disagreement over strategy with
Smith and, 52
extremist brand of evangelism
and, 87
Gallatin election brawl and, 98
hostages and, 171, 179
Jacob Haun and, 162
long march from Ohio and, 55
Millport raod and, 140
Mormon restoration of arms in
Jackson County and, 46
peace negotiations and, 96,
112-113, 167
personality of, 46
photograph of, 49
selected to be the army's general and, 48
Williams, Abraham J., 18
Williams, Frederick, 30-31, 48, 60,
65, 70, 80
Williams, John, 98
Williams, Wiley, 157-158, 173
Willock, David, 101, 158, 160
Wood, Nathaniel, 3-4
Woods, John, 104
Wood, William T., 39, 179

Young, Brigham
church decisions made by a
council and, 185
death of, 198
fleeing to Missouri to escape
arrest and, 71
leadership of, 70
leading the Mormon group to
Illinois and, 182
Mormon army and, 48
moving to Utah and, 201-202
photograph of, 183
resourcefulness of, 50

Zelf, Lamanite warrior chieftain
and, 50

Zion's Camp, 52, 55, 58, 60, 86; see
also Mormon Army

ACKNOWLEDGMENTS

I would like to thank the individuals who helped me with the creation of this work.

To my wife: Without your help and support I would never have succeeded in writing this book. Thank you for reading my manuscript and listening to me even after you'd heard your fill about the Mormon War. I love you and thank you more than you will ever know. To my son and daughter: Thank you for being patient with your Dad even though it would have been more fun to play. May you always have such joy in your hearts. I love you both so much. To Ed and Mary: Thank you for all the support you've lent when I needed it most. You've spent countless hours entertaining my family and even putting up with my bouts of writing stress; you've earned a crown or two.